# What Works?
# A Review of the Efficacy and Effectiveness of Nutrition Interventions

Lindsay H. Allen and Stuart R. Gillespie

United Nations
Administrative Committee on Coordination
Sub-Committee on Nutrition (ACC/SCN)

in collaboration with the
Asian Development Bank (ADB)

### The Asian Development Bank Nutrition and Development Series

This is the first copublication by the ACC/SCN in its Nutrition Policy Series and the Asian Development Bank in its Nutrition and Development Series. The ADB Nutrition and Development Series, begun in 2001, covers the impact of malnutrition in Asia and the Pacific on poverty and depressed human and economic development. The Series stresses three themes: targeting nutrition improvements at poor women and children, with benefits to families, communities, and nations throughout the life cycle; reviewing and applying scientific evidence about nutrition impact for policies, programmes, and developmental assistance that will raise the quality of human resources; and creating opportunities for public, private, and civil sector partnerships that can raise the dietary quality of the poor, and enhance the learning and earning capability of poor children. The Series is intended for ADB member countries, development partners, and scholars interested in applying science and technology to investment decisions.

This copublication was prepared under ADB's RegionalTechnical Assistance 5824—Regional Study of Nutrition Trends, Policies and Strategies in Asia and the Pacific—which was designed and coordinated by Dr. Joseph M. Hunt, ADB's Senior Health and Nutrition Economist, with the support of William Fraser, Manager of the Education, Health and Population Division (East) of ADB, which sponsored the project. For more information, please contact Dr. Joseph M. Hunt, Series Editor: jhunt@adb.org; phone: (632) 632-6830; fax: (632) 636-2407. Address: Asian Development Bank, 6 ADB Avenue, Mandaluyong City, 0421 Metro Manila, Philippines.

Suggested citation form for this report:
ACC/SCN (2001). What Works? A Review of the Efficacy and Effectiveness of Nutrition Interventions, Allen LH and Gillespie SR. ACC/SCN: Geneva in collaboration with the Asian Development Bank, Manila.

ISBN 971-561-388-8
Publication Stock No. 070901

Published by the Asian Development Bank, P.O. Box 789, 0980 Manila, Philippines
E-mail: adbpub@adb.org; website: http://www.adb.org and
ACC/SCN Secretariat, c/o World Health Organization, 20 Avenue Appia, CH 1211 Geneva 27, Switzerland
E-mail: accscn@who.int; website: http://acc.unsystem.org/scn/

# FOREWORD

Improving nutrition in developing countries is both humanitarian and an economic imperative. Yet, despite the gains that have been made, the greater progress that is urgently needed has been hampered by the lack of a systematic evaluation of what works and what does not. A major review of this key issue has been long overdue.

The monograph therefore fills an important gap by providing an overview on which nutrition interventions improve the nutrition status of women and children, with emphasis on the poor in developing countries. The purpose is to define a core menu of proven investment options supported by sound evidence of efficacy. We expect that this review will be a much-consulted reference to support evidence-based nutrition programming in developing countries.

This review takes the perspective of low-income Asia, because the study was commissioned by the Asian Development Bank to inform its policy dialogue with Asian governments. We believe the review will be useful for ADB and all development partners selecting nutrition interventions as stand-alone activities or components in integrated social development projects and programs. Notably, the review draws on global literature and its findings are relevant to all developing countries. The review emphasizes what works and why – for each of the major nutrition problems in Asia: micronutrient deficiencies (vitamin A, iodine and anemia), low birthweight, maternal malnutrition, child growth retardation and arrested cognitive development in early childhood. Supplementation and fortification efficacy and effectiveness trials are reviewed comprehensively. The monograph includes a broader review and impact assessment of food-based approaches to improve maternal and child nutrition. It concludes with recommendations on a core program that passes efficacy and effectiveness tests, and calls for a sensible level of investment in operations research and cost-effectiveness analysis to improve nutrition programming throughout the donor community and national budgets in developing countries.

The decision of the United Nations Sub-Committee on Nutrition and ADB to co-publish the monograph recognizes that Asia is the crucible for improving nutrition of children globally, and nutrition programs must be based on what works. We are committed to further dialogue with the nutrition and development communities to increase support for effective nutrition interventions that will support life-long learning and earning opportunities among Asian children. There is probably no more fundamental way to eliminate poverty than to raise the development potential of children. Nutrition is one of the keys to their proper physical and cognitive development.

Tadeo Chino
President
Asian Development Bank

Namanga Ngongi
Chair
United Nations Sub-Committee on Nutrition

# EXECUTIVE SUMMARY

This review tracks the life cycle impacts of malnutrition in the developing world, highlighting the dynamics of cause and consequence, and then considers what can be done to break the cycle: first from an efficacy perspective, then with regard to large scale effectiveness. The focus is on undernutrition, which may be manifest as stunting, wasting, underweight, foetal growth retardation, low body mass index and various micronutrient deficiencies. The perspective is low income Asia. The review focuses on the five major nutrition problems in Asia and the Pacific region: low birthweight, early childhood growth failure, anaemia, iodine deficiency disorders, and vitamin A deficiency. For each of these, the nature of the problem, its prevalence, distribution, consequences, and causes, are discussed. This is followed by a comprehensive review of existing knowledge of the efficacy of key "nutrition interventions" for preventing or alleviating these conditions. The final two sections review the effectiveness of large scale programmes and the process to be adopted for selecting and prioritizing options.

## Preventing Low Birthweight

Asia has a higher prevalence of low birthweight (LBW) than any other continent, ranging from well over 30% in South Central Asia and Bangladesh to less that 10% in the People's Republic of China (PRC), the Philippines, Malaysia, and Thailand. LBW is strongly associated with undernutrition of mothers. About 60% of women in South Asia and 40% in Southeast Asia are underweight (<45 kg). LBW is probably the main reason why over 50% of the children in Asia are underweight. It also increases the risk of other health and developmental problems. Interventions to reduce the prevalence of LBW should therefore receive very high priority.

Randomized, controlled, efficacy trials to combat LBW have shown the following. Only supplements that provide more energy, rather than more protein, improve birthweight significantly. In populations where protein intake is adequate, high protein supplements (>25% of energy) to pregnant women may even increase neonatal death rates. Maternal supplementation can increase maternal weight gain, infant head circumference and, when there is a serious energy deficit, the length of the newborn infant.

The expected benefits from maternal food supplementation in Asia have yet to be determined but are expected to be considerable. For comparison, in The Gambia, locally produced biscuits providing 1,017 kcal and 22 g protein per day from mid-pregnancy, reduced LBW prevalence by 39%, increased birthweight by 136 g and reduced infant mortality by about 40%. Such improvements in pregnancy outcome can be obtained by encouraging undernourished women to consume more of their normal diet, where possible, and providing appropriate energy supplements, ideally formulated from local foods. Where the normal diet is particularly low in protein or in micronutrients, it is important to ensure that these are also provided as supplements. Women with the lowest weights (from conception to early pregnancy) and the lowest energy intakes are the most likely to benefit. Targeting interventions based on maternal body mass index (BMI), skinfold thickness, and height is unlikely to be as useful as targeting based on weight.

There are conflicting data on whether supplementation during the second trimester or the third trimester is most effective for improving birthweight. It is clear that supplementation during either of these trimesters can reduce the prevalence of LBW. Young maternal age at conception is an additional risk factor for poor pregnancy outcome. Therefore, it is especially important to target interventions to pregnant women are still growing. Continued supplementation that is given to the mother during her subsequent lactation and next pregnancy may cause an even greater improvement in the birthweight of her next child.

Whenever possible, attention should be paid to improving the quality as well as the quantity of food consumed during pregnancy. There is little evidence that supplementation with individual nutrients (including calcium, folic acid, iron, zinc and vitamin A) can improve birthweight, other than possibly through a reduction in preterm delivery. However, micronutrient supplementation of underprivileged pregnant women is extremely important. It can lead to substantial reductions in maternal anaemia and may also reduce maternal mortality, birth defects and preterm delivery. It improves breastmilk quality and infant nutrient stores. Trials are ongoing to test the efficacy of providing supplements containing balanced amounts of multiple micronutrients. In areas of endemic iodine deficiency, adequate maternal iodine status is critical for the prevention of neonatal deaths, LBW and abnormal cognitive and physical development of the infant. Non-nutrition interventions that can improve pregnancy outcome include reducing energy expenditure in physical work, increasing age at conception, malarial prophylaxis, and cessation of cigarette smoking.

## Improving Child Growth

An estimated 70% of the world's stunted children live in Asia, and there has been little recent improvement in this situation. South Central Asia has the second highest prevalence of growth stunting in the world (44%) and the prevalence in South-East Asia (33%) is also high. Growth stunting in childhood is a risk factor for increased mortality, poor cognitive and motor development and other impairments in function. It usually persists, causing smaller size and poorer performance in adulthood. Nutrition intervention trials support the following recommendations.

Exclusive breastfeeding is strongly recommended for the first six months of life. There is probably no advantage to the infant of introducing complementary foods prior to 6 months, especially where the quantity and quality of such foods is inadequate. Breastfeeding should be continued when other foods are added to the infant's diet. In general, the quality of complementary foods is poor compared to breastmilk. The energy density of many gruels, soups, broths, and other watery foods fed to infants in developing countries, is often below the recommended 0.6 kcal/g. Energy intake can be increased by reducing where possible, the water added to foods, and by providing additional feedings. At present, there is insufficient evidence to promote the use of amylases to lower the viscosity of cereals. Adding extra energy in the form of oil or sugar can adversely affect the density of protein and micronutrients in the diet. Even where breastmilk intake is relatively low, the amount of protein in complementary foods is usually more than

adequate. Therefore, adding protein alone or improving protein quality will not improve growth.

Randomized, controlled trials with processed, complementary foods have shown inconsistent impacts on growth. Among nine trials (mostly with infants aged 6 to 12 months), supplements increased weight and length in only three, and weight alone in two more. In the remainder, there was no effect on growth and the expected growth velocity for ages was not attained in any of the studies. The limitations of these trials included: variability in the age at which the intervention started; the composition of the foods and the amounts provided; the extent and replacement of breastmilk; and the baseline nutrition status and morbidity of the infants. Few trials supplied enough micronutrients to permit the children to consume recommended intakes from their diets, plus the supplements. Intervention with food supplements after 12 months is less effective than between 6 and 12 months. However, there is an increased risk of displacement of breastmilk with earlier high intakes of complementary foods, especially before 6 months of age.

In most developing countries, and in some groups in developed countries, the micronutrient content of unfortified, complementary foods is inadequate to meet infant requirements. It is particularly difficult for infants to consume enough calcium, iron, and zinc. Moreover, riboflavin, thiamine, vitamin A, and vitamin $B_6$ intakes are often low. Micronutrient fortification of cereal staples is especially important where these are major constituents of complementary foods. Interventions with single micronutrients have shown the following benefits for children with low intakes and deficiencies: vitamin A, prevention of eye lesions, substantial reduction in mortality from measles and diarrhoea, and increased haemoglobin (Hb) synthesis; iron, improved cognitive and motor development of anaemic infants and children; zinc, improved growth of children who are stunted or have low plasma zinc; iodine, reduced infant mortality and prevalence of goitre, and improved motor and mental function; and vitamin $B_{12}$, improved growth and cognitive function.

Multiple micronutrient deficiencies occur simultaneously. Multiple micronutrient supplements improved height velocity in stunted children in Viet Nam, and infants aged <12 months in Mexico, but had no impact on the growth of children in Peru or Guatemala. Additional trials are underway to compare the benefits of multiple micronutrient and single micronutrient supplementation. Novel approaches to providing multiple micronutrients include a fat-based spread, which has improved growth and Hb in stunted children in one trial, and encapsulated "sprinkles".

Micronutrient intake in young children can be increased by higher consumption of animal products. Among 15 complementary feeding trials, in which dry skimmed milk was included as at least one ingredient, growth in length was significantly increased in 12 trials. However, a trial in which dry fish powder was added to fermented maize, showed no benefits. Animal products, such as chicken liver, could be rich micronutrient sources for infants and children, but controlled trials of their efficacy are still lacking.

## Preventing and Treating Anaemia

Asia has the highest prevalence of anaemia in the world. About half of all anaemic women live in the Indian subcontinent: 88% of them develop anaemia during pregnancy. Vast numbers of infants and children are also affected. Low intakes of absorbable iron, as well as malaria and hookworm infections are the main causes of anaemia. Intervention trials have demonstrated the benefits from improving iron status and reducing anaemia. The greatest benefits are realized in the most severely anaemic individuals.

Randomized, controlled, clinical trials show that iron supplementation of pregnant women improves Hb and iron status, even in developed countries. Efficacy increases with iron doses of up to 60 mg/d. Where iron supplementation has not been effective this has been due predominantly to programmatic constraints such as lack of available supplements, and poor compliance. No conclusions can be made about the benefits of iron supplementation during pregnancy on maternal or foetal health, function or survival. Most trials have been conducted on relatively small numbers of women in developed countries. Severe anaemia during pregnancy is thought to increase the risk of maternal mortality but there have been no controlled intervention trials on this question. An association between anaemia and preterm delivery has been reported in several large studies but most placebo-controlled trials have been unable to confirm that anaemia causes prematurity. Maternal iron supplementation during pregnancy can improve both maternal and infant iron status for up to about six months postpartum. Daily supplementation during pregnancy is more effective than weekly supplementation for preventing anaemia, especially severe anaemia. The total amount of iron consumed is the most important predictor of the maternal haemoglobin (Hb) response. In malaria-endemic areas, antimalarial prophylaxis combined with iron supplementation is particularly important for preventing maternal anaemia and LBW. LBW infants are born with very low iron stores, and these are depleted by 2 to 3 months postpartum. Because breastmilk cannot meet their iron requirements, they should be supplemented with iron, starting at 2 months of age.

Anaemia during infancy can result in long term or permanent impairment of psychomotor function, although more studies are needed. Iron supplementation of anaemic preschool children improves their cognitive and physical development. Improved growth of iron-supplemented preschool children and school children has been observed in some studies but not in others. Anaemia is also associated with lower productivity, even in tasks requiring moderate effort such as factory work and housework. Iron deficiency that has not yet progressed to anaemia may also reduce work capacity. Efficacy trials have shown that iron supplements improve the work performance of anaemic individuals.

Except for iron fortification, there have been few attempts to assess the effectiveness of food-based strategies to improve iron status. Increasing intake of vitamin C, through local foods, is probably an inadequate strategy to improve iron status where iron deficiency is prevalent. Targeting animal products to those with the highest iron requirements, and supporting the production of poultry, small livestock and fish, would increase the intake of absorbable iron and other micronutrients. There are strategies available to increase the iron content of plants through genetic enhancement but the efficacy and effectiveness of this approach have not been evaluated. Fortification of foods with iron has produced improvements in iron status in the following countries: Chile, where nationally distributed dry milk, fortified with ferrous sulphate and vitamin C, lowered the prevalence of anaemia in infants from about 27% to close to zero; Ghana, where electrolytic iron, added to a complementary food, reduced anaemia and iron deficiency; India, where double fortification of salt, with iodine and iron, has the potential to prevent both iron and iodine deficiencies and has been effective for improved Hb concentrations; and Venezuela, with fortification of maize and wheat. The search for better fortificants continues. NaFeEDTA has good potential: when added to sugar in a community trial in Guatemala, it increased Hb and ferritin concentrations. Iron added as NaFeEDTA to soy sauce appears to be well absorbed and is being tested in large scale production and fortification trials in the PRC.

For children and adolescents, weekly delivery of iron supplements improves iron status almost as well as daily delivery. Delivery of weekly iron, through schools, community-based programmes etc., may be a cheap, effective way to prevent iron deficiency. However, daily supplements are still more effective for pregnant women. Supplements containing multiple vitamins and minerals could be more effective for improving Hb response than iron alone, because several nutrients are required for Hb synthesis. Multiple micronutrient deficiencies often occur simultaneously and should be prevented and treated. Multiple micronutrient supplements are now being formulated and tested by international organizations.

## Preventing and Treating Iodine Deficiency

Iodine deficiency disorders (IDD) are a serious problem in Asia. Their prevalence in South-East Asia exceeds that in all other regions of the world. The need to eliminate iodine deficiency is very clear, based on its widespread damaging effects and the large numbers of people affected. There are few randomized, placebo-controlled trials of the effects of iodine supplementation. However, the following conclusions are justified.

Salt iodization is by far the most important population-based intervention to combat IDD and has been efficacious where iodine concentrations in the salt were at appropriate levels at the time of consumption. Efforts toward establishing and sustaining national salt iodization programmes have accelerated over recent years. Effective partnerships have been forged between UN agencies, national and international NGOs, and the salt industry. Globally, 68% of households in countries with IDD, now consume iodized salt. Iodization rates are 70% in South-East Asia and 76% in the western Pacific; following the World Health Organization (WHO) definitions of these regions. These figures reflect household survey data where available; otherwise production level data are used as a proxy.

Cretinism results from maternal iodine deficiency during pregnancy. It can be prevented by supplementing the mother during pregnancy, preferably during the first trimester and no later than the second trimester. Supplementation in late pregnancy, if that is the first time the mother can be reached, may still provide some small benefits for infant function. In one iodine deficient region, iodine supplementation, even in the last half of pregnancy substantially reduced infant mortality and improved birthweight. Iodine deficiency during early life adversely affects learning ability, motivation, school performance and general cognitive function. It is not yet clear whether iodine supplementation, if started during childhood, benefits cognitive function. Neither is it clear whether supplementation improves the growth of children. Giving iodized oil to 6-week old infants caused a 72% reduction in mortality in the first two months. In areas where iodine deficiency is prevalent, it may be useful to administer iodized oil to young infants .

## Preventing and Treating Vitamin A Deficiency

The prevalence of clinical vitamin A deficiency (VAD) is quite low. For the last years in which information is available on children in Asia, it ranged from 0.5% in Sri Lanka to 4.5% in Bangladesh. Other age groups are affected as well, especially pregnant and lactating women. A prevalence of >1% indicates a public health problem. Subclinical VAD is much more common, though the actual prevalence is uncertain owing to a paucity of reliable data at national level. The only national surveys of the prevalence of subclinical VAD in Asia are: 18% for the PRC; 50% for Pakistan; and 10% for the Philippines. These estimates were only for preschool children, and it is highly likely that the prevalence is now less where there have been national supplementation programmes. VAD causes: increased morbidity and mortality of infants, children and pregnant women; poor growth of children; and possibly increased mortality and morbidity of infants infected with HIV. It also contributes to anaemia by interfering with iron transport and utilization for Hb synthesis.

The main cause of VAD is low intake of animal products, many of which contain a large amount of retinol. Beta-carotene is the main provitamin A in plants. Although some plants are very high in beta-carotene, this is generally less well absorbed by humans than retinol. Beta-carotene from fruits and squashes is substantially better absorbed than that from leaves and vegetables in general. Populations with the highest prevalence of VAD consume low amounts of animal products and fruits rich in beta-carotene. Breastmilk is the main sources of vitamin A for infants. Clinical symptoms of VAD are rare in breastfeeding infants during the first year of life even where the prevalence of VAD is high. Poor maternal vitamin A status, and subsequently low breastmilk retinol content is a risk factor for the earlier onset of VAD in infants, as is early cessation of breastfeeding. Infection with *Ascaris lumbricoides* lowers serum retinol concentrations. Deworming has improved the values. Poor absorption of vitamin A may also occur in some types of diarrhoea and fever, during which there is also a higher rate of utilization and disposal of the vitamin. In severe protein-energy undernutrition, retinol binding protein synthesis is impaired. Zinc and iron deficiencies also interfere with the utilization and transport of stored retinol.

Most countries where VAD is known to be a major public health problem have policies supporting the regular supplementation of children. This is an approach of known large scale effectiveness that can reach the subpopulations affected by and at risk of, VAD. Supplementation of women during pregnancy reduces their higher prevalence of night blindness in areas of endemic VAD. Night blindness carries a higher risk of maternal morbidity and mortality. Maternal mortality from pregnancy-related causes was reduced by 40% with weekly vitamin A supplements and 49% with weekly beta-carotene supplements, in an area of rural Nepal with high VAD. These results need to be confirmed by further studies. High dose vitamin A supplements cannot be given safely to pregnant women.

A high dose vitamin A supplement given to infants on the day of birth lowered total mortality during the subsequent 4 months, though a multicentre trial of the efficacy of high-dose vitamin A failed to find an impact on mortality or morbidity during the first year of life. It is likely that the dose given was too low to improve infant vitamin A status for long. Maternal supplementation postpartum can improve both maternal and infant vitamin A status, the latter through higher breastmilk content of the vitamin. Meta-analysis has revealed that high dose vitamin A supplementation reduced mortality from diarrhoea and measles by 23% for infants and for children age 6 months to 5 years. Severe diarrhoea was reduced by low dose vitamin A in one study of severely malnourished children, but the reported benefits of high dose vitamin A on diarrhoea-related outcomes have been variable. Little impact has been found on recovery from acute lower respiratory tract infections. Ongoing research will clarify the benefits of vitamin A supplementation in HIV-infected populations. Evidence to date suggests that supplementation of HIV-positive women may improve pregnancy outcome and that supplementation of infected infants and children can reduce mortality.

Food-based strategies have good potential for preventing VAD. Some of food-based interventions have been implemented on a large scale, but few have been evaluated adequately. Significant progress has been made in understanding how to bring about behavioural change in such programmes, and which food-based strategies are likely to be effective for improving vitamin A status. Food-based approaches need to be pursued more vigorously so that they become a larger part of the longer term global strategy for alleviating VAD. However, the recent finding that the bioconversion of provitamin A in dark green leafy vegetables is less than one quarter of that previously thought, has raised doubts about the degree of efficacy of certain diet modification approaches in improving vitamin A status. Breastfeeding promotion, protection, and support remain an essential component of control programmes for young children, as does infectious disease control, not only through immunization, but also via complementary hygiene and sanitation interventions. There is also an urgent need to expand efforts in fortification, where foods reaching the target population groups are processed or where local fortification is feasible. Fortification of oils with vitamin A is mandatory throughout most of South Asia although this is not often enforced. Control approaches, based on improved availability of vitamin A rich foods and possibly genetic modification of staple foods to enhance vitamin A availability, as with iron, have been slower to develop and more difficult to implement, but progress is being made.

## How Effective are Large Scale Interventions?

Most large scale nutrition interventions can potentially affect most of these problems, though there is an extraordinary dearth of well designed evaluations of community-based nutrition interventions. In this section, a series of guidelines is provided for improving the effectiveness, and ultimately the impact, of key nutrition interventions. These derive from lessons learned with past experience in large scale programmatic settings. The key strategies discussed are growth monitoring and promotion, integrated care and nutrition, communications for behavioural change, supplementary feeding for women and young children, school feeding, health-related services, micronutrient supplementation, and food-based strategies.

## Prioritizing Options

Having discussed both the efficacy evidence and the factors conditioning large scale effectiveness of different interventions, this review concludes with a consideration of the process that needs to be initiated for deciding on the type of action or mix of actions that are most appropriate for combating the problem of undernutrition in different situations. The choice will depend on the actual nature and distribution of the malnutrition problem, its causes, and the type of resources that are available. No single intervention or mix of interventions should ever be prescribed in isolation from a participatory process of problem assessment, causal and capacity analysis, and programme design. Cost-benefit and cost-effectiveness analyses may help in deciding priorities. "Key minimum packages" are discussed. As malnutrition usually results from many factors, there are potential synergies between many actions—carried out by multiple actors across sectors—and that the combined effects of such interventions are often not merely additive, but multiplicative. Programme goals should be prioritized with consideration to the level of a country's development. The review concludes by describing the main elements of successful programme management practices. Community-based nutrition intervention programmes in seven Asian countries are summarized in an Appendix.

# AUTHORS

Lindsay H. Allen, Professor
Department of Nutrition
University of California, Davis
One Shields Avenue
Davis, CA 95616-8669 USA
EMAIL: lhallen@ucdavis.edu

Stuart R. Gillespie, Research Fellow
International Food Policy Research Institute,
2033 K Street, Washington, D.C. 20006-1002 USA
EMAIL:  s.gillespie@cgiar.org

# ACKNOWLEDGEMENTS

The authors are indebted to the following, all of whom took considerable time to read through earlier drafts and prepare useful comments: Barbara Underwood, National Academy of Sciences, Washington DC, USA, Professor H.P.S. Sachdev of the Maulana Azad Medical College in New Delhi, Sri Irawati Susalit of the Bureau for Health and Community Nutrition, BAPPENAS, Jakarta, Indonesia, Mohammed Mannan, Chairman of the National Nutrition Council in Dhaka, Bangladesh and Joseph Hunt, senior nutrition economist of the Asian Development Bank (ADB) in Manila, who was the ADB task master for the regional study "ADB Regional Technical Assistance Project 5824: Regional Study of Nutrition Trends, Policies and Strategies in Asia and the Pacific", under which this review was commissioned. Other team members in this process, who have also offered helpful comments and suggestions along the way, include Suresh Babu, Lawrence Haddad, Susan Horton, Venkatesh Mannar and Barry Popkin. We would also like to thank Ginette Mignot of IFPRI for her help in preparing this document, and Roger Pullin in Manila for copy editing.

# TABLE OF CONTENTS

**List of Tables**

## List of Figures

## List of Boxes

# LIST OF ABBREVIATIONS

| | | | |
|---|---|---|---|
| ACC/SCN | Administrative Committee on Coordination (of the United Nations)/Sub-Committee on Nutrition | DSD | District Secretary's Division (Sri Lanka) |
| ADB | Asian Development Bank | ELC | Early Childhood Learning Centre |
| AGW | *Anganwadi* worker (India) | EPI | Expanded Programme on Immunization |
| AKU | Aga Khan University | EU | European Union |
| ANC | Antenatal care | Fe | Iron |
| ANM | Auxiliary Nurse Midwife (India) | FNB | Food and Nutrition Board |
| ARI | Acute respiratory infection | FWA | Family Welfare Assistant (Bangladesh) |
| AusAID | Australian International Development Agency | GM | Growth monitoring |
| BHA | Butylated hydroxyanisole, an antioxidant used to prevent lipid oxidation | GNP | Gross National Product |
| | | HANDS | Health and Nutrition Development Society (Pakistan) |
| BINP | Bangladesh Integrated Nutrition Project | HA | Height-for-age |
| | | Hh | Household |
| BFHI | Baby-Friendly Hospital Initiative (People's Republic of China and Pakistan) | Hb | Haemoglobin |
| | | HKI | Helen Keller International |
| | | ICCIDD | International Coordinating Committee on Iodine Deficiency Disorders |
| BMI | Body mass index measured as weight (in kg) divided by height (in m) squared. | ICDS | Integrated Child Development Services (India) |
| CASD | Community Action for Social Development (Cambodia) | ICRW | International Center for Research on Women |
| CBC | Communications for behavioural change | ICMR | Indian Council for Medical Research |
| | | IDECG | International Dietary Energy Consultative Group |
| CBNC | Community-based nutrition component (Bangladesh) | IDA | Iron deficiency anaemia |
| CDD | Control of diarrhoeal disease | IDD | Iodine deficiency disorders |
| CF | Conceptual Framework | IEC | Information-education-communication |
| CIDA | Canadian International Development Agency | IFPRI | International Food Policy Research Institute |
| CNC | Community Nutrition Center (Bangladesh) | IMCI | Integrated Management of Child Illness |
| CNO | Community Nutrition Organizer (Bangladesh) | INACG | International Nutritional Anaemia Consultative Group |
| CNP | Community Nutrition Promoter (Bangladesh) | INCAP | Instituto de Nutricion de Centro America y Panama |
| CNW | Community Nutrition Worker (India) | IQ | Intelligence quotient |
| CPCC | National Programme of PEM Control for Vietnamese Children | IRDP | Integrated Rural Development Programme (India) |
| CRSP | Collaborative Research Support Programme | IU | International Units |
| DALYs | Disability-adjusted life years | IUGR | Intrauterine growth retardation |
| DPT | Diphtheria-polio-tetanus immunization | IUGR-LBW | Refers to infant's born at term (>37 weeks) with LBW (see below) |

| | | | | |
|---|---|---|---|---|
| JRY | Food-for-work scheme (India) | | ORT | Oral rehydration therapy |
| JFT | Janasaviya Trust Fund (Sri Lanka) | | PAHO | Pan-American Health Organization |
| LA | Length-for-age | | PAR | Population-attributable risk |
| LBW | Low birthweight | | PDS | Public Distribution System (India) |
| LHW | Lady Health Worker (Pakistan) | | PEM | Protein-energy malnutrition |
| LMP | Last menstrual period | | PHM | Public Health Midwife (Sri Lanka) |
| MCH | Mother and child health | | PI | Ponderal index |
| MICS | Multiple Indicator Cluster Survey (UNICEF/Cambodia) | | PNIP | Participatory Nutrition Improvement Project (Sri Lanka) |
| MIS | Management information system | | PRB | Population Reference Bureau |
| MOH | Ministry of Health (Pakistan) | | RE | Retinol Equivalent |
| MOHFW | Ministry of Health and Family Welfare (Bangladesh) | | RETA | Regional Technical Assistance |
| | | | RR | Relative ratio |
| NAS | National Academy of Sciences (USA) | | SGA | Small-for-gestational-age |
| NCHS | National Center for Health Statistics | | $T_3$ | Triiodothyronine |
| NDTF | National Development Trust Fund (Sri Lanka) | | $T_4$ | Thyroxine |
| | | | TB | Tuberculosis |
| NERP | Nutritional Education and Rehabilitation Programme (Viet Nam) | | TBA | Traditional birth attendant (Pakistan) |
| | | | TGR | Total goitre rate |
| NFA | National Food Authority (Philippines) | | TINP | Tamil Nadu Integrated Nutrition Project |
| NGOs | Nongovernmental organizations | | TPDS | Targeted Public Distribution System (India) |
| NIDs | National Immunization Days | | TSH | Thyroid stimulating hormone |
| NIDDEP | National Iodine Deficiency Disorders Elimination Programme (People's Republic of China) | | UNICEF | United Nations Children's Fund |
| | | | UNU | United Nations University |
| | | | USAID | United States Agency for International Development |
| NNMB | National Nutrition Monitoring Bureau | | USI | Universal salt iodization |
| NMMP | National Mid-Day Meals Programme (India) | | VAC | Vitamin A capsule |
| | | | VAD | Vitamin A deficiency |
| NNNCP | National Nutritional Anaemia Control Programme (India) | | VDC | Village Development Committee (Cambodia) |
| NNPA | National Nutrition Plan of Action (Cambodia) | | VAP | Village Action Plan |
| | | | WA | Weight-for-age |
| NRC | National Research Council (USA) | | WH | Weight-for-height |
| NREP | National Rural Employment Programme (India) | | WHO | World Health Organization |
| | | | WL | Weight-for-length |

# GLOSSARY

| | |
|---|---|
| *Anganwadi* | Courtyard in Hindi. Anganwadi workers are community-based workers in Integrated Child Development Services (ICDS) in India |
| **Bayley score** | Performance on the Bayley tests of motor and mental development |
| **Bitot's spots** | Lesions of the conjunctiva that occur in vitamin A deficiency |
| **Body mass index** | A measure of adult nutritional status, essentially thinness; defined as bodyweight in kilograms divided by height in metres squared ($kg/m^2$) |
| *Dais* | Midwives (Pakistan) |
| **Development quotient** | The conversion of raw scores of development to standardized scores; e.g. for motor or mental development. |
| **Eclampsia** | Maternal convulsions in late pregnancy; one symptom of pregnancy-induced hypertension. |
| **Electrolytic iron** | Iron produced by electrolysis; used for fortification |
| **Elemental iron** | A generic term for iron powders produced by various processes (e.g. H-reduced, electrolytic, carbonyl, atomized) and used as food fortificants. |
| *Grama Niladhari* | Administrative unit (Sri Lanka) |
| **Height-for-age** | An indicator of the degree of stunting of a child (see below), defined as his/her height in relation to the median height of a reference population of that age. |
| **Intrauterine growth retardation** | Birthweight below a given low percentile limit for gestational age (e.g., birthweight less than 10th percentile for gestational age); typically reflects inadequate supply of nutrients and oxygen to the foetus. |
| *Jaggery* | Raw sugar |
| **Low birthweight** | Weighing less than 2,500 grams at birth. |
| **Megaloblastic anaemia** | An anaemia characterized by the presence of large, nucleated red blood cells, as occurs in severe folate or vitamin $B_{12}$ deficiency. |
| **Odds ratio** | The ratio of the odds of a condition or disease in an exposed population to the odds of the same condition or disease in a nonexposed population. |
| **Phytates** | Phytic acid combined with minerals. These constitute 1-2% of the weight of whole grain cereals, nuts, seeds and legumes, and impair mineral absorption from these foods. |
| **Population-attributable risk** | In an exposed population of those who have a condition or disease, the proportion for whom this is attributed to being in the exposed (vs. nonexposed) group. |
| **Ponderal index** | Weight/length$^3$; an indicator of wasting in young infants. |
| **Pre-eclampsia** | Development, during pregnancy, of hypertension with proteinuria and/or oedema. |
| **Prelacteal feeding** | The potentially harmful practice of delaying breastfeeding, and feeding the newborn such foods as milk, honey, or sugar water. These prelacteal feeds are unnecessary and can introduce infection in the baby. They also interfere with the physiology of lactation and delay establishment of breastmilk. |
| **Primagravidae** | Women who are in their first pregnancy. |
| **Raven's progressive matrices** | A non-verbal IQ score that is allegedly free from culture bias. |
| **Relative risk** | The ratio of the probability of a condition or disease in an exposed population to the probability of the same condition or disease in a nonexposed population. |
| *Samurdhi* | A poverty alleviation programme in Sri Lanka |
| **Small-for-gestational-age** | At or below the 10th percentile of a birthweight-for-gestational-age curve |

| | |
|---|---|
| **Stunting** | The anthropometric index 'height-for-age' reflects linear growth achieved pre- and postnatally, with deficits indicating longterm, cumulative effects of inadequacies of nutrition and/or health. Shortness in height refers to a child who exhibits low height-for-age that may reflect either normal variation in growth or a deficit in growth. Stunting refers only to shortness that is a deficit, or linear growth that has failed to reach genetic potential as a result, most proximally, of the interaction between poor diet and disease. Stunting is defined as low height-for-age; i.e., below 2 standard deviations (or 2 Z-scores) of the median value of the National Center for Health Statistics/World Health Organization International Growth Reference for length- or height-for-age |
| **Teratogenic** | Causing abnormal foetal development, such as birth defects. |
| **Thalassaemia minor** | Thalassaemias are inherited disorders in which haemoglobin synthesis is impaired. Thalassaemia minor is the heterozygous form and is usually asymptomatic, with a mild hypochromic, macrocytic anaemia. |
| *Thana* | Administrative district in Bangladesh (see "union") |
| *Thriposha* | Supplementary feeding programme in Sri Lanka |
| **Total goitre rate** | The prevalence of goitre (enlargement of the thyroid gland) in a specific population group, usually expressed as a percentage. Goitre reflects significant iodine deficiency in the population. |
| **Underweight** | The anthropometric index 'weight-for-age' represents body mass relative to age. Weight-for-age is influenced by the height of the child and his or her weight and is thus a composite of stunting and wasting (which makes its interpretation difficult). In the absence of wasting, both weight-for-age and height–for-age reflect the long term nutrition and health experience of the individual or population. General lightness in weight refers to a child having a low weight-for-age. Lightness may represent either normal variation or a deficit. Underweight specifically refers to lightness that is a deficit and is defined as low weight-for-age, i.e.; below 2 standard deviations (or 2 Z-scores) of the median value of the National Center for Health Statistics/World Health Organization International Growth Reference for weight-for-age. |
| **Undernutrition** | A condition in which the body contains lower than normal amounts of one or more nutrients. |
| **Union** | Administrative unit (Bangladesh) |
| **Wasting** | A recent and severe process that has produced a substantial weight loss, usually as a consequence of acute starvation and/or severe disease. Chronic dietary deficit or disease can also lead to wasting. The anthropometric index 'weight-for-height' reflects body weight relative to height. Thinness refers to low weight-for-height and may indicate normal variation or a deficit in weight. Wasting refers to thinness that is a deficit, defined as low weight-for-height, i.e., below 2 standard deviations (or 2 Z-scores) of the median value of the National Center for Health Statistics/World Health Organization International Growth Reference for weight-for-height. The statistically expected prevalence of wasting (as with underweight and stunting) is between 2-3%, given the normal distribution of wasting rates. |
| **Weight-for-age** | An indicator of the degree of underweight of a child (see above), defined as his/her weight in relation to the median weight of a reference population of that age. |
| **Weight-for-height** | An indicator of the degree of wasting of a child (see above), defined as his/her weight in relation to the median height of a reference population of that age. |
| **Z-score** | The deviation of an individual's value from the median value of a reference population, divided by the standard deviation of the reference population. |

# INTRODUCTION

This review tracks the life cycle impacts of undernutrition in the developing world, especially in the low income countries of the Asia-Pacific region. After highlighting the dynamics of cause and consequence, it considers interventions: first from an efficacy perspective, then with regard to large scale effectiveness. Another paper[1] focuses on the problem of overnutrition. These papers were prepared under the Asian Development Bank (ADB) – International Food Research Institute (IFPRI) Regional Technical Assistance Project RETA 5824 on Nutrition Trends, Policies and Strategies in Asia and the Pacific.

Undernutrition may be indicated by foetal growth retardation, low body mass index (BMI), stunting, wasting, underweight, anaemia, and micronutrient deficiencies. Five major nutrition problems in developing countries, with a special emphasis on Asia, are reviewed here: low birthweight (LBW); early childhood growth failure; anaemia; iodine deficiency disorders ( IDD); and vitamin A deficiency ( VAD). For each of these, the nature of the problem, its prevalence, distribution, consequences and causes, are discussed; followed by a review of the efficacy of key nutrition interventions. The effectiveness of large scale programmes is then reviewed, and the process for selecting and prioritizing options discussed.

A nutrition intervention is defined here as one that has the prevention or reduction of undernutrition as at least one of its primary objectives. Such interventions are usually intended to have an impact on the main immediate causes of undernutrition, namely, inadequate dietary intake, poor caring practices, and disease. These determinants are strongly interrelated in a synergistic cycle (Figure 1).

The interventions reviewed here are primarily community-based, although they may or may not be community-driven. They include: breastfeeding promotion; growth monitoring and promotion; communication for behavioural change (CBC), including improved complementary feeding, supplementary feeding, and micronutrient supplementation. Nutrition interventions through health services are also reviewed

briefly. Fortification of essential foods, an approach to micronutrient deficiency, and approaches to improve household food security are also discussed in separate papers[2, 3]. Maternal and child care in the region have also been reviewed[4] and only highlights are reiterated here.

The starting point of this review is a description of the nutrition situation in developing countries, especially in Asia. It concludes with a series of guidelines for maximizing the effectiveness of large scale interventions. Specific issues of coverage, targeting, intensity, programme design, implementation, management, monitoring, evaluation and institutional capacity development are not covered, as these have been dealt with elsewhere[5, 6, 7].

## Undernutrition Throughout the Life Cycle

Undernutrition often starts *in utero* and may extend throughout the life cycle. It also spans generations. Undernutrition occurs during pregnancy, childhood, and adolescence, and has a cumulative negative impact on the birthweight of future babies. A baby who has suffered intrauterine growth retardation (IUGR) as a foetus is effectively born malnourished, and has a much higher risk of dying in infancy. Survivors are unlikely to catch up significantly on this lost growth and are more likely to experience developmental deficits. Moreover, the consequences of being born malnourished extend into adulthood. Strong epidemiological evidence suggests a link between maternal and early childhood undernutrition and increased adult risk of various chronic diseases.

During infancy and early childhood, frequent or prolonged infections and inadequate intakes of nutrients (particularly energy, iron, protein, vitamin A, and zinc) may add to the contribution of IUGR to preschool underweight and stunting. Underlying such immediate causes will be inadequacies in one or more of the three main preconditions for good nutrition: food, care and health. Most growth failure occurs from

**FIGURE 1:   Undernutrition throughout the life cycle**

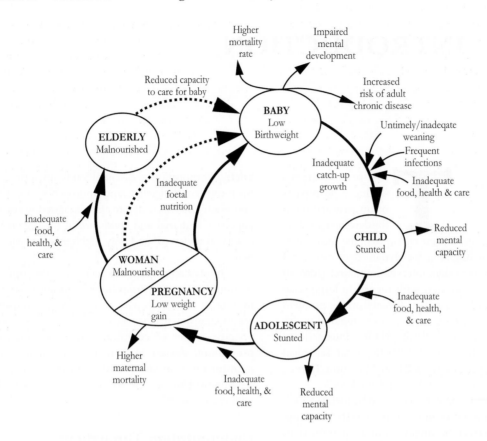

Source:   Adapted from ACC/SCN (2000) *Fourth Report on the World Nutrition Situation.* Geneva: ACC/SCN in collaboration with the International Food Policy Research Institute.

before birth until two to three years of age. A child who is stunted at five years of age is likely to remain stunted throughout life.

Apart from the indirect effects on the mother, micronutrient deficiencies during pregnancy have serious implications for the developing foetus. Iodine deficiency disorders may cause foetal brain damage or stillbirth. Folate deficiency may result in neural tube or other birth defects and preterm delivery, and both iron deficiency anaemia and vitamin A deficiency may have significant implications for the future infant's morbidity and mortality risk, vision and cognitive development.

In adolescence, a second period of rapid growth may serve as a window of opportunity, albeit limited, for compensating for growth failure in early childhood. However, even if the child catches up some lost growth, the effects of early childhood undernutrition on cognitive development and behaviour may not be fully redressed. A stunted girl is likely to become a stunted adolescent and later a stunted woman. Apart from

direct effects on her health and productivity, adult stunting and underweight increase the chance that her children will be born with LBW. And so the cycle turns.

## Research on Interventions to Combat Undernutrition

The research process through which interventions are designed to combat undernutrition is a dynamic and iterative step-by-step process as follows:  i. describe the problem; ii. identify risk factors;  iii. explore the context and identify the determinants; iv. select or formulate possible interventions; v. test interventions in carefully controlled double-blind efficacy trials; vi. formulate public nutrition interventions; vii. assess the efficacy of public nutrition interventions (e.g., through community-based trials); viii. assess the effectiveness of public nutrition interventions (e.g., at the national level); and ix. monitor the adequacy and impact of large scale, public nutrition interventions.

Not all of these steps are needed in every case, but it is important to realize that there is a big difference between steps vii and viii. Efficacy refers to the impact of an intervention under ideal conditions, when the components of the intervention (e.g., food supplements) are delivered directly to all individuals in the target group (i.e., 100% coverage). This is more likely to occur in research with a high level of supervision over delivery of the programme and the careful measurement of outcomes. Such trials demonstrate potential; i.e., what can optimally be achieved. Any new approach to controlling a particular nutrition problem should be subjected initially to efficacy trials, to determine whether a biological impact is actually possible in ideal conditions (step v). Only then should the ensuing steps be taken to introduce the intervention as part of a large scale programme. Effectiveness refers to the impact of an intervention under real world conditions, when programmes are scaled up to reach large populations. Small scale efficacy does not easily translate into large scale effectiveness and impact.

## Conceptual Framework

The life cycle depicted in Figure 1 shows how various nutrition problems, causes, and consequences change and interact over time. To understand better what causes such problems, it is necessary to consider systematically the causes of undernutrition at different levels in society. The widely used food-care-health conceptual framework (Figure 2) illustrates these causes, and their interactions, at three levels: immediate, underlying, and basic. The synergistic interaction between the two immediate causes (inadequate dietary intake and disease) fuels a vicious cycle that accounts for much of the high morbidity and mortality in developing countries. Three groups of underlying factors contribute to inadequate dietary intake and infectious disease: household food insecurity, inadequate maternal and child care, and poor health services in an unhealthy environment. These underlying causes are, in turn, underpinned by basic causes that relate to the amount, control, and use of various resources[8].

**FIGURE 2: Causes of undernutrition in society**

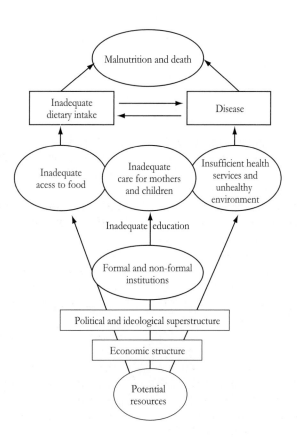

Source:  UNICEF (1990) *Strategy for Improved Nutrition of Children and Women in Developing Countries*.  New York: UNICEF.

This framework is used as an organizing principle for discussions of aetiology and approaches to remedial action. Nutrition-relevant interventions are also designed to impact at the underlying level to combat inadequacies in one or more of the main preconditions (food, care, and health) usually at the household and/or community levels.

Poverty is both a fundamental cause and an outcome of undernutrition. Economic losses from undernutrition include, as percentages of total losses from all causes: foregone human productivity, 10-15%; foregone GDP, 5-10%; and losses in children's disability-adjusted life years (DALYs), 20-25%[9]. Not only is economic growth foregone, but it is foregone for the poor, who need it the most. Nutrition-fuelled economic growth promises to reduce income inequality. Moreover, improved nutrition is a particularly powerful antipoverty intervention because it can be achieved at low cost and it has a lifelong impact. In terms of a propoor, economic growth strategy that is sustainable, investment in nutrition is one of the best options.

# PREVENTING LOW BIRTHWEIGHT

The prevalence of low birthweight (LBW) is higher in Asia than elsewhere[10], predominantly because of undernutrition of the mother before pregnancy, exacerbated by undernutrition during pregnancy. About 60% of women in South Asia and 40% in South-East Asia are underweight (<45 kg), 40% of them are thin, with body mass index (BMI) <18.5, and more than 15% are stunted (<145 cm)[11]. Being of low weight at birth has a profoundly adverse effect on the health and development of the neonate. It is a risk factor for stunting, which starts *in utero* and becomes worse if the diet or health status is inadequate during postnatal development. LBW is probably the main reason why over 50% of the children in South Asia are underweight[12]. The adverse consequences of LBW continue to be manifested during childhood, and are passed on to the next generation when women, who have been chronically undernourished in their past, become pregnant. LBW and subsequent stunting are caused by undernutrition and other health problems, rather than by racial or ethnic differences. Improvements in maternal nutrition and health can increase birthweight, survival and growth of the child, and subsequent size and function (including health, productivity and mental performance) in adult life.

Drawing on much recent work[13], the prevalence, consequences and causes of LBW, and the efficacy of nutrition interventions aimed at preventing LBW are reviewed here. The main focus is on interventions during pregnancy, but approaches to improving adolescent nutrition status are also reviewed. Micronutrient interventions are evaluated from the perspective of their effect on birthweight, rather than on micronutrient deficiency, which is addressed later. Recommendations are made about the nature, timing and targeting of nutrition interventions to improve pregnancy outcome. Many non-nutrition or indirect interventions, such as immunization and sanitation, have significant nutrition effects[9] but these are beyond the scope of this review.

## Definitions and Indicators

Numerous terms have been used to describe infants who are born smaller than is desirable. Many of these are confusing, overlapping, and of limited practical value in developing countries. The focus here is on the most practical and commonly applied terms. LBW is defined as weighing less than 2,500 g at birth. It is one of the most common statistics because it requires a single measurement, weight at birth, and no information about gestational age. There are two main causes of LBW: being born small for gestational age, or being born prematurely. In developing countries, the majority of LBW infants are small but are not born prematurely. Nevertheless, 6.7% of LBW infants are born preterm in developing countries[14].

To deal with the influence of prematurity, a World Health Organization (WHO) Expert Committee proposed the term "IUGR-LBW" ("Intrauterine Growth Retardation – Low Birthweight")[15, 16]. This refers to infants born at term (>37 weeks of gestation) with LBW (<2,500 g). It replaces the older term "small-for-gestational-age" (SGA). It is often difficult or impossible to assess gestational age accurately. For example, using ultrasound rather than the reported date of the last menstrual period (LMP) lowers the estimated prevalence of SGA by about 30 to 50% in developed countries[17, 18]. In Asia, LBW (including preterm infants) estimates are only slightly higher than IUGR-LBW estimates (Table 1).

This means that, for practical purposes, LBW is a valid indicator of the prevalence of IUGR. A regression equation, developed using data from 60 countries where both LBW and gestational age data were recorded[10], can be used to convert LBW to IUGR-LBW. An important caveat is that both the LBW and IUGR-LBW definitions exclude infants who weigh more than 2,500 g at birth, but less than the 3,300-3,500 g birthweight of well nourished infants in developing countries. Many of these "smaller than normal" infants are likely to have been IUGR and will probably suffer adverse functional consequences of their suboptimal weight. The IUGR-LBW category also

TABLE 1: Incidence (%) of low birthweight (LBW) and LBW with intrauterine growth retardation (IUGR-LBW) in some Asian countries

| Country, location | Year | LBW (%) | IUGR-LBW (%) |
|---|---|---|---|
| People's Republic of China, 6 subdistricts of Shanghai | 1981-1982 | 4.2 | 3.4 |
| India, Pune | 1990 | 28.2 | 24.8 |
| Indonesia, Bogor area | 1983 | 10.5 | 8.0 |
| Myanmar, rural and urban | 1981-1982 | 17.8 | 12.7 |
| Nepal, rural | 1990 | 14.3 | 11.8 |
| Nepal, urban | 1990 | 22.3 | 18.2 |
| Sri Lanka, rural | 1990 | 18.4 | 15.8 |
| Thailand, rural and urban | 1979-80 | 9.6 | 6.9 |
| Viet Nam, Hanoi + 1 rural district | 1982-1984 | 5.2 | 4.2 |

Source: Modified from de Onis M, Blossner M, Villar J (1998) Levels and patterns of intrauterine growth retardation in developing countries. *European Journal of Clinical Nutrition* 52: S5-S15.

excludes preterm infants who were IUGR. For these reasons, the IUGR-LBW category substantially underestimates the true magnitude of intrauterine growth retardation. Defining IUGR as a birthweight below the 10th percentile of the international 'birthweight for gestational age' curve[16], has given, on average, incidences that are 14.5% higher than when the IUGR-LBW definition is used[10].

## Wasting or Stunting *in utero*

The foetus undergoes its maximum increase in length at 20-30 weeks of gestation, and in weight during the third trimester[19]. Therefore, the timing of undernutrition *in utero* has different effects on weight and length. Stunted (also called symmetrically or proportionately growth-retarded) infants have a normal ponderal index (PI) (defined as weight/length$^3$) but their weight, length, head and abdominal circumferences are below the 10th percentile of reference values. Wasted (asymmetrically or disproportionately growth retarded) infants have a relatively normal length and head circumference, but their body weights and PIs are low due to a lack of fat, and sometimes of lean tissue. Wasting is thought to result from undernutrition that occurs late in pregnancy, when fat deposition is most rapid. Only 1% of foetal body weight is fat at 26 weeks compared to 12% at 38 weeks. However, stunting may reflect undernutrition throughout pregnancy[14]. The postnatal development and function of wasted newborns is distinctly different from those who are stunted.

## Prevalence of Intrauterine Growth Retardation (IUGR)

In developing countries, IUGR has been estimated to affect between 14 and 20 million infants per year[10], or as many as 30 million[11]. Fourteen million is equivalent to 11% of all births in developing countries[10]. The higher estimates may be closer to reality because most birthweight data are obtained from clinics and, in developing countries, babies born at home are more likely to have LBW. Nevertheless, these estimates provide a useful basis from which to target attention and to allocate resources.

Rates of IUGR-LBW can be categorized as percentages of all births, as follows: low (<5%), moderate (5-10%), high (10-15%) and very high (>15%). For LBW and IUGR-LBW respectively, the highest incidences are found in South Central Asia (28%, 33%). The average prevalence is 11% of births in all developing countries, and about 21% in South-East Asia[10] (Table 2). At the national level, the highest incidences for LBW and IUGR-LBW respectively are: Bangladesh (50%, 39%), India (28%, 21%) and Pakistan (25%, 18%). For other Asian countries, the corresponding data are: Sri Lanka (19%, 13%); Cambodia (18%, 12%); Viet Nam and the Philippines (11%, 6%); Indonesia and Malaysia (8%, 4%); Thailand (8%, 3%), and the People's Republic of China (PRC) (6%, 2%)[10].

TABLE 2:   Estimated incidence (%) and expected numbers of low birthweight (LBW) and LBW with intrauterine growth retarded (IUGR-LBW) infants in developing countries in 2000

| | Incidence (%) (<2,500 g) [b] | LBW Expected No. (thousands) [c] | Incidence (%) (<2,500 g; [3] 37 weeks) | IUGR-LBW Expected No. (thousands) [c] |
|---|---|---|---|---|
| *Africa* [a] | n.a. | n.a. | n.a. | n.a. |
| Eastern | n.a. | n.a. | n.a. | n.a. |
| Middle | 21.3 | 853 | 14.9 | 597 |
| Northern | n.a. | n.a. | n.a. | n.a. |
| Southern | n.a. | n.a. | n.a. | n.a. |
| Western | 17.2 | 1,451 | 11.4 | 962 |
| *Asia* [d] | *18.0* | *13,774* | *12.3* | *9,344* |
| Eastern [c] | 5.8 | 1,250 | 1.9 | 409 |
| South Central | 28.3 | 10,917 | 20.9 | 8,062 |
| South Eastern | 10.3 | 1,190 | 5.6 | 647 |
| Western | 8.3 | 417 | 4.5 | 226 |
| *Oceania* [e] | *15.0* | *29.2* | *9.8* | *19* |
| Melanesia | 15.4 | 29 | 9.9 | 19 |
| Micronesia | n.a. | n.a. | n.a. | n.a. |
| Polynesia | 4.0 | 0.2 | 0.2 | 0.03 |
| **All developing countries** | *16.4* | *17,436* | *11.0* | *11,677* |

[a] The nomenclature of subregions follows that of the United Nations
[b] Source: de Onis M, Blossner M., Villar J (1998) Levels and patterns of intrauterine growth retardation in developing countries. *European Journal of Clinical Nutrition* 52: S5-S15.
[c] Total live births for 2000 are based on the UN (1998) World Population Prospects. New York: United Nations.
[d] Excludes Japan.
[e] Excludes Australia and New Zealand.
n.a. = not applicable because the coverage of live births was < 80%.

## Consequences of Low Birthweight

### Increased Mortality and Morbidity

Whether a newborn infant is stunted or wasted has an important influence on its future development. For example, stunted infants have a higher neonatal mortality than those who are wasted, and also contribute most to poor child survival and development. Wasted infants demonstrate more postpartum weight catch-up[20, 21], whereas stunted infants tend not to catch up to the reference growth norms.

Infants who weigh 2,000-2,499 g at birth have a four-fold higher risk of neonatal death than those who weigh 2,500-2,999 g, and a ten-fold higher risk than those weighing 3,000 - 3,499 g[22]. The more severe the growth restriction within the LBW category, the higher the risk of death. For example, weighing more than 2,500 g but less than 3,000 g at birth, also carries a greater risk for neonatal mortality and morbidity. This is especially true for infants with a low PI[23]. For a given birthweight, being born small because of preterm delivery is a stronger risk factor for perinatal mortality than if the smallness is due to growth restriction[22]. Being born preterm, as well as having LBW carries the strongest risk of mortality[10]. IUGR and LBW infants are more susceptible to hypoglycaemia and to birth asphyxia. In a substantial number of studies they suffered more diarrhoea and pneumonia for a few months after birth[22], explaining in part why LBW is also a risk factor for postneonatal death.

In the few studies from which data are available during the first weeks of life, wasted, LBW newborns experienced more morbidity[21, 23, 24] whereas stunted newborns were more likely to die during this time[25, 26]. This may reflect the greater capacity for the LBW infant to catch up in weight and immune function. The impaired immunocompetence of stunted infants is more likely to persist. In a retrospective study in The Gambia[27], being born during and up to two months after the so-called "hungry season" was a strong predictor of mortality after age 15 years. Being born in the hungry season was also associated with about a four-fold greater risk of dying between the ages of 15 and 45 years, and a ten-fold greater risk of dying between the ages of 35 and 45 years. The deaths were mostly related to infections, or to childbirth in women, and were probably caused by the effects of undernutrition *in utero* on development of the immune system.

## Greater Risk of Stunting

Weight at birth is a strong predictor for size in later life because most IUGR infants do not catch-up to normal size during childhood. In Asian countries, such as Bangladesh, the PRC, India, Pakistan, the Philippines and Sri Lanka, the incidence of LBW predicts the prevalence of underweight during preschool and subsequent years[5].

A review of 12 studies that provided data on the subsequent growth of IUGR infants (preterm infants excluded) revealed that they underwent partial catch-up growth during their first two years of life[28]. After age 2 years, there was little further catch-up and the IUGR infants remained stunted during the rest of their childhood, adolescence and adult life. At 17 to 19 years of age, males and females who were born IUGR-LBW were about 5 cm shorter and weighed 5 kg less than those who were not born IUGR-LBW. Importantly, the magnitude of these differences is similar in developed and developing countries. This suggests that, as a general rule, later undernutrition does not magnify the impact of IUGR. Controlling for maternal height did reduce the influence of birthweight on size at 17-19 years, but birthweight remained a significant predictor. Low maternal height is in itself a reflection of prior undernutrition. Menarche and maturation are probably not delayed by being born IUGR[29].

From a Guatemala longitudinal study[28], data are available on a subset of children followed from birth to adolescence. Although the length Z-scores of the IUGR infants tended to catch up somewhat by 3 years of age, the absolute increments in length were the same for children born IUGR, both with birthweights 2,500 – 3,000 g and 3,000 – 3,500 g. In other words, IUGR children actually grew the same amount during the first 3 years of life as those with a heavier birthweight. The apparent catch-up in Z-scores is an artefact, due to the splayed distribution of these scores: smaller children improved their Z-scores more per unit growth[28]. The above-mentioned studies illustrate that the size and nutritional status of pregnant women are more important than postnatal factors as determinants of the growth of their children in later life.

## Poor Neurodevelopmental Outcomes

LBW infants are more likely to experience developmental deficits. Undernutrition that affects head circumference before 26 weeks of pregnancy has a greater impact on neurologic function than does undernutrition later in pregnancy[30]. The adverse effects of early childhood undernutrition on behaviour and cognitive development may not be fully redressed, even with better diet and care later. In the USA, from a collaborative study on births between 1959 and 1965, the mean IQ scores at four years of age for each birthweight group were: 737-2,000 g, 94; 2,000-2,500 g, 101; and 2,500-3,000 g, 103. A study of the association between IUGR and cognitive development and behaviour in the first six years of life[31] concluded that deficits in performance of the IUGR group began to appear between 1 and 2 years of age. These deficits were larger in high risk subgroups; e.g., those who were born smallest, or when IUGR occurred early in pregnancy. The size of the difference was less at 4 to 7 years of age. However, it is unclear whether IUGR followed by good postnatal nutrition has a measurable effect on cognitive or behavioural development in adolescence, because of dilution by many socio-environmental influences on development[32].

## Reduced Strength and Work Capacity

In the Guatemala longitudinal study[28], males and females at an average of 15 years of age, who were born IUGR, performed significantly more poorly on tests of strength, compared to those born weighing at least 2,500 g[28, 33]. Specifically, they could apply approximately 2 to 3 kg less force to a hand grip dynamometer. The lower work capacity of adults who were IUGR babies is mostly attributable to their lower fat-free mass. IUGR has a serious adverse impact on later work productivity and income generating potential.

## Increased Risk of Chronic Disease

The consequences of LBW probably continue throughout life[1]. The risk of diseases such as hypertension, coronary heart disease, stroke and noninsulin dependent diabetes (together called "syndrome X"), are associated with size, wasting and stunting at birth[34, 35]. The association between adult disease risk and birthweight is seen across the range of birthweights, not just LBW. In developing countries, there is evidence that mortality from infections during early adulthood is higher in individuals who were malnourished *in utero*[27]. IUGR may cause individuals to be programmed differently, as a result of their adaptations to adverse *in utero* environments: the concept of 'foetal programming'[1, 36]. This hypothesis has been challenged[37, 38]. The magnitude of effects of intrauterine and early childhood growth retardation on future disease risks has been recently reviewed[1]. Further work comparing such effects with those of other lifestyle factors is needed.

## Causes of Intrauterine Growth Retardation

Undernutrition is the major determinant of IUGR in developing countries. It has been estimated[39] that about 50% of all IUGR in rural areas of developing countries is attributable to small maternal size at conception (low weight and short stature), and low gestational weight gain. Other important causes include malaria in endemic areas[40] and maternal infections that can cause loss of appetite, higher nutrient losses or requirements, abnormal placental blood flow or structure, or foetal infections[41].

In developed countries, where maternal undernutrition is relatively uncommon, the majority of LBW is caused by premature delivery. Cigarette smoking during pregnancy is the most important factor causing IUGR, followed by low gestational weight gain and low BMI at conception[42]. There is increasing evidence that deficiencies of some micronutrients, such as folic acid, increase the risk of preterm delivery.

## Prenatal Food Supplementation

Many nutrition interventions have been tested for their ability to improve birthweight and other aspects of pregnancy outcome. However, most of these trials had serious limitations: e.g., lack of a control group; failure to randomize treatments; large number of drop-outs; distribution to other household members of foods intended for the pregnant woman; small sample size; or the inappropriate nature of an intervention.

This summary of the efficacy of interventions to improve pregnancy outcome uses the Cochrane Library's Pregnancy and Childbirth Database 2001. Other reviewers have used a similar approach[43]. Cochrane-based systematic reviews are frequently updated, meta-analyses of intervention trials that meet certain criteria, including: random controlled design, prevention of systematic errors, good execution of the intervention; and adequate assessment of outcomes. The design and limitations of each trial are considered and discussed, and may influence the conclusions. Databases on randomized clinical trials have the advantage that they combine data across studies. It has been estimated that a sample size of at least 200 women per group is needed to detect an intervention-induced increase in birthweight of 100 g[44]. Many individual trials do not come close to having an adequate sample size. Combining studies from

different locations also makes the results more generalizable, especially where the outcome is susceptible to nonintervention influences, and where the effect of the intervention is relatively small. This is indeed the case for birthweight and other measures of pregnancy outcome. The results of meta-analyses need to be interpreted with caution, however, keeping in mind that most of the trials have usually been conducted in developed countries, where there is a low prevalence of undernutrition, and that the results may not translate easily into policy decisions.

### Beneficial Nutrition Interventions

In a Cochrane analysis, maternal supplements that provided balanced protein and energy were the only intervention that improved birthweight[45]. These balanced supplements were defined as foods that provided less than 25% of their energy content as protein. No minimum protein content was defined. Fourteen such trials were subjected to analysis. Supplementation was associated with modest increases in maternal weight gain, a small but significant increase in birthweight, and smaller, nonsignificant increases in birth length and head circumference. SGA prevalence was reported in seven of the trials: from Bogota, Colombia; East Java, Indonesia; Harlem, New York City, USA; India; Taipei,China; Thailand; and Wales, U.K. Overall the supplements decreased the prevalence of SGA babies, although this was of borderline significance[45]. Overall there was a 32% reduction in risk of SGA, a 21 g per week higher maternal weight gain and a 32 g increase in birthweight. A significant reduction in stillbirths and neonatal deaths was found in three of the four trials in which it was assessed.

Among these studies, three were carried out in Asia, two of which had very small sample sizes. In India, 20 women of low socioeconomic status were given 417 kcal and 30 g protein daily in the form of 50 g sesame cake, 40 g of *jaggery* (raw sugar) and 10 g oil[46]. There was no intervention in the control group. Birthweights were not significantly different. The means were 2,939 g in the experimental group and 2,676 g in the control group. The SGA prevalence was 0/10 in the experimental group, compared to 5/10 in controls. No data were presented on food intake, so the supplement may have partially substituted for the usual diet rather than adding to it. Reported energy intakes were higher before supplementation. A study in Thailand was also small, involving 43 healthy women at a mean of 28 weeks gestation[47]. They were fed one of two different supplements that each provided an additional 350 kcal and 13 g protein per day as typical foods. The control group received no intervention. Again there was no information on dietary substitution, but mean birthweight was significantly higher in the supplemented women (3,096 g compared to 2,853 g in the controls). The prevalence of SGA was 0/28 in the intervention group compared to 2/15 in the unsupplemented group.

An Indonesian study of 747 clearly undernourished women in East Java, found no significant effect of a supplement on birthweight (2,908 g and 2,948 g in the experimental and control groups respectively) or SGA[48]. The mean birthweights were 2,908 g in the experimental group and 3,948 g in the control group. Women in the experimental group were provided with a supplement containing 465 kcal and 7.1 g protein per day, and those in the control group received 52 kcal and 6.2 g protein per day. The intervention started at 26-28 weeks gestation. In the experimental group, 29/258 infants were SGA, compared to 24/252 in the control group. Again substitution of usual foods by the supplement, and its distribution to other household members, were not assessed. Also, the study was carried out during a period when there was a remarkable improvement in birthweight in East Java, which might have affected the ability of the intervention group to respond, as well as the status of the control group[49].

The Cochrane meta-analysis included the most recent trial in The Gambia[50]. This has caused a resurgence of interest in the benefits of supplementing pregnant women with energy and protein. This trial provides a valuable example of an effective intervention. It was a study of 1,460 different women, with 2,047 births in 28 rural villages. There is no doubt that the women were chronically undernourished, especially during the hungry season when weight loss averaged 3-6 kg due to scarcity of food and heavy energy demands for agricultural work. At recruitment, their average weight was 53 kg and their BMI 21.0. From mid-pregnancy, the women were provided with locally prepared biscuits made from groundnuts, rice flour, sugar, and groundnut oil. These biscuits provided 1,017 kcal, 22 g protein, 56 g fat, 47 mg calcium and 1.8 mg iron per day. Project staff observed their consumption. Control villages were not supplemented. The supplements produced remarkable improvements in pregnancy outcome: average birthweight increased by 136 g; LBW decreased by 39%; and head circumference increased, on average, by 3.1 mm. Length was not affected, nor was gestational age. In the hungry season, the differences were even greater: 201 g for birthweight; 3.9 mm for head circumference; 0.41 cm (significant) for length; and LBW 42% lower. Importantly, a similar seasonal difference was found in an earlier study where supplementation averaged only 430 kcal/day[51].

The more recent trial 50 recorded 40 neonatal (days 1-28) deaths in the control group compared to 25 in the intervention group, but no difference in deaths during the remainder of the first year of life. This is the same community for which being born in the hungry season carries a major excess of premature adult mortality [27].

Why was this study able to show such a large impact of supplementation? Contributing factors probably included the following: the mothers were undernourished and in energy deficit prior to supplementation; the supplement was high in energy and contained a substantial amount of protein; the biscuits were actually consumed by the mothers; and the sample size was large. Interestingly the supplements did not provide much in the way of micronutrients. The women were given routine iron-folate supplements but not multiple micronutrients. It is remarkable that supplementation here did not start until 20-24 weeks of gestation and the women came for their biscuits only on an average of 82 days. Starting sooner might have had an even greater impact. The biscuits were culturally acceptable and produced locally, providing a sustainable method of supplementation.

## Nonbeneficial Nutrition Interventions

It does not appear to be useful to replace dietary energy with supplements that contain more protein. In a Cochrane meta-analysis, three trials were considered in which some of women's usual dietary energy had been "isocalorically" replaced with a balanced (<25% energy as protein) protein-energy supplement . Two of these trials were conducted in Birmingham, England, on 153 and 130 women of Asian descent[52, 53]. In the first of these[52], the supplement provided 273 kcal/day, of which 11% was protein, and both the supplement and the placebo contained vitamins and minerals. In the second[53], the supplement provided 425 kcal/day, 10% as protein, and again both groups were given vitamins and minerals. In both studies, the controls received the same amount of energy but no supplemental protein. The third trial, in Chile, involved 683 low income women, prior to 20 weeks of gestation, who had a low weight-for-height at their first prenatal visit[54]. They were given a high protein (22% of energy), milk-based supplement. The controls had an isocaloric supplement that contained 12% kcal as protein and even more vitamins and minerals than the high protein group. The meta-analysis of these three trials included 966 women, most of whom were from the Chilean study. When protein intake was increased, without raising energy intake, there were trends to lower maternal weight gain and lower birthweight, and a higher risk of SGA births.

There was no effect on gestational age or incidence of preterm birth.

Maternal supplementation with high protein supplements (>25% of the energy content) may affect pregnancy outcome adversely in well nourished populations. Two trials were identified for a Cochrane meta-analysis. In the district of Harlem in New York City, 1,051 women entered a study before 30 weeks of gestation and were provided with a supplement containing 470 kcal and 40 g protein per day, vitamins, and minerals[55]. The control group received a supplement containing 322 kcal and 6g protein per day, plus vitamins and minerals. The second study was based on 25 Indian women of low socioeconomic status in Hyderabad, India. They were employed in manual labour and had low protein and energy intakes at 36 weeks of gestation. The trial provided hospitalization, a hospital diet and a supplement containing 350 kcal/day, 35 g protein, iron and vitamins[56]. The control group received the same treatments except that their supplement did not contain protein. The meta-analysis of the two studies reflected mostly the results of the much larger Harlem trial. The protein supplement resulted in a small, nonsignificantly higher weight gain, a higher (but again nonsignificant) increase in neonatal death in the Harlem group, and no greater foetal growth. There were no differences in infant growth or mental or motor development assessed by the Bayley scale one year later.

## Optimizing Interventions

When designing the most effective nutrition interventions for pregnant women, it is important to know: i) who would benefit most; ii) the stage of pregnancy when the supplement would be most effective; and iii) the optimal nutrient composition of supplemental food. There is limited information available from the literature on all three of these questions, but some general guidelines can be drawn.

### Targeting Supplements to Undernourished Women

A Cochrane meta-analysis[45] concluded that the increment in birthweight due to supplementation was no larger in those women who were undernourished prior to or during pregnancy. However, the group defined as being "undernourished" included women in New York City, and short or thin women in Aberdeen, Scotland. The "well nourished" group included women with marginal diets in Taipei,China who normally consumed 40g protein or less per day. Contrary to the conclusion of the meta-analysis, there is some evidence across individual studies to suggest

that the most undernourished women may benefit most from supplementation, as discussed in the following sections. Discussion of this evidence requires being able to identify women at greatest risk of IUGR. The best predictors are as follows.

### Best Predictors for Women at Greatest Risk of IUGR

#### Prepregnancy Weight

The WHO Collaborative Study on Maternal Anthropometry and Pregnancy Outcomes data[15], collected between 1959 and 1989, on 111,000 women in 25 populations across the world, show that being in the lowest quartile of prepregnancy weight carries an elevated risk of IUGR of 2.5, compared to the upper quartile. A preconception weight of 40 kg (assuming average height is 150 cm) has been proposed as a useful cut-off for predicting IUGR risk in developing countries. This would include more than 50% of women in western India[57] and almost none in the USA. Clearly improving maternal weight prior to conception is a potential strategy to improve birthweight.

#### Attained Maternal Weight at 20, 28 or 36 Weeks of Gestation

Maternal weight during gestation predicts IUGR risk slightly better than prepregnancy weight because it considers weight gain in pregnancy, including the foetus. Comparing women in the lowest quartile of attained weight to those in the highest quartile, the odds ratios for IUGR are 2.7, 3.0 and 3.1 at 20, 28 and 36 weeks of gestation respectively. Including short (below average) maternal height increased the odds ratio to about 3.5, whereas including below-average prepregnancy weight increased the odds ratio to closer to 4.0.

### Additional, Less Useful Predictors of Women at Greatest Risk of IUGR

#### Low Maternal Body Mass Index (BMI)

Body Mass index (BMI) is defined as weight (in kg) divided by height (in m) squared. Maternal BMI is more a reflection of fatness than of lean tissue mass and, of course, correlates strongly with weight. It is certainly true that there is an interaction between maternal BMI at conception, weight gain during pregnancy and birthweight. It is also clear that women with a low BMI and who do not gain adequate weight, are at greatest risk of delivering a LBW infant[58].

Likewise, pregnancy weight gain has a stronger beneficial effect on foetal growth in initially thinner women than in those who are fatter. In the WHO Collaborative Study[15], mothers with a BMI in the lowest quartile were about twice as likely to produce an IUGR infant compared to those in the upper quartile. Thus, low maternal BMI was a poorer predictor of IUGR than either maternal prepregnancy weight or attained weight.

Another limitation of BMI as an indicator of IUGR risk is that fatness influences physiological adaptations to energy available during pregnancy. The thinnest women gain most weight during pregnancy and the fattest gain least. In fact, recommended pregnancy weight gains in the USA[58] and Europe are inversely proportional to BMI at conception. In East Java, Indonesia[59], Pakistan[60], Taipei,China[61] and rural Mexico[62], the highest pregnancy weight gains occurred in the thinnest women. For example, in the Pakistan study, women weighing <45kg postpartum gained 4.5 kg during one reproductive cycle. Those weighing 45-56 kg lost 0.6 kg, and those >56 kg gained 0.6 kg[60]. In the Mexico study, total pregnancy weight gain was strongly negatively related to preconception BMI, skinfolds, and percent body fat (correlation about -0.5), and thinner women also spontaneously consumed more energy during pregnancy[62]. Conversely, for women with a high BMI (>27) at conception, birthweight is practically independent of pregnancy weight gain [58].

These interactions between prepregnancy BMI and gestational weight gain can be explained by the fact that the resting metabolic rate of fatter women is increased dramatically during pregnancy, thereby consuming more energy and leading to a generally lower weight gain[63]. In contrast, the metabolic rate of thin women may even fall in early pregnancy[64]. Their overall energy cost of pregnancy is much lower, and their pregnancy weight gain may be substantially more than that of fatter women.

These physiological responses to maternal BMI probably involve the hormone leptin. Serum leptin concentrations are strongly correlated with maternal BMI prior to pregnancy and in the second trimester[65]. Higher leptin is normally associated with a higher metabolic rate. In contrast, thinner women become more efficient at utilizing dietary energy for weight gain during pregnancy. This is especially true if their energy intake is low; an intervention with a protein-energy supplement in The Gambia did benefit birthweight, but some of the supplemental energy was expended in increased metabolism[64].

Based on these considerations it does not seem useful to choose low BMI as the indicator of IUGR risk, compared to low prepregnancy weight or attained weight. It appears to be low lean tissue mass, rather than low fat mass, that predicts IUGR.

## Pregnancy Weight Gain

The WHO Collaborative Study[15] found that women in the lowest quartile of both low prepregnancy weight, and pregnancy weight gain (to week 20, odds ratio 5.6 ; or to week 36, odds ratio 5.6) were at highest risk of producing an IUGR infant.

Pregnancy weight gains of women in Asia tend to be low. It has been estimated[12] that most women in South Asia gain little more than 5 kg rather than the 10-15 kg gain by women in developed countries. However, there are certain limitations to using weight gain as the only predictor of IUGR risk. Two measures are required. Weight gain is inversely related to BMI so, as discussed above, it will be higher in thinner women as long as the energy-sparing adaptations associated with low fat mass can buffer any concurrent low energy intakes. To complicate the picture further, it has been hypothesized that the degree of maternal undernutrition may affect the response to supplementation[66]. Supplementation of moderately malnourished women produces an increase in birthweight but has little impact on maternal weight gain. However, when seriously malnourished women are supplemented they cannot 'afford' to direct the energy to the foetus and therefore such supplementation improves maternal weight gain more than birthweight[60,67]. This needs to be tested in more studies.

Clearly, energy intakes are so low for many women that the adaptive mechanisms described above cannot prevent low pregnancy weight gain. It has been estimated that women in developing countries who weigh 44-55 kg would deliver an infant with birthweight >3 kg if they gained 10.5 kg during pregnancy[15]. This would be a much higher weight gain than the 5-9 kg range that usually occurs.

## Maternal Height

Maternal height, although it contributes to total maternal mass, has less value than weight or BMI for predicting IUGR[15]. Low height is a good indicator of obstetric complications such as obstructed labour and need for assisted delivery[15]. It is therefore useful to refer short women to appropriate childbirth facilities.

## Timing of Supplementation

Some 20 years ago, the favoured hypothesis was that timing maternal supplementation during the third trimester of pregnancy would be most likely to increase birthweight[14]. The rationale was that foetal fat deposition was fastest during this stage of pregnancy. In earlier trimesters, when maternal fat is increasing fastest, supplementation would be more likely to benefit maternal weight gain. This hypothesis was supported by analysis of pregnancy outcomes in the Dutch famine towards the end of World War II. Women who were in their third trimester during the famine produced babies with the lowest birthweights[68]. In The Gambia, the prevalence of LBW increases the most if the third trimester occurs during the hungry season[51]. The trial of supplementation during pregnancy in Taipei,China found as much improvement in birthweight with supplements given during the third trimester as when given before and throughout pregnancy[69].

Subsequent research contradicts this hypothesis, however, and suggests that nutrition interventions earlier in pregnancy will have the strongest effect on birthweight. In the longitudinal Guatemala intervention study, the amount of fat gained in early pregnancy was the strongest positive predictor of birthweight. A recent analysis of this study revealed that, after adjustment for six potentially confounding factors, each kg of maternal weight gain in the second and third trimesters led to significant increases in birthweight, of 62 g and 26 g respectively[70]. This association between higher maternal weight gain in the second trimester and birthweight was independent of initial maternal size. An even stronger association was seen between gain in maternal thigh fat in mid-pregnancy and birthweight. Mid-pregnancy maternal weight gain and increments in thigh skinfolds were significantly associated with the newborn's length, weight and head circumference and were more strongly predictive of birthweight and other newborn outcomes than were maternal measures in late pregnancy. Similarly, low income teenagers in the USA were almost twice as likely to produce an IUGR infant if they gained inadequate amounts of weight in the first half of pregnancy, regardless of whether their weight gain caught up by the end of pregnancy[71].

It is important to remember that birthweight is clearly not the only important outcome affected by the timing of supplements given to pregnant women. For example, evidence from The Gambia suggests that undernutrition in mid-pregnancy may impair development of the immune system, because infants born two to three months after the hungry season were later seen to have a higher rate of adult morbidity[27].

### Duration of Supplementation

In the Guatemala intervention study, women who were supplemented during one pregnancy, then during lactation and the subsequent pregnancy, produced heavier infants in their second pregnancy

than those who were unsupplemented in their prior pregnancy. In fact, in these short (average height, 151 cm) women, mean birthweight was increased by this continued supplementation to 3,290g, compared to 2,944g in unsupplemented women[72]. These results imply that it is possible to compensate, during her reproductive years, for at least some of the adverse effects of a woman's previous undernutrition. Supplementation of the undernourished mother, before she becomes pregnant, can be expected to improve the outcome of a subsequent pregnancy.

## Micronutrient Supplementation During Pregnancy

Until the late 1990s, little attention was paid to the micronutrient status of pregnant women, except for the constant concern about the high prevalence of maternal iron deficiency. The energy and protein supplements provided in intervention studies often contained some micronutrients but generally failed to include adequate amounts of all important minerals and vitamins. Evidence is beginning to accumulate that the vitamin and mineral status of pregnant women can have major effects on pregnancy outcome. A meta-analysis of the impact of micronutrient supplements in 19 randomized controlled trials[43] concluded that only folic acid reduced the incidence of term LBW. However, only six of the trials were done in regions of the world where micronutrient deficiencies were expected to be a problem. The following evidence supports the importance of micronutrient supplements for pregnant women.

### Supplementation with Single Micronutrients

#### Iron

The prevalence of anaemia in pregnancy is high, especially in poor regions of the world. Therefore, it is difficult, for ethical reasons, to find placebo-controlled trials of iron supplementation in pregnant women. A meta-analysis of the Cochrane database found that iron supplementation significantly reduced the prevalence of haemoglobin (Hb) concentrations below 100 or 105 g/l in late pregnancy[73] but did not affect any other outcomes. Most investigators have looked for associations between maternal Hb and birth outcomes. Several studies have reported an association between low maternal Hb in early pregnancy and increased risk of preterm delivery[74, 75, 76]. In a study of 829 women from Shanghai, the PRC[77], rates of LBW and preterm delivery, but not of IUGR, were higher when maternal Hb concentrations were low (anaemia) or high (poor plasma volume expansion), especially in early pregnancy. This pattern has been observed in other studies. The fact that associations are strongest between preterm delivery and maternal Hb concentrations in early pregnancy may result from the variability in Hb concentration introduced by haemodilution later in pregnancy. In the few randomized, controlled intervention trials where birthweight was measured, three (two in Europe and one in Niger) found no effect and one (in The Gambia, using a folic acid control) found birthweight to be increased whereas gestational age was unaffected[78]. Thus, evidence for an effect of iron supplements on preterm delivery and birthweight is still weak, due to a lack of randomized controlled trials[79, 80].

## Folic Acid

Folic acid is commonly a constituent of iron supplements provided to pregnant women. More data on its prevalence are urgently needed, but there is presently little evidence that folate deficiency is common[79]. This vitamin is present in large amounts in leaves and legumes. A meta-analysis using the Cochrane database concluded that folate supplements increased serum and red cell folate, reduced the prevalence of low Hb concentrations in late pregnancy (odds ratio, 0.61), and possibly increased birthweight[81]. However, a trial in Myanmar and Thailand found no additional improvement in Hb when folic acid was added to iron supplements[82].

In trials in developed countries, and in the PRC[83], folic acid taken prior to conception and during the first six weeks of pregnancy does afford some protection against the occurrence and recurrence of neural tube defects. In the PRC, 400 µg/day folic acid supplements reduced the occurrence of neural tube defects by up to 80%[83]. Folic acid supplements are effective for the substantial number of women who require more folate because their metabolism of this or of related metabolites is different[84]. Periconceptional folic acid supplementation effectively reduced neural tube defects, even in the populations in the USA where the diets of healthy individuals contain relatively substantial amounts of the vitamin. This led to the recent policy of mandatory fortification of wheat flour with folic acid in the USA.

The metabolic cause of neural tube defects is not yet understood but probably involves abnormalities in enzymes that are affected by this vitamin. Women who have given birth to a previous baby with neural tube defects are at much higher risk of this problem recurring in a second pregnancy and should be counselled to take folic acid supplements prior to conception. In general, however, unless such women are identified before they conceive or in the first few weeks after their last menstrual period, providing folic acid in pregnancy is too late to prevent neural tube defects.

At present the most convincing evidence for supplementing women with folic acid later in pregnancy is that it might prevent some cases of preterm delivery and lower the risk of other birth defects. Low serum or red blood cell folate, and subsequently elevated plasma total homocysteine concentrations, are often associated with other pregnancy complications. In low income, mostly African-American women in the USA, those with low folate intakes and low serum folate concentrations at the end of the second trimester had twice the risk of preterm delivery, when potential confounding factors were controlled in the analysis[85]. An analysis of randomized, controlled clinical trials found that folate supplements reduced the risk of antepartum haemorrhage and Caesarean section (one trial each)[86]. A large, retrospective Norwegian study[87] showed that women in the upper vs. lowest quartile of plasma homocysteine concentrations (and presumably more folate deficient) had increased risks as follows: pre-eclampsia, 32% higher risk; preterm delivery, 38% higher risk; and preterm delivery, 101% higher risk.

## Zinc

There has long been interest in the potential for zinc supplements to improve birthweight and pregnancy outcome, because of the important role of zinc in cell division, immunocompetence, and hormone metabolism. Evidence for the efficacy of zinc supplements has, however, been very mixed. Cochrane meta-analyses found no effects of zinc supplementation on labour outcomes or on maternal or foetal mortality or morbidity[88]. A review of 10 zinc supplementation trials conducted up to 1996 showed that birthweight was higher in the supplemented group in four out of 10 trials[44]. Preterm delivery was reduced by zinc in three of the trials, of which two were the same as those showing an improvement in birthweight.

All of these trials were in developed countries except for the Republic of South Africa and India, and most had methodological flaws. The Indian trial, in which 45 mg zinc per day was provided to 168 women, found an improvement in birthweight and less preterm delivery but there was no placebo group[89]. One of the larger trials, that found zinc to be effective, enrolled women in the USA who had below average plasma zinc concentrations, in order to target those with poorer zinc status[90]. In Peru, a well-designed, recent trial using 1,295 women with poor zinc intakes, provided per day 60 mg iron and 250 µg folic acid, with and without 15 mg zinc, starting at 10 to 24 weeks of gestation. Gestational age was assessed with ultrasound and other techniques. There was no impact of the zinc on gestational age, birthweight or length, or any other anthropometric measure[91]. It is not clear how many of these Peruvian women were zinc deficient, but their status would have been marginal at best. Similar results were found in a randomized, placebo-controlled trial on 559 women in the slums of Dhaka, Bangladesh[92]. The supplements were started relatively early, between 12 and 16 weeks of gestation, and provided 30 mg zinc per day. The investigators speculated that the low maternal energy intakes and deficiencies of other micronutrients might have overwhelmed any benefits of zinc. The evidence indicates that supplementing undernourished pregnant women with zinc alone is unlikely to lower the prevalence of LBW.

## Vitamin A

In rural Nepal, women who became night blind near the end of pregnancy had two to three times more urinary tract infections, diarrhoea and dysentery, eating problems, pre-eclampsia and eclampsia, and anaemia[93]. Vitamin A or beta-carotene supplementation reduced perinatal mortality by 44% in a group of more than 2,000 Nepali women[94]. The supplements (7000 μg retinol equivalents, RE) as retinyl palmitate or beta-carotene) were provided weekly prior to conception, throughout pregnancy and into lactation. However, there was no effect on IUGR. Additional studies are needed to show whether these results can be replicated in other situations, and whether supplemental retinol or beta-carotene would be equally effective if started later in pregnancy, when women more typically enter prenatal care. Due to the toxicity of retinol to embryos, pregnant women should be given no more than about 3,000 μg retinol per day.

## Calcium

Calcium supplementation during pregnancy reduces the risk of hypertension, pre-eclampsia and eclampsia, and lowers the blood pressure of the neonate[95]. A Cochrane meta-analysis of randomized controlled clinical trials showed that this effect was strongest in women with lower calcium intakes (<900 mg per day), and that preterm delivery was reduced in women at high risk of developing hypertension. In India, calcium supplementation of women with low calcium intakes substantially reduced the risk of hypertension and eclampsia[96]. It seems that daily supplementation with 1–2 mg calcium is required to produce this response, but this might be worthwhile

attempting in regions where pregnancy-induced hypertension and eclampsia are major causes of maternal mortality.

## Iodine

Maternal iodine deficiency during pregnancy causes cretinism in the neonate, with permanent adverse effects on subsequent growth, general development and cognitive function. A Cochrane meta-analysis examined the effects of maternal iodine supplementation during pregnancy, using three acceptably controlled trials involving 1,551 women[97]. In the two trials conducted in areas with severe iodine deficiency, the Democratic Republic (DR) of Congo (formerly Zaïre) and Papua New Guinea, iodized oil injection produced a significant (about 30%) reduction in deaths during infancy and early childhood[98, 99]. The DR Congo trial showed that the injection was effective even when given in mid-pregnancy. Based on this meta-analysis, it was concluded that additional placebo-controlled trials to test the benefits of iodine supplementation on pregnancy outcome are no longer ethically justifiable. More information on iodine interventions is provided below.

## Supplementation with Multiple Micronutrients

There is considerable interest at present in moving towards the use of multiple micronutrient supplements. In developing countries, where diets are of poor quality and infections and parasites impair the absorption or increase losses of several nutrients, and where women are repeatedly depleted by pregnancy and lactation, it is usual for individuals to be deficient in several nutrients simultaneously. HIV-infected individuals may also have low serum concentrations of several vitamins and minerals[100]. When HIV-positive, pregnant women in Tanzania were given multiple micronutrients, compared to a placebo, this reduced LBW by 44%, births before 34 weeks of gestation by 39% and IUGR by 43%[101]. In low income women in the USA, multiple micronutrient supplements in the first two trimesters of pregnancy halved the risk of preterm delivery, although this was not a randomized controlled trial[102]. Additional trials of the benefits of multiple micronutrients for pregnancy outcome are ongoing in Bangladesh, Mexico, and Tanzania. The results of these studies will be important in decisions over whether or not to adopt a multiple micronutrient supplementation strategy for pregnant women in developing countries. Some concerns have been raised about this approach in India[103]. An important consideration is that improving maternal micronutrient stores during pregnancy will increase the concentration of many of these nutrients in breastmilk, and prevent maternal depletion during lactation. The nutrients that should receive greatest priority are thiamine, riboflavin, vitamins $B_6$ and $B_{12}$, vitamin A, iodine and selenium. These nutrients have been termed "Priority I" for the lactating woman, because: a) maternal status and intake affects their concentration in breastmilk; b) low intakes from breastmilk can have adverse effects on the infant; c) the concentration of these nutrients in breastmilk can be readily improved by increasing maternal intake; and d) for most of them, foetal storage is relatively low and the infant is particularly dependent on an adequate supply in breastmilk[104].

# Non-Nutritional Interventions During Pregnancy

A comprehensive review of 24 non-nutritional pregnancy interventions found that only two improved birthweight[105]. These were smoking cessation, which improved birthweight and lowered term LBW by about 20%, and antimalarial prophylaxis. Data from 11 trials, on more than 3,000 women in endemic areas for malaria, showed the strongest effect of antimalarials on primagravidae, where birthweight increased by 112 g[106].

It is inappropriate to conclude that non-nutritional interventions are not effective for reducing LBW. Very few trials have been attempted in malnourished populations and indeed few logical interventions have been tested in randomized, controlled trials. On a group or population basis, such interventions will make a difference only if they improve adverse factors or behaviour that affect a substantial proportion of the population [population-attributable risk (PAR)], and that cause a substantial increase in the relative risk (RR) of an adverse outcome (such as IUGR)[42]. This explains in part why smoking and antimalarial prophylaxis are effective interventions.

There has been some research on whether prolonged standing or strenuous work is associated with IUGR. Many studies found no association, although some did; e.g.[107, 108, 109]. In a large analysis of 7,722 pregnancies in the USA, work outside the home by pregnant women in the third trimester was associated with birthweights 150 to 400 g lower and more placental infarcts, compared to women who remained at home[108]. Working had the strongest negative association with foetal growth in mothers who were underweight at conception, had low pregnancy weight gain, and whose work required standing. Low placental blood flow was offered as an

explanation. In Asian countries, large numbers of women work very hard during pregnancy. This makes their energy requirements harder to meet and increases the risk of energy deficit and IUGR. Advice to protect the pregnant woman from excessive activity, especially during late pregnancy, should be tested for its effects on birthweight[110].

# Adolescent Nutrition

## Adolescent Growth

During adolescence, growth in height accelerates, driven by hormonal changes, and is faster than at any other time in the individual's postnatal life, except in the first year[111]. More than 20% of total growth in stature and up to 50% of adult bone mass are achieved during adolescence[112]. Nutrient requirements are significantly increased above those in the childhood years.

Among girls, the "growth spurt" or peak growth velocity occurs normally about 12-18 months before menarche (onset of menstruation), at some time between 10 to 14 years. Growth in stature continues, however, for up to 7 years after menarche. Maximal adult height in women may thus be attained as early as 16 years or, particularly for populations with high rates of undernutrition, as late as 23 years[113]. Moreover, for several more years after growth in height is complete, the pelvic bones are still growing. This is a process that is crucial for reducing the risk of obstructed labour[114]. The development of the birth canal is not fully completed until about 2-3 years after growth on height has ceased[115], whereas peak bone mass is not achieved until the age of 25 years[116].

Better nourished girls have higher premenarcheal growth velocities and reach menarche earlier than undernourished girls. The latter grow more slowly but for longer, because menarche is delayed. In India[117], both peak weight and height velocities were delayed by 18 months for children who were stunted at age 10 years. Ultimately, these two factors tend to balance out and total height achieved during adolescence (not necessarily attained adult height) may be similar for well nourished and undernourished adolescents[118, 119]. The adult height finally attained may still differ as a result of pre-existing childhood stunting. The delay in menarche is thought to be partly related to low iron stores in childhood[120].

## Adolescent Pregnancy

For nutrition, the important aspect of the abovementioned findings is that underweight, adolescent girls are growing for longer, and thus may not finish growing before their first pregnancy. In

India, for example, up to 67% girls were classified as being at obstetric risk (by weight and height criteria) in their 15th year as compared to about 20% in their 19th year[121]. In a report on 242 adolescent pregnancies (10-18 years) from Gorakhpur in Uttar Pradesh, India[122], LBW and prematurity rates were 67% and 33%, respectively. The corresponding figures for mothers below 17 years of age were 83% and 33%, respectively.

Viewing these statistics against data on the age of marriage in India, the potential for severe maternal undernutrition and heightened LBW risk becomes clear. In six large, north Indian states, the mean age of marriage of rural girls was 13.8 years, and their age of conception 15.3 years[123]. In general, at least 25% of adolescent girls in the developing world have had their first child by age 19 and a great many more shortly thereafter[124]. In many countries, the proportion of unmarried adolescents becoming pregnant is at an all-time high[125].

Research has shown that adolescents who are still growing are likely to give birth to a smaller baby than mature women of the same nutrition status[126, 127]. This is probably due to competition for nutrients between the growing adolescent and the growing foetus[120, 128] and poorer placental function[129] which in turn increases the risk of LBW and neonatal mortality[130]. In addition, concurrent pregnancy and growth have a particularly detrimental effect on micronutrient status of adolescent girls, after controlling for energy intake and other confounding effects[128]. Calcium status is a particular concern, because the bones of adolescents require calcium for growth at a time when foetal needs for bone growth are also high.

Adolescent pregnancies also confer a higher risk of maternal and infant mortality and preterm delivery. As with other women, these risks are further elevated in adolescents when birth care is inadequate. In India, it was found that children born to teenage mothers were 40% more likely to die in their first year than those born to women in their twenties[131]. Among five countries in Asia the corresponding figure was 50%[132]. In Bangladesh, maternal mortality ratios for 15 to 19-year-olds have been found to be twice as high as those for 20 to 24-year-olds[133]. The younger the adolescent, the greater the risk. In Jamaica and Nigeria, for example, women under 15 years were up to eight times more likely to die around the time of delivery than those in the 15-19 years age group[133]. Risks are further heightened by the fact that pregnant, adolescent girls are less likely to use antenatal and obstetric services.

There are fewer studies and less consensus on the risks of lactation to adolescents[134], although there is suggestive evidence of a greater weight loss during lactation[135] and poorer breastmilk production[136] among adolescents, as compared to adult women. It has been suggested[137] that there is a higher loss of bone minerals among lactating adolescents, though these findings have been challenged[138].

With respect to attained adult height (or capacity to achieve genetic potential for size), a very strong association was found in India with under-five height status and to a lesser degree with weight status in the school-age group (5-10 years) [117]. Stunting in early childhood is thus likely to persist into adulthood; as corroborated by studies of the International Center for Research on Women (ICRW)[139] (see below).

## Adolescent Nutritional Status

Adolescent anthropometry at specific chronological ages varies significantly worldwide[119]. Many of the differences are attributable to variations in timing of the growth spurt. There is a dearth of detailed work on the specific cut-offs, predictive values and PARs of adolescent anthropometric indices[127]. Moreover, there are no reference data that are widely applicable to pregnant adolescents.

The most notable set of studies to date on adolescent nutritional status were carried out by the ICRW. Male and female prevalence of stunting, thinness and anaemia among adolescents were compared as part of a multicountry study[139]. Their findings, summarized here, are revealing. The prevalence of stunting or short stature (% below the 5th percentile National Center for Health Statistics/ World Health Organization height-for-age reference) was between 27 and 65% in nine of the 11 studies. The stunting process occurs in early childhood, when rapid growth is supposed to occur. These children were stunted as they came into adolescence and their height-for-age did not improve across the eight years of adolescence. Gender differences were neither common, nor consistent where they did exist. Among eight studies, only two (Benin and Cameroon) showed worse male stunting, and only one (India ) showed worse female stunting.

Thinness (percentage below the 5th percentile NCHS/WHO BMI-for-age) was highly prevalent (23-53%) in only three of the eight studies and, surprisingly, boys appeared to have at least twice the prevalence of girls in seven of the studies. BMI, unlike height, improved during adolescence for all girls, whatever their initial nutrition status at 10 years, but only among boys with low BMI at 10 years. This "improvement" may, however, be an artefact of late maturation, delaying the growth spurt in these developing-country adolescents as compared to the USA reference population. Moreover, the greater prevalence of thinness among boys suggests they were more delayed, relative to their reference data, than girls were relative to theirs. This interpretation is supported by the observation that the linear growth of boys, unlike that of girls, had not stopped by age 19 years.

Anaemia was the greatest nutrition problem and was highly prevalent (32-55%) in four of six studies in which it was assessed. There was no gender difference in three of four studies in which it could be assessed. In the fourth study (Ecuador), more boys were anaemic than girls. Prior to the ICRW study, little research had been done on anaemia during adolescence, although its mean prevalence among adolescent girls in developing countries had been estimated at 27%[140]. Adolescent girls lose more iron through menstruation, but adolescent boys may need more per kg weight gained, because they build up relatively more muscle. The surprising gender difference in thinness may be because anaemia constrains the weight gain of boys more than that of girls. As adolescent growth slows, however, the iron status of boys improves; whereas that of girls tends to worsen, with more serious future consequences.

Adequate nutrition during adolescence implies adequacy of dietary intake and/or body stores of both macro- and micronutrients, with respect to the activity level of the individual. Dietary studies in adolescents have shown serious shortfalls in intakes. Among 13-15 year old girls in Haryana, India, for example, mean intakes of energy, protein, iron, riboflavin, niacin and vitamin A were all well below recommended intakes[141]. The widespread cultural constraints on the freedom of postmenarcheal girls to leave their home may limit their access to seasonal fruit, commercially-prepared foods, or other significant sources of dietary diversity[142], while gender discrimination in intra-household food allocation may also limit their intake. Few studies have attempted to relate adolescent micronutrient status to LBW risk. With regard to activity level, adolescent girls are often already employed in full-time labour carrying out high intensity tasks. It is at this time that they begin to be given more responsibility for the multiple tasks culturally defined as female.

## Can Adolescents Catch-Up Incomplete Childhood Growth?

The question whether adolescents catch up incomplete childhood growth caused by undernutrition was studied by various authors; e.g. [143, 144]. Four studies were carried out on undernourished children from poor families who were adopted, by age five, into middle-class families[145]. These adoptees did catch up lost

growth to some extent but not completely, even under optimal conditions. Such partial catch-up reflects the accelerated growth rates in adolescence and can also involve a longer period of fast adolescent growth when biological maturation is delayed because of previous undernutrition.

A study was made on the effects of adoption of poor Indian infants (81% LBW) into wealthy Swedish families soon after birth[146]. There was marked catch-up growth in childhood: mean stunting prevalence dropped from 62% to 20% after two years. However, the individual height and weight differences among these children at birth persisted into childhood. The mean adult height attained (154 cm) by the adopted Indian girls was just 1 cm greater than the mean height of poor adult women living in India, and significantly less than that for more affluent women in India (159 cm). Girls who were stunted when adopted in infancy, were also significantly shorter in adulthood than their peers who were not stunted at the time of adoption. The improved early childhood growth in these adopted girls hastened menarche considerably and shortened the period of rapid premenarcheal growth. This has been summarized thus: "what was gained in the swing (accelerated growth in childhood) was more than lost in the roundabout (shortening of overall duration of growth due to earlier onset of puberty)" [147]. Note, however, that only 8% of these adopted girls attained heights of less than 145 cm, with risks of obstetric complication, as compared to over 15% of women throughout Asia[148] and 12-25% of women in India[149].

In addition to these studies of adoptees, there have been longitudinal studies (without interventions). In three out of four such studies[143, 150, 151] there was partial catch-up. The fourth[144] failed to show any catch-up. A cross-sectional study of a Kenyan population, living in adverse circumstances, found partial catch-up growth during adolescence, without a specific intervention[118]. The catch-up was due largely to delayed maturation.

Overall, there remains little evidence that growth retardation suffered in early childhood can be significantly caught up in adolescence. There are no known studies to determine whether growth-retarded children respond, with catch-up growth during adolescence to nutrition and health interventions[127]. When maturation is delayed in children who are malnourished on entering adolescence, the delay is usually for less than two years[117], possibly not enough to compensate significantly for lost growth in childhood. Stunted children are more likely than nonstunted children to become stunted adults, while they remain in the same environment which gave rise to the stunting. Growth failure in early childhood manifested by stunting, may therefore be irreversible to a large extent[145]. Moreover, even if adolescent catch-up growth could be stimulated by an intervention and stunting thereby reduced, this would not necessarily also rectify all the problems of earlier undernutrition, for which stunting is merely a marker. For example, a reduction in stunting would probably reduce obstetric risk due to small maternal size, but would not necessarily reverse the effects of early childhood stunting on cognitive function. This has been shown in a recent study in the Philippines[152]. Some catch-up growth was achieved between the ages of 2.0 and 8.5 years, among children who were up to two years of age, but their cognitive deficits persisted[152]. Early childhood stunting and its functional correlates can be addressed together only if the environment in which the young child grows is improved at that time; i.e., within the first two years of life[145].

In a study of the reproductive lives of girls born during the Dutch famine and with adequate growth during childhood, it was shown that they gave birth to a higher proportion of IUGR babies than other Dutch cohorts[153, 154]. IUGR may produce some prenatal insults to the foetal reproductive system that damages future reproduction, manifesting itself a generation later. In India, early childhood stunting among young girls was correlated significantly with the birthweights and mortality risk of their infants[155].

In a Guatemalan study on adult women, whose nutrition status had been measured at three years of age, nearly 67% of severely stunted and 34% of moderately stunted three-year-old girls became stunted adult women[156]. Moreover, the prevalence of LBW was nearly doubled in infants of women who had suffered severe stunting (< -3 Z-scores) at three years of age, compared to those who were not stunted (> -2 Z-scores) at the same age. Women who had experienced greater growth retardation during childhood also had smaller body frames as adults, and were thus at greater risk of obstructed labour.

Examination of national anthropometric data, showed a strong correlation between prevalence of underweight in children under five years of age in the 1970s and the prevalence of underweight in adult women in the 1980s[148]. Furthermore, there were strong associations between underweight in adult women and LBW (1980), and between LBW (1988) and under-five child underweight (1990). These correlations are again broadly indicative of the tendency for smallness to be perpetuated across generations. Small girls do seem likely to become small women who have small babies. McCarrison may have been right, over 50 years ago when he said: *"The satisfaction of nutritional needs in pregnancy begins with the antenatal lives of the mothers of our race"* (quoted[157]).

# Intervening in Adolescence

Of the main factors found to be related to LBW risk, three - namely, the height and weight of the woman at the time of conception and her iron status and intake - would suggest the potential for improvement during adolescence. Let us examine feasible options.

## Improving Dietary Intake

There is very limited evidence for partial catch-up during the adolescent growth spurt (see above) and studies have yet to be undertaken to find out whether intervening would promote additional catch-up. It has been suggested that three important questions be asked before a food intervention (the most common) is considered[139]. First, how much height could be gained? The only study that comes close to answering this[158] showed that growth hormones were elevated in premenarcheal participants of a food intervention (i.e., there was the potential for faster growth). Height changes were not measured.

Second, is menarche hastened and, if so, what are the implications? If a food intervention succeeds only in hastening menarche and thus reducing the period of fastest growth (e.g.[145, 146]), it may not increase height by much. If this possibility is avoided, by delaying the intervention until after menarche, can further pelvic growth be achieved in this later period of slower growth? A study in India has suggested not[117]: dietary intake after menarche was not associated with adolescent growth. Even if greater attained heights were possible with either of these two options, would this benefit the woman or future child?

Third, how much fat is gained simultaneously? Raising attained height, through a food intervention, would also increase body weight, including fat stores[139]. This would be advantageous to the thin and stunted adolescent, but might lead to overweight among girls who, though stunted, are not thin during adolescence. The ICRW studies[139] together suggest the need for caution here because, by age 18-19 years, few girls were thin, as assessed by BMI-for-age.

Existing knowledge therefore suggests that height gain during adolescence might not be feasible as a nutrition objective. In 1993, an International Dietary Energy Consultative Group (IDECG) workshop on the causes and mechanisms of linear growth retardation concluded that there was: *"no evidence that intervention at the time of puberty has any special effect on linear growth and in any case it would not be justifiable to delay intervention until such a late stage. The time for intervention is early childhood, when growth is first becoming retarded"* [159].

Nevertheless, there are important potential benefits other than linear growth, from improving dietary intake. These include weight gain among thin adolescent girls, and improved micronutrient (particularly iron and folate) status, to improve their wellbeing in the present as well as their nutrition status during any subsequent pregnancy.

Adolescents have special needs and face particular challenges during pregnancy. Behaviour and culture, in addition to the nutrition and biological factors, influence the outcomes of adolescent pregnancies. In many cultures, adolescent girls are responsible for the majority of household duties, including caring for younger siblings, carrying water, and preparing meals for the family, among whom they are the last to eat. During pregnancy, these responsibilities become an even greater burden on the still growing adolescent girl, who may not be able to consume enough food to meet her energy needs. Pregnant adolescents may be less likely to admit they are pregnant and thereby may deny themselves proper nutrition and food. They may also delay seeking antenatal care for various reasons: lack of money; lack of power to make decisions regarding personal health; and poor treatment from health providers who are not sensitized to provide the particular care that pregnant adolescents require[160].

There may be, however, particular opportunities for improving the nutrition status of adolescents. Their dietary practices may be more flexible than those of adults; and they may have fewer cultural constraints or restrictive taboos. School enrolment of female adolescents is usually higher than antenatal care coverage, facilitating coverage of supplementation schemes.

Promotion of a balanced diet during adolescence need not wait for the results of a longitudinal study. However, there would be value in investigating the effectiveness of food supplementation in raising prepregnant nutrition status among thin and stunted adolescent girls. Significant gains in height are unlikely, but it would be useful to know whether any significant gains in weight are achievable, among thin girls of low BMI-for-age, and by what means. Micronutrient status also could be investigated as an outcome. An example of a useful research design might be a longitudinal study to investigate the growth of three groups of adolescent girls: a) no intervention; b) food intervention; and c) food intervention, plus iron and folic acid supplementation and/or multivitamin-mineral supplementation.

## Improving Iron and Folate Status

The one clear area for likely benefits of a nutrition intervention is improving iron and folic acid status.

This improves current nutrition status, as well as increasing iron stores for girls who may soon become pregnant. Borderline iron stores before conception are the main cause of iron deficiency anaemia during pregnancy[120]. Given the difficulty of identifying early pregnancy, it might be too late to prevent neural tube defects if folic acid supplementation is delayed until pregnancy is known.

Most efforts have focused on controlling anaemia in pregnant women who can be reached through the health system. There is also a need for a more *preventive* approach: raising the iron stores of women before they become pregnant. The iron requirement of adolescent girls is: *"very difficult, if not impossible to satisfy even with good quality, iron-fortified diets"* [161]. Weekly supplementation of iron deficient non-pregnant women in California, USA, with 60 mg iron + 250 µg of folic acid for 7 months (30 tablets) was effective for controlling iron deficiency anaemia and improving iron status. The positive effect of iron supplements, especially if given daily[162] on iron stores is relatively temporary (about 6 to 12 months) so supplementation is best continued up to the time of conception and throughout pregnancy[163].

A preventive, life cycle approach needs to be community-based, using different avenues for reaching different groups, including adolescent girls. New approaches should be monitored, evaluated and documented so that others can learn from success. Schools, health clinics, youth clubs and the media are all avenues through which such interventions can be promoted. Boys should be involved as well as girls, given the high rates of anaemia found in the multicountry ICRW study[139].

## Delaying First Pregnancy

The first pregnancy should be delayed at least until adolescent growth has finished. Approaches might include: incentives to delay marriage until after 19 years of age; incentives for girls to stay in school; and disincentives to early sexual activity for boys and girls below 18 years of age. Article 1 of the Convention on the Rights of the Child[164], defines under 18-year-olds as "children", and should be used for vigorous advocacy on this issue.

However, a study of 19 countries, in which there has been at least a half-year rise in the average age of women at marriage, shows that there was no parallel increase in the time elapsed between marriage and first birth[165]. Urgency to marry and have children early is related to the precariousness of the status of girls rather than to fertility goals. The links between poverty and early childbearing in developing countries have been largely neglected, both in research and policy-making.

Laws and regulations should facilitate the availability of contraceptives to adolescents, and their use. Health agencies need to ensure access to confidential reproductive and sexual health information and services, protected by law. Information-education-communication (IEC) approaches for adolescents should be designed by adolescents, so as to be made more relevant. Peer motivation should be used to reinforce messages.

At a more basic level, the empowerment of women through sustained raising of their social, economic and educational status, would result in more value being placed on women's productive and social roles in society as opposed to reproductive roles. Improved education status, through staying in school, would also increase receptivity to family planning programmes. In India, approaches to raising the status of adolescent girls are being explored within the Integrated Child Development Services (ICDS) programme. These approaches involve vocational training, as well as direct nutrition support, and education geared to delaying marriage, but they have not yet been evaluated.

In summary, the most successful interventions will be those that provide a package of care to address the social and behavioural challenges faced by pregnant adolescents, in addition to providing nutrition education and antenatal care[166]. In developing countries, however, interventions must address the special needs of pregnant adolescents while developing long term strategies that focus on improving the nutrition status of girls during childhood, delaying marriage and first pregnancy, keeping girls in school, and empowering women.

## Summary and Conclusions

Asia has a higher prevalence of low birthweight (LBW, <2500 g) than any other continent, ranging from well over 30% in South Central Asia and Bangladesh. Much lower rates, <10%, are seen in the PRC, Thailand, the Philippines and Malaysia. The prevalence of LBW is strongly associated with the relative undernutrition of mothers in the region; about 60% of women in South Asia and 40% in South-East Asia are underweight (<45 kg). LBW is probably the main reason why over 50% of the children in Asia are underweight. It also increases the risk of other health and developmental problems. Interventions to reduce the prevalence of LBW should therefore receive very high priority.

The conclusions that can be drawn from randomized, controlled efficacy trials include the following.

- Only supplements that provided more energy caused a significant improvement in birthweight. Although the protein in these supplements provided up to 25% of the energy, the results of at least one study suggest that supplements containing no protein can increase birthweight. In that study, the supplement did contain some micronutrients, the intake of which covaried with energy intake. In populations where protein intake is adequate, providing high protein supplements (>25% of energy) to pregnant women may even increase neonatal death rates.

- Maternal supplementation can also increase maternal weight gain, infant head circumference and, when there is a serious energy shortage, the length of the newborn infant.

- The magnitude of the expected benefit from maternal supplementation in Asia remains to be determined but is expected to be considerable. The largest, well designed trial was conducted in The Gambia. From mid-pregnancy, locally produced biscuits providing 1017 kcal and 22 g protein per day reduced LBW prevalence by 39%, and increased birthweight by 136 g. In the season when maternal energy intake was most inadequate supplementation reduced LBW by 42% and increased birthweight by 201 g. The infant mortality rate fell by about 40%. Women in The Gambia are generally heavier (53 kg on average at enrollment) than those in many parts of Asia. This may provide some protection against LBW, but they may be more seriously energy deficient during the hungry season.

- For undernourished women, or those who have a low body weight (<40 kg), these improvements in pregnancy outcome could be obtained by encouraging them to consume more of their normal diet where possible, and/or providing appropriate energy-containing supplements. The supplements should ideally be formulated from local foods. Clearly any supplements should be consumed by the mother and not by other family members.

- Where the normal diet is particularly low in protein, or as is often the case, low in micronutrients, it is important to ensure that these nutrients are also provided as supplements.

- If targeting is desired, women with the lowest weight (at conception through early pregnancy) and/or lowest energy intakes may be most likely to benefit. Targeting interventions based on maternal BMI, skinfold thickness or height is unlikely to be more useful than targeting based on weight.

- There are conflicting data on whether supplementation during the second trimester vs. third trimester is most effective for improving birthweight. However, it is clear that supplementation during either trimester can reduce the prevalence of low birthweight. In The Gambia, supplementation did not start until 20-24 weeks of gestation and the biscuits were consumed for only 82 days on average. The total amount of energy provided by supplements during pregnancy is likely to be the most important factor, so that supplementation for the longest possible time becomes more critical where the amount of daily energy provided by supplements is lower.

- Young maternal age at conception is an additional risk factor for poor pregnancy outcome so that it is also important to target interventions to those who are still growing.

- Continued supplementation of the mother during her subsequent lactation and pregnancy may cause an even greater improvement in the birthweight of her next child.

- Whenever possible attention should be paid to improving the quality as well as the quantity of food consumed during pregnancy. There is little evidence from randomized controlled trials that supplementation with individual nutrients (including iron, zinc, folic acid, vitamin A and calcium) can improve birthweight, unless this is through a reduction in preterm delivery. However, supplementation of underprivileged pregnant women with micronutrients is certainly extremely important and can lead to substantial reductions in maternal anaemia, may reduce maternal mortality, birth defects and preterm delivery, and improve breastmilk quality and infant nutrient stores. Trials are ongoing to test the efficacy of providing supplements containing balanced amounts of multiple rather than single micronutrients.

- In areas of endemic iodine deficiency, adequate maternal iodine status is critical for the prevention of neonatal deaths, low birthweight and abnormal cognitive and physical development of the infant.

- Non-nutritional interventions that can improve pregnancy outcome include reducing energy expenditure in physical work, increasing age at conception, malarial prophylaxis and cessation of cigarette smoking.

# IMPROVING CHILD GROWTH

During the first two or three years after birth, children in developing countries grow more slowly than those in wealthier regions of the world. It is difficult for them to regain this lost growth potential in later years, especially if they remain in the same environment. In the previous section, it was shown that undernutrition of the mother at conception and during pregnancy has a strongly adverse influence on early growth of her foetus, which is then a risk factor for subsequent growth stunting of the infant and young child. However, there is no doubt that feeding practices during the first years of life also have an important influence on the nutritional status, growth and function of the young child.

This section starts by describing the growth patterns of infants and children in developing countries, the regional prevalence rates of stunting, underweight, and wasting and the causes and consequences of these outcomes. This is followed by consideration of recommended child feeding practices in the first years of life and the type of problems encountered during the period of complementary feeding. The latest evidence on the efficacy of approaches aimed at improving complementary feeding is reviewed, followed by the impact of micronutrient supplementation interventions on growth. While the focus here is on infants and preschool children, because of their greater vulnerability to undernutrition and the special problems of feeding young children, many of the general principles described below apply equally well to older children.

## Growth Patterns of Infants and Children

It is universally accepted that anthropometry is the most useful tool for assessing the nutrition status, and risks of poor health and survival of infants and young children. The current international reference data[127] are far from perfect. They were obtained by measuring infants between 1929 and 1975 in the USA. These reference infants were predominantly formula-fed, and from non-representative genetic, geographical and socioeconomic backgrounds. Well nourished breastfed infants generally grow more rapidly than formula-fed infants (and thus more rapidly than the growth reference) during the first 2 to 3 months of life. However, they then grow more slowly than the growth reference between 3 and 12 months. These expected differences in growth, related to the type of early feeding, should considered when comparing the growth of exclusively breastfed infants to the growth reference. After 12 months of age, the disparity in growth between well nourished breastfed infants and the growth reference is no longer seen. The National Center for Health Statistics (NCHS) published revised growth charts in May, 2000, based on more recent surveys in the USA[167]. However, these surveys included few infants who were breastfed for more than a few months. The new reference values for weight-for-age (but not height-for-age) towards the end of the first year of life are substantially higher than those for infants who were exclusively breastfed for 4 months then partially breastfed thereafter[168]. The growth references will be revised, after the completion of a multicentre, international, infant growth study that is being coordinated and supervised by the WHO[169].

Three anthropometric indices are commonly used to assess infants and children: length-for-age (LA) or height-for-age (HA), weight-for-age (WA), and weight-for-length (WL) or weight-for-height (WH). Length is usually measured before a child is two years old, and height thereafter. Reported changes in growth rates or size at around 2 years are sometimes an artefact of the discontinuity of the growth curves at this age.

Growth data are usually expressed as Z-scores, calculated as the deviation of the value for an individual from the reference population at that age, divided by the standard deviation for the reference population. Z-scores correct for differences in age among a group of children. Low LA or HA (stunting) is usually an indication of long term undernutrition. Low WA is a less useful measure because it can be caused by stunting, accompanied by low, normal, or larger than normal amounts of fat and muscle. Low

WL or WH (wasting) may be the result of recent undernutrition that has caused tissue loss but has not yet affected stature.

## Stunting

The WHO has established ranges that can be used to classify populations on the basis of the prevalence of stunting. Stunting is defined as more than 2 standard deviations below the median value of the NCHS/WHO International Growth Reference for length- or height-for-age[127]. For children less than 5 years old, a low prevalence of stunting is <20%, whereas 20-29% indicates a medium prevalence, 30-39% a high prevalence, and ≥40% a very high prevalence. Stunting usually becomes more prevalent after 3 months of age. The rate of decline in Z-scores starts to slow down at around 18 months and is very gradual after 24 months. Height Z-scores usually stop declining after around 3 years of age.

The global prevalence of stunting in children under 5 years averages about 33% in developing countries, but varies widely among them[11]. South Central Asia has the second highest prevalence of stunting in the world (44%), exceeded only by East Africa (48%). West Africa (35%), South-East Asia (33%), Central America (24%), North Africa (20%), the Caribbean (19%) and South America (13%) follow in order of prevalence. Data are not good enough to permit estimates to be made for East and West Asia[11]. Asia is home to about 128 million (70%) of the world's 182 million stunted children aged under 5 years. The prevalence in South Central and South-East Asia was about 5% lower in 2000 than it was in 1995. This is encouraging, but at the present rate it will take many decades to reduce the prevalence of stunting in Asia to acceptable levels. Nine countries in Asia (shaded in Table 3) have a very high prevalence of stunting. An analysis of global data revealed that higher per capita energy availability, female literacy, and gross national product (GNP) were the most important factors explaining national differences in stunting[170].

Because stunting is a cumulative process, the percent of stunted children increases with age. Such increases in stunting prevalence with age do not necessarily indicate that the nutrient intake and status of the children are worse at two years of life than earlier, although they often are. Rather, it reflects the cumulative nature of stunting.

## Underweight

The global prevalence of low WA, defined as more than 2 standard deviations below the NCHS/WHO international growth reference WA median, is substantially lower than that of stunting. In other words, undernutrition in early life is more typically manifested as stunting than as low weight. Underweight is a function of short stature, low tissue mass, or both. Although it is more difficult to interpret, WA is often used to screen for undernutrition because it does not require measurements of height. It is important to recognize that WA data underestimate substantially the number of malnourished children.

The WHO classifications of the prevalence of underweight are: <10%, low prevalence; 10-19%, medium; 20-29%, high; and ≥30%, very high. The global prevalence is 26.7%. South Central Asia has the highest prevalence in the world (43.6%). In South-East Asia it is 28.9% and in Asia overall, 29.0%[11]. The national patterns and differences in underweight adequacy are similar to those for stunting (Table 3). Most (72%) of the underweight children in the world live in Asia, especially in South Central Asia. The fall in prevalence of underweight in Asia from 1995 to 2000 was 3-4%, about the same as the decline on a global basis. As with stunting, the prevalence of low WA also increases with age.

## Wasting

Wasting is defined as more than 2 standard deviations below the NCHS/WHO international growth reference weight-for-height median. It is usually caused by a relatively recent illness or food shortage that induces acute and severe weight loss, although chronic undernutrition or illness can also cause this condition. The prevalence of wasting is much lower than that of stunting or underweight. The expected prevalence in developing countries is 2-3%. When wasting rises to about 5%, mortality rates increase substantially[127]. In Asia, the overall prevalence is 10.4%, and is highest in South Central Asia (15.4%), 10.4% in South-East Asia, and lower in East Asia (3.4%). Data are not yet available for West Asia. The global prevalence is 9.4% for developing countries. The prevalences in South Central Asia (15.4%) and West Africa (15.6%) are the highest in the world.

## Causes of Poor Growth

The most common immediate causes of poor growth of humans in developing countries include: poor maternal nutrition status at conception and undernutrition *in utero*; inadequate breastfeeding; delayed complementary feeding, inadequate quality or quantity of complementary feeding; impaired absorption of nutrients due to intestinal infections or parasites; or combinations of these problems (Figure 3).

**TABLE 3:** Prevalence (%) of stunting and underweight in preschool children and corresponding gross national product (GNP) per capita in the Asia-Pacific region [a]

| Country | Year(s) of survey | 1998 GNP per capita (US $) | Stunting [b] % | Underweight [c] % |
|---|---|---|---|---|
| Afghanistan | 1997 | < 760 | 47.6 | - |
| Bangladesh | 1996-97 | 350 | 54.6 | 56.3 |
| Bhutan | 1986-88 | < 760 | 56.1 | 37.9 |
| Cambodia [d] | 1996 | N/A | 56.0 | 52.0 |
| People's Republic of China | 1992 | 750 | 31.4 | 17.4 |
| Fiji Islands | 1993 | 2110 | 2.7 | 7.9 |
| India | 1992-93 | 430 | 51.8 | 53.4 |
| Indonesia | 1995 | 680 | 42.2 | 34.0 |
| Kazakhstan | 1995 | 1310 | 15.8 | 8.3 |
| Kiribati | 1985 | 1180 | 28.3 | 12.9 |
| Kyrgyzstan | 1997 | 350 | 24.8 | 11.0 |
| Lao PDR | 1994 | 330 | 47.3 | 40.0 |
| Malaysia | 1995 | 3600 | - | 20.1 |
| Maldives | 1995 | 1230 | 26.9 | 43.2 |
| Myanmar | 1994 | < 760 | 44.6 | 42.9 |
| Nepal | 1996 | 210 | 48.4 | 46.9 |
| Pakistan | 1990-91 | 480 | 49.6 | 38.2 |
| Papua New Guinea | 1982-83 | 890 | 43.2 | 29.9 |
| Philippines | 1993 | 1050 | 32.7 | 29.6 |
| Solomon Islands | 1989 | 750 | 27.3 | 21.3 |
| Sri Lanka | 1993 | 810 | 23.8 | 37.7 |
| Thailand | 1987 | 2200 | 21.5 | 25.3 |
| Tonga | 1986 | 1690 | 1.3 | - |
| Uzbekistan | 1996 | 870 | 31.3 | 18.8 |
| Vanuatu | 1983 | 1270 | 19.1 | 19.7 |
| Viet Nam | 1994 | 330 | 46.9 | 44.9 |

Source: WHO (1999) Global Database on Child Growth and Malnutrition. Forecast of Trends. Geneva: Nutrition Division, WHO.

Notes: [a] Shaded cells (stunting) show the countries with the highest rates of stunting (>40%) for which 1990s data are available. Shaded cells (GNP) show the poorest countries (GNP per capita <US$760). There is clearly a strong association.

[b] Stunting - The anthropometric index 'height-for-age' reflects linear growth achieved pre- and postnatally, with deficits indicating longterm, cumulative effects of inadequacies of nutrition and/or health. Shortness in height refers to a child who exhibits low height-for-age that may reflect either normal variation in growth or a deficit in growth. Stunting refers only to shortness that is a deficit, or linear growth that has failed to reach genetic potential as a result, most proximally, of the interaction between poor diet and disease. Stunting is defined as low height-for-age; i.e., below 2 standard deviations (or 2 Z-scores) of the median value of the National Center for Health Statistics/World Health Organization International Growth Reference for length- or height-for-age.

[c] Underweight - The anthropometric index 'weight-for-age' represents body mass relative to age. Weight-for-age is influenced by the height of the child and his or her weight and is thus a composite of stunting and wasting (which makes its interpretation difficult). In the absence of wasting, both weight-for-age and height–for-age reflect the long term nutrition and health experience of the individual or population. General lightness in weight refers to a child having a low weight-for-age. Lightness may represent either normal variation or a deficit. Underweight specifically refers to lightness that is a deficit and is defined as low weight-for-age, i.e.; below 2 standard deviations (or 2 Z-scores) of the median value of the National Center for Health Statistics/World Health Organization International Growth Reference for weight-for-age.

[d] Cambodian national data are from the 1996 UNICEF Multiple Indicator Cluster Survey for 6 to 59 month-old children.

**FIGURE 3:** The inadequate dietary intake – disease cycle

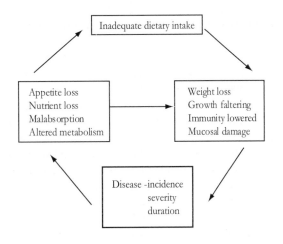

Source:   Tomkins A, Watson F (1989) *Malnutrition and Infection.* ACC/SCN State-of-the-Art Series Nutrition Policy Discussion Paper No. 5. Geneva: ACC/SCN.

## Interactions Between Undernutrition and Diseases

Undernutrition is almost always the result of combinations of diseases and dietary inadequacies interacting in a mutually reinforcing manner (Figure 1). Undernutrition lowers immuno-competence and increases the risk and severity of infection. Inadequate dietary intake may cause death without the influence of any disease, and disease (e.g., measles or malaria) may cause death even in well nourished children. However, the most common cause of death is the combination of inadequate dietary intake and disease. Disease may affect dietary intake (i.e., through anorexia) and inadequate dietary intake may cause disease through contamination.

These interactions between inadequate dietary intake and disease, in the form of a vicious cycle, have been referred to as the "malnutrition-infection complex". Strictly speaking, however, it is a complex between the two immediate causes, with undernutrition being the outcome. This complex remains the most prevalent public health problem in the world today.

The interactions of nutrition and infection with regard to individual infections and defined nutrients are now better known. For example, protein-energy malnutrition increases the duration of episodes of diarrhoea. The importance of interactions between VAD and a number of infectious diseases (notably measles) are now becoming clear. VAD also affects epithelial membranes, and thus relates to respiratory tract infections and to diarrhoea. Deficiencies of other

micronutrients, even when clinical signs are not present, exert an influence through such routes as lowered immunocompetence (e.g., iron deficiency) and integrity of epithelial tissues. Zinc may also have a general effect on infectious disease, again at least partly through the immune system.

Inadequate dietary intake can cause weight loss or growth failure in children and leads to low nutrition reserves. Almost all nutrient deficiencies are probably associated with a lowering of immunity. There may be progressive damage to the mucosa, lowering resistance to colonization and invasion by pathogens, particularly in protein-energy and vitamin A deficiencies. Lowered immunity and mucosal damage are the major mechanisms by which defenses are compromised. Under these circumstances, diseases will have potentially increased incidence, severity, and duration.

The disease process itself exacerbates loss of nutrients, both by the host's metabolic response, and by physical loss from the intestine. These factors exacerbate undernutrition, leading to further possible damage to defense mechanisms. At the same time, many diseases are associated with a loss of appetite and other possible disabilities, further lowering the dietary intake. Although other relationships play a part, this cycle summarises many of the most important relationships. It accounts for much of the high morbidity and mortality, under the circumstances of high exposure to infectious diseases and inadequate diet, that characterize many poor communities. The complex nature of the interaction has meant that it is very difficult to unravel and to distinguish cause from effect. Indeed, the understanding of which specific nutrient deficiencies contribute most to the high prevalence of stunting and wasting in developing countries is still relatively poor. This as well as the influence of non-nutrition factors explains, in part, why it has been so difficult to design effective intervention strategies.

## Consequences of Poor Growth

Poor growth is strongly associated with risk of mortality. From a review of 28 community-based studies in 12 Asian and Sub-Saharan African countries, it was estimated that about 45 to 65% of child deaths are due to severe (<60% of median WA) plus moderate (60-69% of median WA) and mild (70-79% of median WA) undernutrition[171]. A WHO analysis of six longitudinal studies revealed a strong association between severity of WA deficits and mortality rates: 54% of deaths of children under 5 years in developing countries were accompanied by low WA[127].

Undernutrition's impact on illness, disability and death probably is substantial, and probably underestimated. The World Bank[172] attributed between 20 to 25% of the global burden of disease in children to undernutrition, and 15.9% of total global (DALYs) to "malnutrition". The latter figure represents 18% of total developing world DALYs, 22.4% of Indian DALYs, 5.3% of DALYs in the PRC and 14.5 percent of other Asian countries and islands DALYs[173]. The definition used for "malnutrition" in such estimates was narrow. For example, the direct impacts of micronutrient deficiencies other than iron, vitamin A and iodine are not included, neither are the direct health consequences of overnutrition. Moreover, the estimates of the indirect impacts of undernutrition as a contributing risk factor for illness and death were partial and conservative: restricted to children, and to protein-energy malnutrition and vitamin A deficiency. If these other factors were to be included, they would not be perfectly additive, but would probably add substantially to overall contribution of malnutrition to global DALYs of 15.9%. Some commentators have made informal estimates that suggest the complete contribution of all forms of malnutrition could be as high as 50% of the global burden of disease[174].

When children reach the age of 3 years, their nutrient requirements fall, they become less vulnerable to stunting, and their diet usually improves. As a consequence, the growth rate of stunted children then becomes fairly normal. They remain short, but do not continue to become shorter relative to the growth reference. Although there may be some growth catch-up of stunted children in adolescence, related to their delayed maturation and more time for growth, this does not usually compensate for failure to grow in early childhood[28] (see above). Stunted children have caught-up growth substantially when adopted into environments in which they have become well-fed and healthy, or have recovered from a chronic illness[159]. The short stature of adults in developing countries is largely the result of poor growth during the first three years of life. In Guatemala, supplementation in early childhood improved the stature, fat-free mass and work capacity of adolescents and young adults[175, 176]. Specifically, adolescent males who had been supplemented with a high protein-energy supplement during early life were 0.8 cm taller, 1.3 kg heavier, had a 1.2 kg greater fat-free mass and a 0.38 L/min higher maximum oxygen consumption than those who had been given a low energy, no protein supplement. Similar results were found for females.

Undernutrition in early childhood is often associated with poor cognitive and motor development. In a meta-analysis, LBW (whether caused by IUGR or prematurity) predicted a 6-point reduction in IQ during school age[177]. Most of the data were from developed countries. The impact is probably stronger in poor environments. Children who have been severely undernourished in early childhood suffer a later reduction in IQ of as much as 15 points[178]. In Guatemala, supplementation in early childhood improved reading and vocabulary scores in adolescence and young adulthood, but did not affect performance on the Ravens Progressive Matrices test[179, 180]. Psychosocial stimulation, in addition to supplementation, can improve the development quotient of young children, with the maximal effect obtained by a combination of both[181] ( Figure 4). Improved early nutrition and care can compensate in part for undernutrition *in utero*.

In addition to the adverse effects of early undernutrition (*in utero* and in early infancy) on brain development, there is a complex interaction between the apathy and relative inactivity of undernourished young children and their stimulation by their environment[182]. In a longitudinal study in Cebu, Philippines, children who were stunted between birth and 2 years had significantly lower cognitive ability when tested at age 8 to 11 years[152]. The earlier that children became stunted, the more the severe their stunting, and the greater their impairment in later cognitive ability. Much of the shortfall in test scores was caused by the stunted children's later age of enrollment in school, poorer attendance and greater repetition of school grades. Stunted children may be treated differently because they are smaller and appear to be younger, and they may appear to their parents to be less alert and less ready for schooling[182]. Schooling acts as a buffer against the effects of poverty and malnutrition on intellectual function[183].

## The Fundamental Importance of Care

Care, as it came to be defined during the 1990s, refers to the behaviour and practices of caregivers (mothers, siblings, fathers, and child care providers) who provide the food, health care, psychosocial stimulation and emotional support necessary for the healthy growth and development of children[4, 184]. These practices and the ways in which they are performed (with affection and with responsiveness to children) are critical to survival, growth, and development of children. They translate food security and health care into a child's well being (Figure 2). It is impossible for caregivers to provide this care without sufficient resources, such as time, energy and money.

A Care Initiative Manual, developed by the United Nations Children's Emergency Fund (UNICEF)[185], lists

FIGURE 4:   Development quotients of stunted children with various treatments, compared to those for nonstunted children and controls

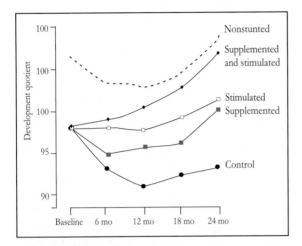

Source: Grantham-McGregor SM, Powell CA, Walker SP, Himes JH (1991) Nutritional supplementation, psychosocial stimulation and mental development of stunted children: the Jamaican study. *The Lancet* 388: 1-5.

six care practices, with subcategories, and three kinds of resources needed for good child care. For example, mothers are often advised to increase the frequency of feeding, but they may have too much work to have the time for giving an additional feed, and may find themselves blamed for providing inadequate care.

Care practices and resources for care are important not only for the good nutrition status of children, but also for their growth and development. They have been recognized as the building blocks of UNICEF's integrated approach to young children, called "Early Childhood Care for Survival, Growth and Development" [186]. The six care practices are described briefly here, before a detailed discussion of care practices in breastfeeding and complementary feeding.

First, care for women requires behaviour in the family to support women, including making sure that they receive adequate prenatal care and safe delivery, and have equal access to education. Second, food preparation takes enormous amounts of the time and effort of caregivers. Adequate stoves lessen the exposure of women to indoor air pollution. Third, hygiene practices have long been recognized as critical for child nutrition. Fourth, home health practices are important, including the diagnosis of illness in the home, preventative health care, protection from pests, and prevention of accidents. Fifth, good psychosocial care is needed, including warmth, verbal interaction and encouragement of learning, which improved cognitive

development of children (Figure 4), and is related to complementary feeding styles. Feeding, including breastfeeding and complementary feeding, is the sixth care practice. This is discussed in the following section, and the large scale effectiveness of care interventions is discussed in the penultimate section.

The significance of care practices for the nutrition status of children was investigated for 475 low-income households in Accra, Ghana, that had a child between 4 and 36 months of age[187]. Based on a recall questionnaire, a 'care practices' scale was constructed. The scale reflected breastfeeding patterns, timing of complementary feeding, food quality, and two questions related to feeding practices: whether anyone helps the child to eat? (28 % said no); and whether the caregiver "does anything" if the child refuses food? (21 % do nothing). There was a significant association between scores on the care practices scale and stunting and underweight of the children. Interestingly, care practices were unrelated to children's height-for-age if their mothers had secondary education, but care practices were highly related to children's nutrition status if mothers had only primary or less education. The effect of income was insignificant, when controlling for maternal schooling and care practices. This would suggest that less educated mothers should be targeted for special messages about care.

## Exclusive Breastfeeding

Frequent, exclusive breastfeeding is important in the early weeks of lactation in order to stimulate optimal milk production. "On-demand" feeding leads to earlier maximal milk production than feeding on a fixed schedule. The introduction of any other foods or fluids, including water, is likely to reduce the infant's demand for breastmilk, and to interfere with the maintenance of lactation, ending with early termination of breastfeeding. No fluids other than breastmilk are required by the young infant. When infants are given solid foods, or even nonmilk fluids, the prevalence of diarrhoea is much higher due to contamination of the bottles or food[188, 189]. During diarrhoea and fever, breastfed infants will continue to consume breastmilk but will reduce their intake of complementary foods and fluids[190]. From a nutrition perspective, it is important to recognize that any other foods will displace at least some breastmilk, especially in the first six months of life[191]. Because breastmilk is generally higher in most nutrients than other foods available to young infants, nutrient intake will be lower when other foods are introduced too early. Many other biological, nutrition and psychological advantages to breastfeeding have been described in detail elsewhere[192, 193].

Exclusive breastfeeding is recommended for the first 6 months of life[194]. Reviewers of evidence as to whether 4 or 6 months is the best age to introduce complementary foods, concluded that there was no advantage to starting before six months[191]. In Honduras, there was no improvement in growth when SGA, breastfed infants were given hygienically prepared, nutritious, complementary foods at 4 months compared to 6 months[195]. Although growth and morbidity were not higher when complementary foods were introduced at 4 vs. 6 months, this may be explained by the fact that the foods used in this study were hygienically prepared and stored. However, there are still few data from controlled studies that compare the merits of starting supplementation at 4 or 6 months.

## Complementary Feeding

Complementary feeding is defined as the period during which foods or liquids are provided along with continued breastfeeding. Complementary food is the term used to describe any nutrient-containing foods or liquids, other than breastmilk, that are given to young children during the period of complementary feeding[191]. Complementary food includes special "transitional" foods that are prepared especially for the infant and, increasingly as the child becomes older, the same foods that are consumed by other members of the household.

### Recommendations for Complementary Feeding

A recent review of current recommendations for complementary feeding revealed some similarities, as well as many differences, among national and international organizations[168]. The similarities include: the need for a gradual transition from soft foods to family foods; starting complementary feeding some time between 4 and 6 months of age; and introducing cereals first and avoiding offering cow's milk until 9-12 months of age. The differences include: mention or lack of mention of the need for iron-fortified foods, specific vitamin A sources, meat, poultry, fish, and vitamin - mineral supplements; and the recommended number of meals. The need to reinforce the importance of continued breastfeeding is often overlooked. There is a critical need for international guidelines that provide advice about best feeding practices (including breastfeeding) during the first years of life. WHO has recently published such guidelines for the WHO European Region[196].

As a general rule, the nutrient intake of the young child deteriorates when complementary foods start to substitute for breastmilk. Complementary feeding is poorly done in many developing countries, due to lack of information about what foods are appropriate, how much should be given, how they should be given, and their inadequacy in quantity and quality, among other problems. WHO commissioned a major review of these questions[191]. A brief summary of the relevant conclusions follows here.

### Estimating the Amount of Nutrients Needed in Complementary Foods

The WHO report[191] provides estimates of the amount of nutrients that should be consumed in complementary foods. The approach used was to estimate the usual intake of each nutrient from breastmilk, for infants consuming low, average and high amounts of breastmilk between 6 and 24 months of age. The usual intakes were calculated as the average reported volumes of breastmilk consumed in developing (and separately in developed) countries, and average values for the nutrient content of human milk. The nutrient intakes estimated in this way were then subtracted from the recommended intakes for each nutrient, producing an estimate of the amount of each nutrient that is needed from complementary foods. If desired, these values, (Table 4) can be modified by substituting country-specific, recommended nutrient intakes or breastmilk composition data. It should be emphasized that the following calculations were based on estimates of the nutrient content of breastmilk of women in developed countries (except for vitamin A) due to lack of adequate information from developing countries. This means that the contribution of breastmilk to the infant's intake of some nutrients has been overestimated, and the need for these nutrients from complementary foods has been underestimated, where maternal undernutrition has reduced the breastmilk content of these nutrients.

The nutrient requirements (with variations depending on age) from complementary foods, for infants that consume average intakes of breastmilk after the age of 6 months, are as follows: energy, 50-70%; protein, 20-45%; vitamin A, 5-30%; thiamine, 50-80%; riboflavin, 50-65%; calcium, 60%; vitamin $B_6$, 75-88%; zinc, 85%; and almost 100% for iron. Importantly, almost no vitamin $B_{12}$, C, or folate is needed from complementary foods if some breastmilk is consumed, because breastmilk is so high in these vitamins. An important caveat here is that maternal undernutrition can easily reduce the content of vitamin $B_{12}$ in breastmilk. Breastmilk also makes a very important contribution to meeting the vitamin A requirements of the infant, although maternal vitamin A depletion will also lower the content of this vitamin in breastmilk.

TABLE 4:   Estimated daily amounts of nutrients needed from complementary foods, by age of infants, and usual breastmilk intake in developing countries

| Nutrient | 6-8 months Breastmilk intake (mL) | | | 9-11 months Breastmilk intake (mL) | | | 12-23 months Breastmilk intake (mL) | | |
|---|---|---|---|---|---|---|---|---|---|
| | Low 350 | Avg. 666 | High 982 | Low 253 | Avg. 611 | High 969 | Low 145 | Avg. 558 | High 971 |
| Energy (kcal) | 465 | 269 | 73 | 673 | 451 | 229 | 1002 | 746 | 490 |
| Protein (g) | 5 | 2 | 0 | 7 | 3 | 0 | 9 | 5 | 1 |
| Vitamin A (µgRE) | 164 | 13 | 0 | 214 | 42 | 0 | 313 | 126 | 0 |
| Folate (µg) | 0 | 0 | 0 | 9 | 0 | 0 | 35 | 3 | 0 |
| Niacin (mg) | 3 | 3 | 3 | 5 | 4 | 4 | 8 | 7 | 7 |
| Riboflavin (mg) | 0.3 | 0.2 | 0.1 | 0.3 | 0.2 | 0.1 | 0.5 | 0.4 | 0.3 |
| Thiamine (mg) | 0.1 | 0.1 | 0 | 0.2 | 0.2 | 0.1 | 0.5 | 0.4 | 0.3 |
| Vitamin $B_6$ (mg) | 0.26 | 0.21 | 0.17 | 0.27 | 0.22 | 0.17 | 0.28 | 0.23 | 0.17 |
| Vitamin $B_{12}$ (µg) | 0 | 0 | 0 | 0.1 | 0 | 0 | 0.3 | 0 | 0 |
| Vitamin C (mg) | 10 | 0 | 0 | 14 | 0 | 0 | 23 | 8 | 0 |
| Vitamin D (µg) | 6.8 | 6.6 | 6.5 | 6.9 | 6.7 | 6.5 | 7 | 6.7 | 6.4 |
| Vitamin K (µg) | 9.2 | 9 | 8 | 9.4 | 9 | 8 | 9.6 | 9 | 8 |
| Calcium (mg) | 421 | 336 | 252 | 449 | 353 | 256 | 301 | 196 | 92 |
| Copper (mg) | 0.2 | 0.1 | 0.1 | 0.2 | 0.1 | 0.1 | 0.4 | 0.3 | 0.2 |
| Iodine (µg) | 19 | 0 | 0 | 30 | 0 | 0 | 51 | 10 | 0 |
| Iron (mg): | | | | | | | | | |
| low bioavailability | 21 | 21 | 21 | 21 | 21 | 21 | 12 | 12 | 12 |
| medium bioavailability | 11 | 11 | 11 | 11 | 11 | 11 | 6 | 6 | 6 |
| high bioavailability | 7 | 7 | 7 | 7 | 7 | 7 | 4 | 4 | 4 |
| Magnesium (mg) | 62 | 51 | 41 | 70 | 58 | 46 | 79 | 66 | 53 |
| Phosphorus (mg) | 348 | 306 | 263 | 362 | 314 | 266 | 246 | 193 | 141 |
| Selenium (µg) | 3 | 0 | 0 | 5 | 0 | 0 | 11 | 4 | 0 |
| Zinc (mg) | 2.5 | 2.2 | 1.9 | 2.6 | 2.3 | 2.1 | 2.7 | 2.4 | 2.1 |

Source:   Adapted from Brown KH, Dewey KG, Allen LH (1998) *Complementary feeding of young children in developing countries: a review of current scientific knowledge.* Geneva: WHO.

Nutrient density (Table 5) refers to the amount of a given nutrient per 100 kcal of food, and is calculated from the ratio of the amount of each nutrient needed from complementary foods to the amount of energy needed from complementary foods. Nutrient density is an important consideration because it is not high enough in many of the foods available for complementary feeding. This means that the intake of nutrients from such foods will be inadequate, even when the infant's energy needs are met.

**TABLE 5:** Desirable nutrient density of complementary foods (per 100 kcal) by age of infants, and usual breastmilk intake in developing countries

| Nutrient | 6-8 months Breastmilk intake (mL) | | | 9-11 months Breastmilk intake (mL) | | | 12-23 months Breastmilk intake (mL) | | |
|---|---|---|---|---|---|---|---|---|---|
| | Low 350 | Avg. 666 | High 982 | Low 253 | Avg. 611 | High 960 | Low 145 | Avg. 558 | High 971 |
| Protein (g) | 1.1 | 0.7 | 0 | 1 | 0.7 | 0 | 0.9 | 0.7 | 0.2 |
| Vitamin A (µgRE) | 35 | 5 | 0 | 32 | 9 | 0 | 31 | 17 | 0 |
| Folate (µg) | 0 | 0 | 0 | 1 | 0 | 0 | 3 | 0 | 0 |
| Niacin (mg) | 0.6 | 1.1 | 4.1 | 0.7 | 0.9 | 1.7 | 0.8 | 0.9 | 1.4 |
| Riboflavin (mg) | 0.3 | 0.2 | 0.1 | 0.3 | 0.2 | 0.1 | 0.5 | 0.4 | 0.3 |
| Thiamine (mg) | 0.1 | 0.1 | 0 | 0.2 | 0.2 | 0.1 | 0.5 | 0.4 | 0.3 |
| Vitamin $B_6$ (mg) | 0.05 | 0.08 | 0.23 | 0.04 | 0.05 | 0.08 | 0.03 | 0.03 | 0.04 |
| Vitamin $B_{12}$ (µg) | 0 | 0 | 0 | 0.01 | 0 | 0 | 0.03 | 0 | 0 |
| Vitamin C (mg) | 2.2 | 0 | 0 | 2.1 | 0 | 0 | 2.3 | 0 | 0 |
| Vitamin D (µg) | 1.5 | 2.5 | 8.9 | 1 | 1.5 | 2.8 | 0.7 | 0.9 | 1.3 |
| Vitamin K (µg) | 2 | 3.3 | 11 | 1.4 | 2 | 3.5 | 1 | 1.2 | 1.6 |
| Calcium (mg) | 91 | 125 | 345 | 67 | 78 | 112 | 30 | 26 | 19 |
| Copper (mg) | 0.04 | 0.04 | 0.14 | 0.03 | 0.02 | 0.04 | 0.04 | 0.04 | 0.04 |
| Iodine (µg) | 4 | 0 | 0 | 4 | 0 | 0 | 5 | 1 | 0 |
| Iron (mg): | | | | | | | | | |
| low bioavailability | 4 | 8 | 28 | 31 | 5 | 9 | 1 | 2 | 2 |
| medium bioavailability | 2 | 4 | 15 | 2 | 2 | 5 | 1 | 1 | 1 |
| high bioavailability | 1 | 2 | 9 | 1 | 1 | 3 | 0 | 1 | 1 |
| Magnesium (mg) | 13 | 19 | 56 | 10 | 13 | 20 | 8 | 9 | 11 |
| Phosphorus (mg) | 75 | 114 | 360 | 54 | 70 | 116 | 25 | 26 | 29 |
| Selenium (µg) | 0.6 | 0 | 0 | 0.7 | 0 | 0 | 1.1 | 0.5 | 0 |
| Zinc (mg) | 0.5 | 0.8 | 2.6 | 0.4 | 0.5 | 0.9 | 0.3 | 0.3 | 0.4 |

Source: Adapted from Brown KH, Dewey KG, Allen LH (1998) *Complementary feeding of young children in developing countries: a review of current scientific knowledge*. Geneva: WHO.

## Improving the Nutrient Content of Complementary Foods

### Increasing Energy Intake

It is difficult to interpret associations between energy intake and growth. When energy intake from foods is low, the intake of many other nutrients will also be inadequate. Experiments in which the energy content of infant formulae was varied, while keeping the protein content constant, indicate that energy deficiency affects growth in weight but not in height, at least in the short term[197, 198]. Intervention studies, supplying energy alone as additional fat or a high energy food, have not found a consistent effect on growth. In Papua New Guinea, energy supplements increased the weight gain and fatness of school children, but not their linear growth[199, 200]. In contrast,

a high energy food (310 kcal/day) given to undernourished Indian children increased both their height and weight gain[201].

Many complementary foods have a low energy density. The recommended energy density of complementary foods fed three times a day to infants consuming average amounts of breastmilk, is 0.6 kcal/g at 6-8 months, increasing to 1.0 kcal/g at 12 –23 months. If the intake of breastmilk is low, the energy density may need to be 0.8-1.2 kcal/g. In contrast to these recommendations, the energy density of many gruels, soups, and broths fed to children in developing countries is below 0.3 kcal/g. The number of daily feedings of these watery foods may already be high, in which case it would be best to increase their energy density, rather than the number of feeds per day[191].

Energy density can be increased by reducing the viscosity of cereals with amylases. These can be purchased commercially or made by germinating local cereals. This strategy has achieved mixed results. Although an amylase-treated, cereal porridge can be fed more rapidly and needs less added water, such foods are slightly more expensive and take longer to prepare. They also carry a higher risk of bacterial contamination if home-produced amylases are used. Amylase treatment increased energy intake in only five out of eight studies[191]. Concerns about the microbiological safety of foods treated with amylase, and the lack of clear efficacy of increasing energy intake, suggest that extensive promotion of amylase treatment approach is not justified at this time.

Another approach, often recommended to increase energy density is to add fats or sugars to complementary foods. However, adding oils or sugars to foods aggravates the problem of already low nutrient density. For example, it has been calculated that adding one teaspoon of oil to 100 g of maize gruel in West Africa would reduce protein density from 8.9 to 3.3% of energy, and iron density from 0.5 to 0.2 mg/kcal[191].

## Increasing Protein Intake

In most situations, the protein intakes of infants are adequate[202], especially if they are consuming some breastmilk[191, 203]. Trials with infant formulas revealed that changing energy intake, while holding protein intake constant and adequate, affected the weight (fatness) of infants rather than their linear growth[197]. In the INCAP longitudinal study in Guatemala[204], there was no added benefit from providing infants and preschool children with good quality protein compared to energy alone. Protein was given here as *atole*, a gruel prepared from dried skim milk and cereal. Energy intake was the strongest predictor of both linear growth and weight increase[204]. However, the supplements did contain some micronutrients and thus the intake of these covaried with energy intake. Moreover, the supplemented children remained severely stunted, even though many of them consumed more energy than their requirements and their protein intakes were two to three times higher than recommendations[205]. In the Nutrition Collaborative Research Support Programme (CRSP), linear growth faltering was prevalent in preschool children in Egypt, Kenya and Mexico, even though their intakes of protein and essential amino acids were adequate[202].

The preceding discussion does not mean that protein intake is always adequate in the period of complementary feeding. Situations that contribute to a low protein intake are: low breastmilk intake; the use of low protein, starchy staples, such as cassava;

overreliance on foods high in sugars and fats; and low food intake in general.

## Processed Complementary Foods

Starting in the 1960s, and up to the 1980s, there was considerable interest in developing and testing mixtures of ingredients, especially cereals and legumes that would improve the quantity and quality of protein in complementary foods. For example, this was a major focus for the Protein Advisory Group of the United Nations, which advised agencies, such as UNICEF, on appropriate formulations. Some of these weaning foods were be designed, processed, mixed and packaged at the country level; e.g., *Incaparina* in Guatemala made from processed corn and cotton seed flour, vitamins and minerals; and *Thriposha* in Sri Lanka, made from corn and soybeans. Others were developed in the community (e.g., weaning formulas in Thailand prepared from roasted rice, beans, plus ground nuts or sesame) or at home (e.g., *Sarbottam Pitho* made from roasted legumes, wheat and/or corn and/or rice in Nepal) [206]. In addition to combining cereals and legumes, these complementary formulations recommendations usually recommended the addition of fruit and vegetables in the home, to provide nutrients such as vitamins A and C. However, there was little attempt to estimate and to provide the required amounts of micronutrients.

The earlier formulations met with limited success. Problems encountered included: relatively high cost for many households, especially those with the most undernourished children; lack of availability in rural areas; poor marketing; and sometimes, poor texture or flavour. Also, the importance of micronutrients for child growth and development had not been recognized, so that these mixtures tended to be nutritionally incomplete.

There has been some resurgence of interest in promoting processed, complementary foods[207]. Reasons for this include: the trend to urbanization, which creates demand for purchased foods that are easy and quick to prepare; the availability of improved, simple technology for production of blended cereals at the community level, which lowers the cost and improves the sustainability of supply; and the ability to fortify these foods with micronutrients. Production of such foods can generate income for women. The cost of buying fortified products to improve dietary quality may be less than adding other foods, such as animal products.

These foods should not be promoted for use by infants less than 6 months old if there is any risk that they will interfere with breastfeeding. The desirable characteristics of processed complementary foods have been described by several authors; e.g. [208, 209]. The nutrient content (protein, fat, and micronutrients) of processed foods varies widely and is often not consistent with the amounts or densities of nutrients such as those recommended in Tables 4 and 5. There is an urgent need to pay more attention to the composition of these foods and to the bioavailability of their micronutrients. Different formulations may be needed for younger infants (who have higher nutrient requirements per kg body weight) compared to older preschool children. The Codex Alimentarius states that fortified foods should contain at least two thirds of the recommended intake of specific micronutrients per 100 g of dry food[210].

## Improving the Micronutrient Content (Quality) of Complementary Foods

For practical purposes, the term "poor dietary quality" usually implies that a diet is low in micronutrients and/or that the micronutrients are not well absorbed; i.e., poor bioavailability.

### Increasing the Consumption of Animal Products

One strategy for improving the amount and bioavailability of micronutrients is to increase consumption of animal products. Animal products are high in most micronutrients, and many minerals and vitamins are better absorbed from milk, meat and eggs than they are from plant-derived foods. Unfortunately, children in developing countries often receive only small amounts of foods that contain animal products, if any. Most animal-based foods contain more fat than plant-based foods. This makes them more energy dense, as well as being a good source of fat soluble vitamins and essential fatty acids. Animal products usually contain more retinol, vitamins D and E, riboflavin, calcium and zinc per 100 kcal of energy content, and are the only source of vitamin $B_{12}$. Animal products are the only foods that have high enough iron, zinc, calcium and riboflavin densities to provide the daily requirements of these micronutrients in complementary foods. This is especially true between 6 and 12 months of age, when only liver can be consumed in amounts large enough to meet recommended iron intakes[191]. Some types of animal products (meat, fish, and poultry) contain more iron and zinc than cereals, and in a form which is several times more absorbable than in iron and zinc from plants[211, 212]. However, consumption of animal products is culturally unacceptable in some areas.

There has been interest in improving the quality of complementary foods by adding locally available animal products, as well as specific fr vegetables, to the usual cereals, staples and legumes that are fed to young children in developing countries. A higher intake of animal products has been associated with better growth in some studies. In Peru, higher intakes of breastmilk, animal products in foods, and complementary foods in general all promoted growth between 12 and 15 months of age[203]. In rural Mexico, the main predictor of children's size and growth between 18 and 30 months of age was maternal size and the children's intake of animal products[213]. The smallest children had the smallest mothers and the lowest intake of animal products. In Kenya and Egypt, animal products were also predictors of available zinc, iron, and vitamin $B_{12}$ intakes, as well as child size and growth[214].

A dramatic example of the effects of witholding animal products from infants and young children is provided by studies of macrobiotic diets in the Netherlands. This example is particularly valuable because macrobiotic diets are somewhat similar to the diets of children in developing countries, and indeed are better than many. They consist primarily of cereals (mainly rice), vegetables, legumes, and marine algae, small amounts of cooked fruit and occasional fish. No meat or dairy products are used. Compared to omnivorous controls, the Dutch macrobiotic children consumed less protein, fat, calcium, riboflavin, vitamin $B_{12}$ and vitamin C. The adverse effects of these diets were clear even though these children were raised in sanitary environments and relatively good socioeconomic conditions. Birthweights were about 3,290 g in the macrobiotic group, significantly lower than the 3470 g in the controls. Birthweights were related to the household's usual consumption of fish and dairy products. The growth of children on macrobiotic diets followed the reference line until 4 months, at which point length gain declined dramatically (to a rate of 13.2 cm/year compared to 16.7 cm/year in controls) until it stabilized at 16 months[215]. There was no later catch-up. Weight gain followed a similar pattern but there was some catch-up after 2 years. WH was normal. Children from families consuming dairy products three times a week grew better than those who rarely consumed them. The macrobiotic infants showed numerous biochemical abnormalities and nutrient deficiencies, including: iron, with consequent anaemia; riboflavin deficiency; rickets; and vitamin $B_{12}$ deficiency[216]. Their gross motor development, speech and language development were delayed[217]. Recent publications show that the vitamin $B_{12}$ status and cognitive function of these children was still impaired in early adolescence, in spite of the fact that parents heeded advice to feed animal products, starting at 6 years on average[218].

Due to their good acceptability by infants and children, and their relatively low cost, milk products have often been provided to young children in order to improve the quality of their diets. In 12 out of 15 intervention trials (Table 6), consumption of milk resulted in improved growth relative to controls[219]. Another approach has been the addition of locally available animal products to plant-based diets. However, the addition of dry fish powder to a fermented maize porridge, or to a blend of beans, groundnuts, and maize did not improve the growth or micronutrient status of Ghanaian children who were given these foods between 6 and 12 months of age[220].

Given the poor economic situation of many households in developing countries, is it reasonable to recommend that their children consume more animal products? For some, this may not be a practical solution. There is, however, increasing awareness that animal products are likely be the only unfortified foods that can provide enough micronutrients to children, and that it is feasible to increase their consumption. Viable strategies, in many situations, include: educating the mother to target small amounts of animal products (such as liver) to her youngest children; encouraging consumption of cheaper animal products (e.g., eggs, fish, dried milk); and supporting home production of small animals, fish and birds. Additionally, fermented milk products may be an excellent source of nutrients for children, and are more amenable than fresh milk to non-refrigerated storage.

## Improving the Content and Bioavailability of Nutrients in Plant-Based Complementary Foods

The micronutrients that are most difficult to obtain in sufficient quantity from complementary foods in general, and especially from plant-based complementary foods, are: absorbable iron and zinc; calcium; vitamin A; and sometimes riboflavin. Vitamin $B_{12}$ is found only in animal products and breastmilk. Efforts are ongoing to increase the bioavailability of iron and zinc from complementary foods, using techniques such as germination and fermentation, to reduce the content of phytates. For example, these are being evaluated in Malawi (R. Gibson, personal communication).

Giving infants and young children coffee or tea to drink can have an adverse effect on iron status, because these drinks contain polyphenols that inhibit iron absorption. In a controlled intervention trial in Guatemala, discontinuing the usual coffee intake of preschool children improved their response to iron supplements[221]. If teas are given to young children

between meals, there is less interference with iron absorption if they are given with meals.

The absorption of iron from cereals and legumes can be improved by consuming more vitamin C in the same meal. The implications of this interaction for complementary feeding have been described as follows[222]. The vitamin C should be included in or given with the meals which contain most iron, or consumed within an hour of such meals. The addition to, or fortification of, a meal with 50 mg vitamin C approximately doubles the amount of iron that an infant can absorb. It may be difficult to provide this amount of vitamin C from fruit, juices or vegetables, but even smaller amounts will cause some improvement in iron absorption. Vitamin C produces the greatest increase in iron absorption when complementary foods (e.g., soy, whole maize, lentils, unpolished rice) are high in inhibitors such as phytates, but obviously has little effect if the foods are low in iron. The iron status of infants will improve if vitamin C is added to iron-fortified, formulated infant foods or dry milk[223].

Risk factors for the early onset of VAD in infancy and childhood include: early weaning or a low intake of breastmilk; poor vitamin A status of the mother and subsequently low concentrations of the vitamin in breastmilk; and low intake of animal products rich in retinol[224]. However, the vitamin A requirements of infants and young children can be met from plant sources alone[225]. Dark green, leafy vegetables are less effective, although useful, sources of vitamin A, because their beta-carotene is less well absorbed than that of fruit[226]. Food-based interventions that have successfully improved vitamin A status are reviewed below in the section on Preventing and Treating Vitamin A Deficiency.

### Fortification of Complementary Foods with Micronutrients

It is difficult to meet all of the micronutrient needs of infants and young children through home-based foods. A review of 23 complementary food combinations used in developing countries, including some animal products, revealed that although most of them could supply enough energy and protein, none had enough iron and few had enough zinc[227]. Animal products supply more of these nutrients but only few, such as liver, have a high enough densities to meet requirements[191]. Even in developed countries, the diets of young children would be too low in iron without supplementation; and therefore many cereals and other complementary foods are fortified with iron, even where diets are usually of high quality. Iron deficiency anaemia (IDA) is still a problem for infants in many developed countries[228].

TABLE 6: Intervention trials with complementary foods

| REGION / Country | N | Initial age (months) | Duration of Intervention (months) | Intervention | Impact on Growth | Impact on Micronutrient Status |
|---|---|---|---|---|---|---|
| **AFRICA** | | | | | | |
| Sudan[a] | 628 | 6-26 | 3-6 | DSM vs. beans | + height (DSM group) | NA |
| D.R.Congo[b] | 120 | 4 | 3 | V/M fortified blend (cereal, soy, milk, oil) vs. none | NS | NA |
| Ghana[c] | 208 | 6 | 6 | Weanimix, Weanimix with V/M, Weanimix with fish powder, fermented maize with fish powder vs. cross-sectional comparison group | NS among intervention groups; + weight & + height in intervention groups vs. comparison group | + Vit A + ferritin (in V/M group only): NS (Hb, riboflavin, Zn) |
| Sénégal[c] | 110 | 4 | 3 | V/M fortified blend (cereal, soy, milk, oil) vs. none | + height | NA |
| **ASIA-PACIFIC** | | | | | | |
| Indonesia[d] | 113 | 6-20 | 3 | High energy snacks | + weight; NS height | NA |
| New Caledonia[c] | 90 | 4 | 3 | V/M fortified blend (cereal, soy, milk, oil) vs. none | NS | NA |
| Papua New Guinea[e] | 43 | 6-12 | 12 | DSM, peanut butter, soy or none | NS | +Hb ( DSM group) |
| People's Republic of China[f] | 164 | 6-13 | 3 | V/M fortified vs. unfortified rusk | NS | +Hb -Vitamin E NS (Vitamin A, riboflavin, Fe and indices) |
| Thailand[g] | 205 | <36 | 12 | High fat biscuit, V/M fortified | NS | NA |
| **EUROPE** | | | | | | |
| Denmark[h] | 41 | 8 | 2 | High-meat vs. low-meat foods | NS | + Hb; NS (Fe and Zn indices) |
| **LATIN AMERICA** | | | | | | |
| Colombia[i] | 170 | Trimester III | 39 | DSM, with high protein vegetable mix, Fe, and vitamin A | + height from 6 mo, + weight from 3 mo | NA |
| Guatemala[j] | 330 | 3 | 33 | "Incaparina" (cereal, legumes, milk) vs. sugar drink (some V/M in both). | + height, + weight | NA |
| Jamaica[k] | 127 | 9-24 | 12 | Milk formula + DSM vs. none | + height, + weight, + head circumference | NA |
| Bolivia[c] | 127 | 4 | 3 | V/M fortified blend (cereal, soy, milk, oil) vs. none | NS | NA |

Sources: Adapted from Brown KH, Dewey KG, Allen LH (1998) Complementary feeding of young children in developing countries: A review of current scientific knowledge. Geneva: WHO; and Dewey KG (2001). Approaches for improving complementary feeding of infants and young children. Background paper for the WHO/UNICEF Technical Consultation on Infant and Young Child Feeding, Geneva: WHO. (In press). Additional sources are:

[a] Vaughan JP, Zumrawi F, Waterlow JC, Kirkwood BR (1981) An evaluation of dried skimmed milk on children's growth in Khartoum province, Sudan. Nutrition Research b 1:243-252.

[b] Simondon KB, Gartner A, Berger J, Cornu A, Massamba JP, San Miguel JL, Misotte I, Simondon F, Traissac P, Delpeuch F, Maire B (1996) Effect of early, short-term supplementation on weight and linear growth of 4-7-mo-old infants in developing countries: A four-country randomized trial. American Journal of Clinical Nutrition 64. 537-545.

[c] Lartey A, Manu A, Brown KH, Peerson JM, Dewey KG (1999) A randomized, community-based trial of the effects of improved, centrally processed complementary foods on growth and micronutrient status of Ghanaian infants from 6 to 12 mo of age. American Journal of Clinical Nutrition 70: 391-404.

[d] Husaini MA, Karyadi L, Husain Sandjaja YK, Karyadi D, Pollitt E (1991) Developmental effects of short-term supplementary feeding in nutritionally-at-risk Indonesian infants. American Journal of Clinical Nutrition 54: 799-804.

[e] Becroft T, Bailey KV (1965) Supplementary feeding trial in New Guinea highland infants. Journal of Tropical Pediatrics and African Child Health 11:28-34.

[f] Liu DS, Bates CJ, Yin TA, Wang XB, Lu CQ (1993) Nutritional efficacy of a fortified weaning rusk in a rural area near Beijing. American Journal of Clinical Nutrition 57: 506-511.

[g] Gershoff SN, McGandy RB, Nondasuta A, Tantiwongse P (1988) Nutrition studies in Thailand: effects of calories, nutrient supplements, and health interventions on growth of preschool Thai village children. American Journal of Clinical Nutrition 48: 1214-1218.

[h] Engelmann MDM, Sandstrom B, Michaelsen KF (1998) Meat intake and iron status in late infancy: An intervention study. European Journal of Clinical Nutrition 67: 26-33.

[i] Lutter CK, Mora JO, Habicht J-P, Rasmussen KM, Robson DS, Herrera MG (1990) Age-specific responsiveness of weight and length to nutritional supplementation. American Journal of Clinical Nutrition 51: 359-364; and Mora J, de Paredes B, Wagner M, de Navarro L, Suescun J, Christiansen N, Herrera MG (1979) Nutritional supplementation and the outcome of pregnancy. I. Birthweight. American Journal of Clinical Nutrition 32: 455-462.

[j] Martorell R, Habicht J-P, Rivera JA (1995) History and design of the INCAP longitudinal study (1969-77) and its follow-up (1988-89). Journal of Nutrition 125: 1027S-1041S; and Schroeder DG, Martorell R, Rivera JA, Ruel MT, Habicht J-P (1995) Age differences in the impact of nutritional supplementation on growth. Journal of Nutrition 125: 1051S-1059S.

[k] Walker SP, Powell CA, Grantham-McGregor SM, Himes JH, Chang SM (1991) Nutritional supplementation, psychosocial stimulation, and growth of stunted children: The Jamaican study. American Journal of Clinical Nutrition 54: 642-648.

DSM = dry skimmed milk; Hb = Hb; N = sample population size; NA = not assessed; NS = not significant; V/M = vitamins and minerals; + = significant increase; - = significant decrease.

## Efficacy Trials of Complementary Foods

Randomized trials of the effects of processed complementary foods on nutrition status and development have produced mixed results. Most trials involved infants between 6 and 12 months of age. The results of trials published since 1988 were summarized in the WHO report[191] and newer trials have also been summarized by Dewey[168] (Table 6).

The trials reviewed in the two reports were conducted in Papua New Guinea[229], Sudan[230], Thailand[231]; Colombia[232]; Guatemala[156, 233]; Indonesia[234]; Jamaica[235]; PRC[236], Bolivia, the D.R. Congo, New Caledonia and Sénégal[237]; Ghana[220], and Denmark[238]. The overall conclusions derived from these trials include the following:

- The trials varied considerably in terms of the age at which the intervention occurred, the composition of the complementary foods, the baseline nutritional status of the infants; and the extent of breastfeeding.
- In three trials (Guatemala, Colombia and Jamaica) the supplement increased weight and length; in Indonesia and Sénégal, only weight was increased.
- Most of the supplements contained dry milk, with or without cereals. There was no obvious relationship between composition and outcomes.
- The critical age for intervention appears to be between 6 and 12 months, with diminishing benefit during the next 1 to 2 years.
- The supplemental foods provided a substantial amount of energy, on average twice the amount that was actually consumed by the infants (intake was 120 to 458 kcal/day). Displacement of breastmilk, and therefore net increase in energy intake, was not measured in any of the studies. Displacement is more likely when the complementary foods are given prior to six months of age[239], and may explain the lack of response of infants supplemented from 4 to 7 months in the D.R. Congo, and the positive response of already-weaned infants in Jamaica and Colombia.
- Some trials provided foods to the mother during pregnancy, then to the child. There is some evidence that infants born to women supplemented during pregnancy have greater weight and length gains even before they themselves start consuming the complementary food[240, 241], but more studies are needed to confirm this possibility.
- Few studies provided adequate micronutrients or assessed the impact on micronutrient status.

Multiple micronutrient fortification or supplementation had variable effects on status in the few studies in it was measured.
- Hb was increased by unfortified foods alone in Papua New Guinea, the PRC, Denmark, Vietnam and The Gambia, but not in Ghana.
- In none of the studies reviewed for the WHO report[191] did children attain the expected growth velocity for age. This was not checked for the remainder of the studies. There are many possible reasons for this including the long term effects of *in utero* undernutrition.

## Micronutrient Supplementation to Improve Growth

There have been numerous randomized, placebo-controlled trials of the effects of single nutrient supplements on the nutrition status and development of infants and children. To the extent that they are actually consumed, supplements improve, in most cases, the body stores of the specific micronutrient. The most important question is whether such supplementation improves functional outcomes: such as growth, vision (in the case of vitamin A), morbidity or mortality, or cognitive and motor development. The following discussion primarily deals with the impact of supplements on growth. The impacts of iron and vitamin A supplements on other functions are reviewed further in the sections on Preventing and Treating Anaemia and Preventing and Treating Vitamin A Deficiency.

### Iron

In developing countries, iron deficiency occurs early in infancy, and approximately 50% of infants are iron deficient by the end of their first year of life[11]. This may be an overestimate, based on recent data indicating that the Hb cut-off indicating anaemia in infants is set too high[242]. Nevertheless, there is ample evidence that iron deficiency is common during infancy. There is mixed evidence for an improvement in growth of anaemic preschool and school children when they are given iron supplementation. Iron supplements increased the weight gain of anaemic children in four studies in Indonesia, Kenya, and the USA[243]. Height gain was not measured in two of the studies. It was significantly improved in one, and not improved in the other. One possible explanation for this inconsistency is that the studies were too short to detect effects on linear growth. They were designed to measure rapid changes in Hb concentrations.

For infants, recent placebo-controlled intervention trials in Sweden and Honduras found that iron supplementation from age 4 to 9 months (1 mg/kg/day; i.e., half the dose recommended by WHO for infants age 6 to 24 months) significantly reduced length gain (on average by 0.4 cm) during this period[244]. Iron-supplemented infants who had higher baseline ferritin concentrations (>60 µg/L) had more diarrhoea than those in the placebo group. Clearly more work is needed in this area before routine iron supplementation for young infants can be recommended.

## Zinc

Zinc deficiency is probably widespread in developing countries, although its prevalence is uncertain due to a lack of simple status indicators. It is caused by: low intakes of animal products; diets high in phytates, which inhibit zinc absorption; and losses due to diarrhoea. Randomized, controlled trials of zinc supplementation for children have produced varying degrees of growth response. For example, short children in the USA grew faster when supplemented with 5 mg zinc/day for 12 months[245], and 3- to 5-year-old children in rural Ecuador responded to 10 mg/day zinc with faster height gain within six months[246]. Stunted Guatemalan infants also responded to zinc supplements with faster linear growth[247]. In contrast, a trial that provided 20 mg/day zinc to preschool children in rural Mexico for 12 months found no improvement in weight or height[248]. A meta-analysis of 25 studies revealed that there was an overall small, but highly significant, impact of zinc supplements on height, but only in children with initial HA Z-scores less than –2.0[249]. Weight also increased slightly yet significantly, but only in those children with initially low plasma zinc concentrations. No variations were detected in response due to age at treatment. There may be other benefits of zinc supplementation for children, including: a reduction in the duration and severity of diarrhoea, observed in Guatemala, India, Mexico, Papua New Guinea, Peru and Viet Nam[250]; persistent diarrhoea and dysentery, in India[251]; and acute lower respiratory infections, in India[252].

## Vitamin A

Supplementation of infants and children less than 5 years old with vitamin A is routinely achieved in most developing countries by administration of oral capsules, often delivered through the Expanded Programme on Immunization (EPI) of WHO, and through "National Vitamin A Days"[253]. This reduces ocular symptoms of vitamin A deficiency, as well as mortality from measles[254], and improves Hb synthesis. However, randomized, controlled trials in Peru, Ghana and India failed to show any benefit on mortality or morbidity, of providing high doses of vitamin A through the EPI during infancy. Moreover, the vitamin A status of the infants was little improved[255]. The doses of vitamin A provided may have been too low[256].

Children with mild xerophthalmia in West Java, Indonesia had slower rates of weight and height gains than nonxerophthalmic children[257]. This and other observations have suggested that modest improvements in growth might be an additional benefit from vitamin A supplementation of deficient children. This has been observed in some randomized, controlled studies[258, 259], but not in all e.g., [260, 261, 262]. In a recent Indonesian trial, only children with initially low serum retinol concentrations (<0.35 µmol/l) responded to a supplement of 100,000 IU to 200,000 IU of vitamin A[263]. In the 4 month intervention, the supplemented children's height and weight gain were, on average, 0.39 cm and 152 g more than those in the placebo group. Children younger than 24 months responded only if they were consuming no vitamin A from breastmilk. It appears that vitamin A status may affect linear growth. The conflicting results among studies might be explained by failures to take into account the initial vitamin A status of supplemented children and the extent of deficiencies of other micronutrients required for growth. Improving vitamin A status is justified, however, even if it does not improve growth.

## Calcium

A review of calcium intervention studies[264], found that four out of six failed to find an impact on growth. The two trials with a positive effect were conducted 60 years ago in a school for children of low to middle socioeconomic status, in India. The children were aged 3 to 6 years, and 6- to 12-years[265]. Most calcium intervention studies have been done on prepubescent children. Even in 8- to 12-year-old school children who were consuming very small amounts of calcium (average, 342 mg/day) in The Gambia, increasing calcium intake to 1,056 mg/day, through supplements for 12 months, caused no improvement in weight or height gain compared to a placebo group[266]. However, the supplemented children did improve their bone mineral content and had lower serum osteocalcin, indicating reduced bone resorption. Current thinking is that bone mineralization during growth is the major determinant of peak bone mineral content in adulthood, and that this protects against osteoporosis in later life. Concern about adequate calcium intakes in childhood is certainly justified, even if these do not affect growth.

## Iodine

Severe iodine deficiency causes substantial linear growth retardation. Marginal deficiency is associated with shorter stature[267]. Some of the associations seen in early childhood might be explained by a residual effect of poor maternal iodine status during pregnancy, which reduces birthweight. The provision of iodized oil prior to conception increases birthweight[268]. However, growth was not restored to normal when iodized oil was given to children in a region of Ecuador with endemic iodine deficiency[269] or to goitrous school children in Bolivia[270]. As discussed further below, the other benefits of iodine supplementation of deficient infants and children include reduction in the spectrum of IDD and in infant mortality.

## Multiple Micronutrients

Single micronutrient deficiencies are probably unlikely in children aged less than 3 to 5 years[271, 272], and several micronutrient deficiencies are implicated in growth failure. It is therefore reasonable to assume that supplements containing multiple micronutrients will have the largest impacts on growth and function. There is currently substantial interest by international organizations, such as UNICEF and WHO, in testing the effects of multiple micronutrient supplements. As is true in the case of supplementation with iron alone, the main limitations to their adoption seem to be programmematic, such as delivery and compliance, rather than cost. The additional micronutrients add little to the overall price of supplements. A multiple micronutrient supplement might be more attractive to consumers than an iron supplement alone. However, some micronutrients need to be consumed daily or every few days in order to improve status; whereas iron, vitamin A and folic acid supplements may improve nutrient status if taken once a week.

Several multiple micronutrient formulations, appropriate for children during the period of complementary feeding are now being tested in malnourished populations, though relatively few trials have been completed and published. In Viet Nam, multiple micronutrient supplements (containing iron, vitamins A and C and zinc) improved the rate of linear growth and reduced anaemia in preschool children, when given for 3 months either weekly or as a larger dose three times per week[273]. The iron, vitamin A and zinc status of the supplemented children was also better than that of the controls, who received iron supplements only. In Mexico, children aged 8 to 14 months were randomly assigned to a multiple micronutrient supplement or a placebo for 12 months[274]. There was no significant effect on weight.

Length gain was 0.3 Z greater in the supplemented children, but only if they were less than 12 months of age at the start of the intervention. In Peru, a trial compared supplements that contained zinc alone with supplements providing zinc and micronutrients[275]. The inclusion of micronutrients appeared to increase the relative risk of dysentery, whereas zinc alone reduced the prevalence of cough. In Guatemala, infants were randomly assigned to one of four groups for 8 months, starting around 6 months of age. The treatment groups were given: multiple micronutrients with whey protein concentrate; multiple micronutrients with bovine serum concentrate; bovine serum concentrate alone; and whey protein concentrate alone. There were no differences in length gain among the groups[276]. Further trials with multiple micronutrient supplements for young children are in progress in South Africa, Peru and Indonesia, using a new supplement formulated by UNICEF and other agencies.

A novel product that shows potential is a fat-based spread that contains multiple micronutrients (Nutriset, Paris, France). This product has been useful in emergency relief situations and for recovery of malnourished children[277]. Further efficacy trials with such products are urgently needed. The advantages of Nutriset include: very low water content, which reduces interactions among micronutrients as well as bacterial growth; high acceptability by preschool children (infants have not yet been tested); high energy density; improved carotene and fat soluble vitamin absorption, due to its fat content; and the fact that enzymes such as amylase can be added to reduce viscosity when the product is added to cereals. Its production does not require sophisticated technology and it can be produced locally, using foods such as peanuts as the base. It is available in single serving sachets, as well as in larger containers.

The micronutrient spread has been tested for its effects on catch-up growth and anaemia in children living in a permanent refugee camp in Algeria[278]. Prior to supplementation, this population was dependent on rations (predominantly wheat flour, rice, other cereals, and a small amount of canned fish) that provided slightly more than half of the energy and protein requirements for adults, slightly under half of their iron, vitamin C and thiamine requirements, and 6% of their vitamin A requirements. The intervention was targeted to stunted children (HA below -2 Z-scores). For 6 months, 364 children, aged 30 to 64 months, were provided daily with 50 g of the fortified supplement, or the supplement without micronutrients, or nothing (controls). All the children were treated for parasites with metronidazole. The 50 g of supplement provided about 300 kcal and 5 g

**TABLE 7:  Interventions with multiple micronutrients**

| Country | N | Initial age (months) | Duration of Intervention (months) | Interventions | Impact on Growth | Impact(s) on micro nutrient status |
|---|---|---|---|---|---|---|
| The Gambia[a] | 125 | 6-18 | 12 | Fe + vits; Zn + vitamins; vitamins only; none | ns | + Hb |
| Guatemala[b] | 259 | 6 | 8 | BSC + V/M, V/M, BSC or placebo | ns | ns |
| Mexico[c] | 319 | 8-14 | 12 | V/M vs. placebo | + height (in children aged < 12 months initially) | (vitamins A and E) |
| Peru[d] | 412 | 6-36 | 6 | Zn + V/M, Zn alone, or placebo | ns | nr nr |
| Viet Nam[e] | 163 | 6-24 | 3 | Fe, Zn, and vitamins A and C, weekly or daily, or placebo | + height (only in stunted children) | + Hb, + vitamin A, + Zn |

Sources:  [a]  Lartey A, Manu A,  Brown KH, Peerson JM, Dewey KG (1999) A randomized, community-based trial of the effects of improved, centrally processed complementary foods on growth and micronutrient status of Ghanaian infants from 6 to 12 mo of age. *American Journal of Clinical Nutrition* 70: 391-404.

[b]  Brown KH, Santizo MC, Begin F, Torun B (2000) Effect of supplementation with multiple micronutrients and/or bovine serum concentrate on the growth of low-income, peri-urban Guatemalan infants and young children. *Federation of American Societies for Experimental Biology Journal* 14: A534.

[c]  Rivera JA, Gonzales-Cossio T, Flores M (2001).  Multiple micronutrient supplementation improves the growth of Mexican infants. (Submitted for publication). *American Journal of Clinical Nutrition.*  (In press).

[d]  Penny ME, Brown KH, Lanata CL, Peerson JM, Marin RM, Duran A, Lonnerdal B, Black RE (1997)  Community-based trial of the effect of zinc supplements with and without other micronutrients on the duration of persistent diarrhoea, and the prevention of subsequent morbidity. *Federation of American Societies for Experimental Biology Journal* 11: A655.

[e]  Thu BD, Schultink W, Dillon D, Gross R, Leswara ND, Khoi HH (1999) Effect of daily and weekly micronutrient supplementation on micronutrient deficiencies and growth in young Vietnamese children. *American Journal of Clinical Nutrition* 69: 80-86.

Notes:   BSC = bovine serum concentrate; Hb = haemoglobin; N = Sample population size; ns = not significant; nr = not yet reported; + = increased; V/M = vitamin and mineral.

protein/day; substantial daily amounts of iron (11 mg) and zinc (about 10 mg), and about half the daily requirements for calcium and the major vitamins and minerals, except for vitamin A. The supplement contained no vitamin A, which was instead provided in capsules. The height velocity in those receiving the fortified supplement was about 6 mm/month: significantly higher than for those receiving unfortified supplement or no supplement at all (5 mm/month).  The prevalence of anaemia fell from about 75% initially to less than 10% in the fortified supplement, but remained above 50% in the unfortified and control groups. There were significant reductions in diarrhoea, acute respiratory infections and fever episodes in the supplemented children.

The positive impact of this study may have been influenced by the following. The children were initially stunted, anaemic, and presumably deficient in multiple micronutrients. They liked the supplement very much, so compliance was high.  Moreover, its consumption was supervised.  The supplement supplied substantial amounts of micronutrients and the intervention lasted for 6 months. Importantly, only the micronutrient-fortified supplement, and not the macronutrients in an equivalent amount of unfortified supplement, was effective at improving growth and reducing anaemia.

A novel strategy that is being developed and tested is the use of micronutrient "sprinkles". These are vitamin-mineral mixtures in which the micronutrients apsulated, or coated with lipids or other reduce adverse interactions among the nutrients (for example, iron can destroy vitamins A and E in a mixture of these nutrients). Sprinkles are available in single-dose sachets that can be added once a day to any food or liquid given to the infant. Iodine, iron, vitamin A, and zinc can be combined in this way. In Ghana, a trial of this approach, in anaemic 6- to 24-month-old children, concluded that iron added to food in sprinkles (which contained iron and vitamin C) was as available as that in ferrous sulphate drops (S. Zlotkin, personal communication). Further trials are underway with additional micronutrients and the measurement of functional outcomes.

## Summary and Conclusions

South Central Asia has the second highest prevalence of growth stunting in the world (44%), and the prevalence in South-East Asia is also high (33%). An estimated 70% of the world's stunted children live in Asia, and there has been little recent improvement in the situation. Growth stunting in childhood is a risk factor for increased mortality, poor cognitive and motor development and other impairments in function. It usually persists, causing smaller size and poorer performance in adulthood. Nutrition intervention trials support the following recommendations.

- Exclusive breastfeeding is strongly recommended for the first 6 months of life.
- There is probably no advantage to the infant of introducing complementary foods prior to 6 months, especially where the quantity and quality of such foods is inadequate.
- Breastfeeding should be continued when other foods are added to the infants diet. In general the quality of complementary foods is poor compared to breastmilk.
- The energy density of many gruels, soups, broths, and other watery foods fed to infants is often below the recommended 0.6 kcal/g. Energy intake can be increased by reducing the water added to foods where possible, and/or providing additional feedings. At present there is insufficient evidence to promote the use of amylases to lower the viscosity of cereals. Adding extra energy in the form of oil or sugar can adversely affect the density of protein and micronutrients in the diet.
- Even where breastmilk intake is relatively low, in most situations the amount of protein in complementary foods will be more than adequate so that adding protein alone or improving protein quality will not improve growth.

- Randomized controlled trials of the effects of processed complementary foods have shown a mixed impact on growth. Most of the trials included infants 6 to 12 months. In three, the supplement increased weight and length; in two (including Indonesia) only weight was improved; and in another four (including Thailand) there was no effect on growth. In no study did children attain the expected growth velocity for age.
- Intervention after 12 months is less effective than between 6 and 12 months. However, there is an increased risk of displacement of breastmilk when intakes of complementary foods are high, especially before 6 months of age.
- Limitations of these trials include variability in the age at which the intervention started, the composition of the foods and the amounts provided, the extent and replacement of breastmilk, and the baseline nutritional status and morbidity of the infants. Few of these complementary feeding trials supplied enough micronutrients to permit the child to consume recommended intakes from the diet plus supplements.
- In most developing countries and even in wealthier regions, the micronutrient content of unfortified complementary foods is inadequate to meet infant requirements. It is particularly difficult for infants to consume enough iron, zinc, or calcium, and vitamin A, riboflavin, thiamine and vitamin $B_6$ intakes are often low. The intake of vitamin $B_{12}$ will be inadequate if maternal deficiency has reduced breastmilk concentrations and the infant consumes low amounts of animal products.
- Interventions with single micronutrients have shown the following benefits for children with low intakes and/or a deficiency of the respective nutrients: vitamin A prevents eye lesions, causes a substantial reduction in mortality from measles and diarrhoea, and increases Hb synthesis; iron improves cognitive and motor development of anaemic infants and children; zinc improves growth of children who are stunted or have low plasma zinc; iodine reduces infant mortality and goitre prevalence and improves motor and mental function; vitamin $B_{12}$ improves growth and cognitive function.
- Because multiple micronutrient deficiencies tend to occur simultaneously, there is interest in the benefits of providing supplements that contain multiple micronutrients. Multiple micronutrient supplements caused some improvement in height growth rate in stunted Vietnamese children and in Mexican infants aged <12 months, but had no impact on growth in Peru or Guatemala.

Additional trials are underway to confirm whether multiple micronutrients improve child nutritional status, health and development more than single micronutrients. Novel approaches to providing multiple micronutrients include a fat-based spread which improved growth and Hb in one trial in stunted children, and encapsulated "sprinkles" which are undergoing further trials.

- Micronutrient intake can also be improved by targeting animal products to young children. The consumption of higher amounts of animal products was associated with better growth and micronutrient status in several studies. A review of 15 complementary feeding trials in which dried milk was included as at least one ingredient revealed that growth in length was significantly increased in 12 of these. The control groups either received no intervention, energy or some micronutrients. The one trial with dry fish powder showed no benefits of adding it to fermented maize. Increasing meat intake improved Hb in Danish infants. Meats such as chicken liver could be rich micronutrient sources for infants and children, but controlled trials of their efficacy are lacking.

- Micronutrient fortification of cereal staples is especially important where these are major constituents of complementary foods.

# PREVENTING AND TREATING ANAEMIA

naemia is defined as a low Hb concentration in blood, or less often, as a low haematocrit, the percentage of blood volume that consists of red blood cells. The limits which define anaemia are shown in Table 8[279]. Nutrition anaemias are caused when there is an inadequate body store of a specific nutrient needed for Hb synthesis.

**TABLE 8:  Haemoglobin (Hb) limits used to define anaemia[a] based on WHO/ UNICEF/UNU (1996) recommendations**

| Age or gender group | Hb below (g/L) | Haematocrit below (%) |
|---|---|---|
| Children 6 months -5 years | 110 | 33 |
| Children 5-11 years | 115 | 34 |
| Children 12-13 years | 120 | 36 |
| Nonpregnant women | 120 | 36 |
| Pregnant women | 110 | 33 |
| Men | 130 | 39 |

Source: Stoltzfus RJ, Dreyfuss ML (1998) *Guidelines for the Use of Iron Supplements to Prevent and Treat Iron Deficiency Anemia*. Geneva: International Nutritional Anaemia Consultative Group/UNICEF/WHO.
[a] These definitions are for populations living at sea level. To adjust for altitude, make the following additions to the values for Hb and haematocrit respectively: 3,000-3,999 ft (914 – 1,218 m) +2.0, +0.5; 4,000-4,999 ft (1,219 – 1,523 m) +3.0, +1.0; 5,000-5,999 ft (1,524 – 1,827 m) +5.0, +1.5; 6,000-6,999 ft (1,828 – 2,133 m) +7.0, +2.0.

Anaemia is usually caused by lack of iron, the most common nutrient deficiency. Iron deficiency anaemia (IDA) is typically diagnosed by low Hb, accompanied by biochemical evidence of iron deficiency, such as low serum ferritin concentration. Hb response to iron supplementation can also be used to confirm that the anaemia was caused by iron

deficiency. Women and children have a higher prevalence of nutrition anaemias than men. Even in developed countries, about 20 to 30% of women of reproductive age have little or no stored iron. Malaria and hookworm, the major non-nutrition risk factors for anaemia, affect both men and women.

In addition to iron, several other micronutrients are important for Hb synthesis. VAD is a significant factor in many cases of anaemia and can contribute to incomplete Hb recovery after iron supplementation. Vitamin $B_{12}$ deficiency is common in many regions, and folic acid deficiency has been reported in some areas. A relatively severe deficiency of either of these two vitamins can cause anaemia by impairing red blood cell synthesis. Riboflavin deficiency also occurs commonly in some regions, and impairs iron absorption. The relative contributions of these vitamin deficiencies to anaemia can be determined by comparing Hb response to supplementation with iron alone, or in combination with the other nutrients, although there is little information on this. Anaemia has multiple adverse effects on human function. These are independent of the other consequences of specific nutrient deficiencies.

## The Prevalence of Anaemia and of Iron Deficiency

The World Health Organization[196] estimated that about 40% of the world's population (more than 2 billion individuals) suffer from anaemia. The groups with the highest prevalence are: pregnant women and the elderly, about 50%; infants and children of 1-2 years, 48%; school children, 40%; nonpregnant women, 35%; adolescents, 30-55%; and preschool children, 25%. Because few countries have collected representative data on the prevalence of anaemia, and because much of the information is from clinic records or small surveys, national or regional estimates of anaemia are not very precise. Nevertheless, it is apparent that the prevalence of anaemia in developing countries is about four times that of developed countries. Current estimates for anaemia in developing and developed countries respectively are: for pregnant women, 56 and 18%; school children, 53 and 9%; preschool children, 42 and 17%; and men, 33 and 5%[196].

The WHO has suggested the following classification of countries with respect to the level of public health significance of anaemia: a prevalence of <15% is "low", 15-40% is "medium" and >40% is "high". Asia has the highest rates of anaemia in the world. About half of the world's anaemic women live in the Indian subcontinent, and 88% of them develop anaemia during pregnancy. The situation in Asia has not improved in recent years[11].

Anaemia occurs at a late stage of iron deficiency, after stores are depleted. The prevalence of iron deficiency, which is usually detected by low serum ferritin concentrations, is estimated to be from 2.0 to 2.5 times the prevalence of anaemia. There are few data on the actual prevalence of iron deficiency in developing countries because of the resources required to measure the necessary biochemical indicators. In population groups with a high prevalence of anaemia, however, almost all individuals will be iron deficient, except possibly if the anaemia is caused predominantly by malaria.

## Causes of Anaemia

Inadequate absorption of dietary iron is the main explanation for the much higher prevalence of anaemia in the developing countries of Asia and other regions, except where it is caused by infections such as hookworm and malaria. The best sources of dietary iron are meat, fish and poultry. These foods have a major influence on iron status, but intakes are low among poor people or when such foods are avoided for religious or cultural reasons. They contain more iron than cereals, dairy products, fruit or vegetables, and about 40% of their iron content is in the haem form, of which about 25% is absorbed. Only about 2-5% of the total iron is absorbed from cereals and legumes, and cereals contain much less iron than meat, fish or poultry[211].

At certain periods in life, iron requirements are particularly high, and therefore less likely to be met. Iron requirements are highest for pregnant women: 1.9 mg/1,000 kcal of dietary energy in the second trimester and 2.7 in the third. The figures for other groups are: infants, 1.0; adolescent girls, 0.8; adolescent boys, 0.6; nonpregnant women, 0.6; preschool and school children, 0.4; and adult men, 0.3[212]. Assuming that individuals within a household eat a similar diet, those with the highest iron

requirements are at highest risk of becoming iron deficient. Women have a substantially higher prevalence of anaemia than men, because about half of their iron requirement is needed to replace iron losses in menstruation. This explains why most women in developing countries, and many in developed countries, enter pregnancy with depleted iron stores. Their high iron requirements, for maternal tissue synthesis and for transfer to the foetus, exacerbate their iron deficiency, as do: blood losses at delivery; short (less than 2 year) interpregnancy intervals; adolescent pregnancy; and multiple births.

In infancy, risk factors for anaemia include premature clamping of the umbilical cord[280] and maternal iron deficiency during pregnancy. In a comparative study of 6 month-old, exclusively breastfed infants in Honduras and Sweden, ferritin concentrations of the Honduran infants were half those of the Swedish infants, presumably illustrating the lower accumulation of iron *in utero* by the Honduran group[242]. The iron content of breastmilk is low and cannot supply enough for the full-term infant after the age of 6 months. Therefore, prolonged breastfeeding, as well as inadequate amounts of absorbable iron in complementary foods, explains the peak prevalence of anaemia between about 9 and 18 months of age. About half of the infants in developing countries become anaemic by 12 months[282].

In many countries, the prevalence of anaemia declines substantially starting at about two years of age, because iron requirements for growth fall after the first year of life. However, where intake of animal products is low, and parasites common, prevalence of anaemias may still be high. In adolescence, anaemia again becomes common: girls start to lose iron in menstrual blood, and both boys and girls deposit iron in lean tissue. Because adolescent boys gain more lean tissue than girls, the prevalence of anaemia may be similar between the genders.

A major cause of anaemia is infection with malaria or other parasites. *Plasmodium falciparum* is the primary cause of severe malaria in regions of the world where malaria is endemic. In tropical Africa, for example, malaria and anaemia explain the majority of visits to heath centres. In Tanzania, malaria causes about 60% of the anaemia, and iron deficiency only 30%[78].

An Expert Consultation on the determinants of anaemia, organized by the Micronutrient Initiative (MI) in September 1997, led to the design of a life cycle risk matrix as an aid in analyzing the etiology of anaemia. Such a matrix could also be used for deciding on appropriate action at each lifecycle stage[281].

## Consequences of Anaemia

Anaemia impairs human function at all stages of life. Severe anaemia during pregnancy is thought to increase the risk of maternal mortality. A review of 21 studies[282] showed that anaemia explained 23% of the maternal mortality in Asia and 20% in Africa. However, these studies were retrospective and when anaemia is associated with mortality, both of these outcomes could be caused by a third problem, such as infection. There have been no large scale, placebo-controlled, prospective intervention studies to test the effect of iron supplementation on maternal mortality, partly for ethical reasons. Severe maternal anaemia, with Hb < 8 g/L, is almost certainly a greater mortality risk factor than mild or moderate anaemia[283].

Pregnancy anaemia has been reported to be associated with preterm delivery and a subsequently LBW in many studies[80]. For example, in a study of low income, predominantly adolescent women in the USA, IDA (but not anaemia without iron deficiency) predicted a 3-fold greater risk of preterm delivery[76]. The Hb concentrations of 829 Chinese women, at 4 to 8 weeks of pregnancy, predicted their risk of preterm delivery. The relative risks for preterm birth, by g/L of Hb, were: 2.52 for $\geq$130 g/L; 1.11 for 120-129 g/L; 1.64 for 100-109 g/L; 2.63 for 90-99 g/L; and 3.73 for 60-89 g/L[77]. However, the effect of iron status on actual duration of gestation has been measured in only two randomized, placebo-controlled, intervention trials, in France and in Finland. In neither did iron supplementation reduce preterm delivery or affect the duration of gestation[284, 285]. However, none of the women was severely anaemic and the severity of anaemia in general was far less than is usual in pregnant women in developing countries. As discussed further below, there is no strong evidence that anaemia in pregnancy causes LBW.

Associations between Hb concentration and psychomotor performance have been demonstrated at all stages of life. Although iron is required for the function of several brain neurotransmitters, an Expert Consultation[286] concluded that only anaemia, and not iron deficiency without anaemia, impairs the mental and motor development, and the behaviour of infants. A review of studies on the effect of iron deficiency on children's cognitive development concluded that there is sufficient evidence to show that iron supplementation of anaemic children aged >2 years improved their development, but that it remains uncertain whether supplementation of anaemic children <2 years old is beneficial[287]. Another concern for anaemic children is that they have a higher absorption of toxic heavy metals such as lead and cadmium, so they are at greater risk in polluted environments[288].

Anaemia has long been known to impair work performance, endurance and productivity[289]. In Indonesian women, Hb concentrations have been related to performance, even in tasks requiring only moderate activity. Anaemic women produced 5% less in factory work, and did 6.5 hours less housework per week[290]. In addition, iron deficiency impaired the work capacity of young American women, independently of Hb concentration[291]. It appears that iron deficiency does not have to progress to anaemia to affect work performance. Therefore, iron deficiency and anaemia may adversely affect the work performance of an even larger proportion of the world's population than that which suffers from anaemia.

## Efficacy Trials of Iron Supplementation

### Supplementation in Pregnancy

The WHO recommends that all pregnant women be supplemented with 60 mg iron daily, in a pill that also usually contains 400 µg folic acid[279]. This is the recommendation in most of the developing and many industrialized countries. Because of current concern about the apparent lack of effectiveness of large scale iron supplementation programmes intended to control pregnancy anaemia[212, 292, 293], it is important to know whether supervised, randomized, placebo-controlled, iron supplementation trials can prevent or treat anaemia and iron deficiency in pregnancy.

It is usually considered unethical to withhold iron during pregnancy where there is a high prevalence of anaemia. Therefore, randomized, controlled trials are rare, especially in developing countries. A recent meta-analysis included nine randomized, placebo-controlled, clinical trials of routine iron and folate supplementation in 5,449 pregnant women[294]. The women were recruited before 28 weeks of gestation and all had initial Hb concentrations >100 g/L. The usual dose was around 100 mg elemental iron plus 350 µg folic acid. The iron-folate supplements raised or maintained concentrations of serum iron and ferritin, and serum and red blood cell folate. There was a substantial reduction in the number of women with Hb concentrations <100 and <105 g/L in late pregnancy. No conclusions could be drawn about the effects of this supplementation on other maternal or foetal outcomes because few data were collected on these. An important limitation of these studies is that only three out of the nine trials in the analysis, at least two of which were in regions where malaria is endemic, were undertaken in areas where anaemia is a serious public health problem. However, this meta-analysis showed that iron supplementation improved maternal iron status, even in relatively well nourished populations. Another meta-analysis, using 24 randomized, controlled trials in developing countries, found that supplementation clearly reduced anaemia[295].

Other important information emerged from a Cochrane meta-analysis[294]. Hb and iron status improved with iron doses up to 60 mg/day and supplementation lasting up to 20 weeks. Longer term, small doses of iron were more effective than short term, large doses. These conclusions about the effects of timing and duration are supported by newer evidence. A meta-analysis of randomized, controlled iron supplementation trials that compared the efficacy of iron given daily or weekly[296], concluded that daily supplementation was most effective for preventing anaemia, especially severe anaemia during pregnancy. Given the short period during which pregnant women usually take supplements, and the high demands for iron during pregnancy, iron supplements should be given daily, if they are to have maximum impact on Hb and iron status. However, weekly doses certainly improve these measures as well. An analysis of supplementation trials in Tanzania confirmed that the total amount of iron consumed during pregnancy is the most important predictor of Hb response[297]. Likewise, in Bangladeshi pregnant women, Hb response per 60 mg iron tablet was the same whether the dose was taken daily or weekly. Most of the Hb response was produced by the first 20 tablets, and Hb plateaued after 40 tablets[298].

Among 21 randomized, controlled, iron intervention trials, in which the effect of iron treatment on birthweight was assessed, only trials in India[299] and The Gambia (for those women who took at least 80 iron pills)[78] found birthweights to be higher in the treatment group. Associations between both low and high Hb concentrations in gestation and LBW have been observed in many nonintervention studies; i.e., a U-shaped relationship between Hb and birthweight. However, given the lack of efficacy of iron supplementation on birthweight in most trials, these associations are probably artefacts of poor plasma volume expansion (for high Hb) or medical problems such as infection or haemorrhage (for low Hb).

Maternal iron status in pregnancy does influence the iron stores of the infant postpartum. In most association and intervention studies, in which maternal iron status in gestation and infant iron status postpartum were measured, cord blood ferritin was related to maternal Hb or ferritin, whereas maternal and infant Hb concentrations were rarely correlated[79]. Maternal iron supplementation in gestation may improve infant iron stores for some months after delivery. The iron status of iron-supplemented French women in late gestation remained correlated with the iron status of their infants at 2 months of age[284]. Infants born to anaemic mothers in Spain were almost six times as likely to become anaemic at 12 months of age, compared to infants born to nonanaemic mothers controlling for feeding practices, morbidity and socioeconomic status[300]. The logical conclusion is that maternal iron supplementation in pregnancy may provide the infant with some protection from iron deficiency postpartum. This is an important consideration, given the high prevalence of anaemia that develops during the first year of life, and its potentially permanent or long term effects on child development.

An additional benefit of iron supplementation during pregnancy is the opportunity to improve maternal iron stores postpartum. In Finland[301], and Niger[302], iron supplements during pregnancy increased maternal stores for 6 months postpartum compared to controls. This could reduce the risk of anaemia during lactation and in a subsequent pregnancy.

A combination of antimalarial prophylaxis and iron supplementation is particularly important for preventing maternal anaemia and LBW in areas where malaria is endemic[279]. In regions of endemic VAD, the simultaneous provision of low dose (for safety reasons) vitamin A supplements is likely to improve the Hb response of anaemic women to iron supplementation[303].

## Iron Supplementation of Infants and Preschool Children

LBW infants are born with lower iron stores, and have higher iron requirements for growth. Their iron requirements cannot be met from breastmilk, and their iron stores are depleted by 2 to 3 months postpartum. The global recommendation is to supply such infants with supplemental iron drops starting at 2 months of age[304].

Randomized, placebo-controlled, efficacy trials with infants reveal that iron supplementation significantly improves Hb and ferritin concentrations. However, the usual age of onset of anaemia in infancy is controversial, in part because of uncertainty about setting Hb limits for anaemia. This is illustrated by randomized, controlled supplementation studies in Honduras and Sweden. The investigators supplied 1 mg iron/kg to infants between 4 and 9 months of age, or between 6 and 9 months[242]. The infants were all exclusively breastfed until 6 months of age and partially breastfed thereafter. Although the Honduran infants had substantially lower ferritin concentrations at baseline, the provision of iron supplements between 4 and 6 months increased Hb and ferritin concentrations equally in the two countries. This suggests that these responses were not due to iron deficiency. Supplements given from 6 to 9 months improved Hb and ferritin in Honduras, but only Hb in Sweden. A higher prevalence of diarrhoea in the iron-supplemented group gave cause for concern. The results of this study imply that the current Hb cut-off set for anaemia in infancy may be too high and the prevalence of anaemia in young infants overestimated. More needs to be learned about the appropriate age for starting iron supplementation in infancy, and the Hb and ferritin limits that signify true deficiency.

Several placebo-controlled intervention trials have demonstrated that iron supplements increase Hb concentrations of preschool children in developing countries. These include trials in Indonesia on children aged 12 to 18 months[305] and in Viet Nam[273]. In Indonesia, a home-based, weekly supplement was effective for increasing Hb concentration and reducing anaemia from 37% (placebo control) to 16%[306]. The supplements were 30 mg iron, given to children age 2 to 5 years, once a week, by their mothers.

Not all iron intervention trials succeed in improving the Hb concentration of young preschool children. A randomized, controlled efficacy trial was conducted in rural Mexico, for which 220 children were recruited between 18 and 36 months of age[307]. At baseline, about 70% of the children had anaemia, accompanied by iron deficiency. For a year, under supervision, the children were provided with either 20 mg iron/day or a placebo. Hb concentrations were slightly significantly higher after 6 months of supplementation with iron but, surprisingly, there was no significant difference after 12 months in Hb concentrations between the iron-supplemented and the placebo groups. Hb concentrations improved as the children became older, but 30% of them remained anaemic at 12 months in spite of normalization of ferritin concentrations. The lack of Hb response to iron supplementation was not obviously due to parasites or morbidity. Because the children suffered from multiple micronutrient deficiencies and those who did increase their Hb in response to iron supplements seemed to be generally better nourished, it is possible that other micronutrient deficiencies were limiting the Hb response to iron.

There has been only one trial to compare the efficacy of iron to improve Hb concentrations when given in a multiple micronutrient supplement, compared to when given as iron alone. In a region of rural Mexico where several micronutrient deficiencies occur simultaneously in preschool children, groups with low Hb concentrations were given iron alone, iron plus vitamin $B_{12}$, iron plus multiple micronutrients, or a placebo, every other day for 4 months. At the end of the study, Hb response was significantly greater in the iron alone or iron plus vitamin $B_{12}$ groups than in the multi-micronutrient group[308]. A placebo-controlled trial on preschool children in Viet Nam measured response to daily iron supplements (8 mg/day) that also contained vitamin A and zinc[273], but there was no iron-alone control. The prevalence of anaemia fell from 51% at baseline to 6% after the 3-month intervention, when it was significantly less than the 43% in controls. A third group of these children took supplements containing higher levels of these nutrients (including 20 mg iron) once a week. The prevalence of anaemia fell from 48% at baseline to 9% after 3 months. The HA of children in both of the supplemented groups improved significantly compared to the placebo group. The authors concluded that consumption of the supplement once a week would be sufficient to reduce anaemia and to improve vitamin A and zinc status in this group.

There have been very few studies of the long term effects of IDA during infancy, and its reversibility by iron supplementation. An Expert Consultation[286] concluded that iron therapy for infants and children aged <2 years did not improve deficits in mental or motor performance, whereas iron supplementation for preschool children (2 to 4 years) was able to reverse the functional impairments. However, as described below, there have been very few intervention trials on infants and young children. At around 5 years of age, the cognitive performance of Costa Rican children was apparently still impaired, if they had been anaemic during infancy[309]. It is not yet certain that iron supplementation during infancy can reverse these effects. Iron supplementation , started at age 12 to 23 months, did not improve the developmental scores of anaemic Costa Rican children[310]. In contrast, iron supplementation did successfully reverse the motor and mental performance deficits of Indonesian children aged 12 to 18 months[305]. The mental and motor performance of infants in the USA was better at 9 and 12 months when they were raised on iron-fortified formula (12.8 mg/L) compared to a regular formula (1.1 mg/L)[311]. However, these differences disappeared by the time the children reached 15 months of age.

More than 22 countries have adopted iron supplementation of infants and preschool children as a public health policy[293]. The recommendation is to provide 12.5 mg of elemental iron plus 50 µg folic acid per day from age 6 months to age 12 months in regions where the anaemia prevalence is <40%, and from age 6 to 24 months where the prevalence of anaemia is

> 40%[279]. It is important that LBW infants receive this dose from 2 months of age up to 12 months. In reality, however, there are few national programmes to prevent or to treat anaemia in infants. India and some Caribbean countries are exceptions. Constraints include poor compliance, the relatively high cost of the iron solutions and droppers, and the lower stability of solutions, compared to tablets[312].

## Iron Supplementation of School Children and Adolescents

A substantial amount of evidence confirms that iron supplementation of anaemic school children improves their school performance, verbal and other skills[286]. Iron supplementation of Israeli girls, aged 16 to 17 years, reduced tiredness and improved their ability to concentrate[313]. In the USA, iron deficient but non-anaemic girls, aged 13 to 18 years, had better verbal learning and memory abilities after 2 months of iron supplementation in a randomized, controlled trial[314]. In India, boys and girls, aged 15 to 18 years, improved their cognitive function after iron supplementation[315].

In Kenya, when iron supplements were provided to school children on school days for 32 weeks, there was a significant increase in weight, WH, arm circumference and skinfold thickness compared with the placebo group[316]. Hb levels also improved significantly.

As it has become increasingly apparent that it is difficult, if not impossible, to correct anaemia fully by iron treatment during pregnancy alone, more attention is being paid to the need to provide adolescent women with either daily, or weekly, low dose iron supplements. This strategy may prevent them being anaemic and iron deficient when they become pregnant, as long as the supplements are given for long enough and close enough to conception; however, where the usual intake of dietary iron is low, supplementation will still need to be continued during pregnancy[163]. Treatment of pregnant Nigerian adolescents with iron, folic acid and antimalarial prophylaxis, increased maternal height and lowered the incidence of cephalopelvic disproportion[115].

## Frequency, Duration and Prioritization of Iron Supplementation

One of the main obstacles to obtaining good compliance of participants in iron supplementation programmes has been the perceived need to consume the supplements every day for at least a few months at a time. During the past few years, there has been considerable interest in the possibility that iron supplements do not have to be given as frequently as once a day to be effective. If this is correct, it opens many new possibilities for supplementation programmes. Costs could be reduced and compliance increased if supplements were provided once a week; for example, to children in schools, on the weekly day of rest, linked to religious events, or distributed by the community. These strategies may afford the possibility of preventing iron deficiency rather than the usual situation of trying to treat anaemia.

A recent meta-analysis[296] compared the efficacy of weekly and daily iron supplementation for improving Hb and serum ferritin concentrations. The three main conclusions were as follows. Both daily and weekly iron supplementation are efficacious as long as compliance is good: an important and exciting finding that creates new opportunities for programmeme delivery. Under almost all conditions and particularly where there was less control over the dose being consumed, daily supplementation was more effective than weekly: this, presumably, is because missing a weekly supplement will have a greater adverse effect on iron status than missing one or several daily supplements. The duration of supplementation was not an important determinant of efficacy, except in pregnancy, with its high demands for iron and short window of supplementation, in which case daily supplements are more effective.

Because efficacy trials usually improve Hb and iron status, the poor effectiveness of some iron supplementation programmes is likely to be caused predominantly by other barriers to compliance including: lack of perceived benefit of taking the supplements, by the intended recipients and by health care providers; perceived or actual side effects such as diarrhoea or constipation, which are unlikely unless the dose exceeds 60 mg/day; poor supply or limited access to supplements; and unattractive packaging etc.[212]: see also section on Effectiveness of Micronutrient Supplementation; iron (below).

With regard to prioritization of vulnerable groups for iron supplementation, current recommendations from the International Nutritional Anaemias Consultative Group (INACG), WHO and UNICEF[279] are that the main priority groups are pregnant and postpartum women and children aged 6-24 months, because of their greater risk of deficiency and the greater likely benefits of supplementation. Where anaemia is highly prevalent (usually considered to be >40%), supplementation would also benefit women of reproductive age, preschool children, school children, and adolescents. In these target groups, the decision to supplement will depend most likely on feasibility. This might be highest in a day-care or school setting for children and adolescents or in the workplace for women.

In populations with a high prevalence of anaemia, almost all women and children are iron deficient. This argues for universal supplementation. Where severe anaemia is relatively common (2% or more of a population group) then its detection and treatment in primary health care facilities is necessary, to prevent morbidity and mortality from severe anaemia[279].

Where resources are very limited, it will be necessary to prioritize supplementation prior to conception, which is difficult, and from as early as possible in pregnancy, and then through lactation, infancy, and early childhood. These stages should be approached as a continuum, with the most vulnerable period being from preconception to age 2-3 years. The specific situation dictates the setting of priorities and the level of investment. Where LBW prevalence is very high, then addressing this must be a priority.

## The Role of Other Micronutrients in Anaemia

Vitamin A deficiency (VAD) also causes anaemia. When adult male volunteers in the USA were depleted of vitamin A, their Hb concentrations fell from about 150 to <110 g/L within 12 months[317]. Treating this anaemia with iron alone had no effect, whereas vitamin A plus iron readily restored Hb concentrations. In general, the Hb concentration of VAD individuals increases by about 10 g/L when vitamin A supplements are provided[318].

Riboflavin deficiency may be quite common in developing countries where intake of animal products is low, and especially during seasons when there is less intake of vegetables. It has been estimated[319] that 90% of adults in China were riboflavin deficient. There is a lack of information the prevalence of deficiency in other Asian countries. The few data on its prevalence in other countries include: 50% for elderly persons in Guatemala[320]; 77%, among anaemic, lactating women in Guatemala[321]; and almost 100% of pregnant and lactating women in The Gambia[322]. The high riboflavin requirements of pregnant and lactating women may put them at the highest risk of deficiency. Riboflavin deficiency lowers Hb concentrations, probably by impairing iron absorption[323]. It may also reduce synthesis of Hb, and cause storage iron to be trapped in ferritin. In efficacy trials, riboflavin supplements improved Hb response to iron supplementation in Gambian men and lactating women who were iron and riboflavin deficient[324, 325], and children in the former Yugoslavia[326]. Supplements containing both riboflavin and iron increased serum ferritin concentrations more than iron alone, in anaemic, lactating Guatemalan women[321].

Severe folic acid or vitamin $B_{12}$ deficiencies can cause anaemia, but it is not clear to what extent the global prevalence of anaemia is influenced by such deficiencies. Folic acid has long been included in iron supplements for pregnant women on the assumption that this will treat folic acid deficiency anaemia. There is, however, little evidence that folic acid deficiency is a public health problem in many developing countries. No abnormal values for serum or red blood cell folate concentrations were reported in Thailand[327], Guatemala[328], or Mexico[329]. This may be explained by the considerable amount of folate in foods such as legumes, leafy greens and fruit, that are consumed in large amounts in developing countries. Moreover, in a WHO collaborative study in Myanmar and Thailand, there was no incremental effect on Hb of adding folic acid to iron supplements for pregnant women[82]. Small, nonsignificant increases in Hb, have been reported in pregnant women in Africa[330], India[331, 3332], Myanmar[333], and Thailand[334]: usually when folate plus iron supplements were compared to supplementation with iron alone. Increasingly, the inclusion of folic acid in iron pills for pregnant women is targetted at reducing neural tube defects in the small segment of the population who are genetically at risk for this problem. However, for folic acid supplements to be effective against these defects, they must be consumed prior to or up to six weeks after conception. Most pregnant women do not enter care during this time window. Other reasons to include folic acid in iron supplements include a probable reduction in risk of preterm delivery[43] and the association between elevated plasma homocysteine in pregnancy and a variety of adverse pregnancy outcomes[87]. Folic acid supplementation often lowers plasma homocysteine concentrations. Folic acid should also be administered to LBW or premature infants, because they are at greater risk of developing folate deficiency and megaloblastic anaemia. Folic acid improves Hb and folate status in such infants[335].

As with folic acid deficiency, a severe deficit of vitamin $B_{12}$ results in megaloblastic anaemia. There are, however, limited data on the global prevalence of vitamin $B_{12}$ deficiency. This vitamin, also called cobalamin, is found only in animal products. No forms of cobalamin found in plants or bacteria are biologically active in humans. Therefore, a low intake of animal products is certainly a risk for vitamin $B_{12}$ deficiency. There are also some common situations in which absorption of vitamin $B_{12}$ from food is impaired to the point that deficiency ensues; for example, gastric atrophy from *Helicobacter pylori* infection, which is common in the elderly, and overgrowth of bacteria in the small intestine. One third of individuals of all ages have been reported to have vitamin B$_{12}$ deficiency in Mexico[336] and Guatemala[337]. Deficiency is common in the elderly, even affecting about 22% of elderly in the USA and Europe[338]. Its prevalence is undoubtedly higher in developing countries, where animal product intake is low and the prevalence of *H. pylori* is even more common. About 38% of Guatemalan elderly had severe deficiency[339]. More information is needed on the prevalence of vitamin B$_{12}$ deficiency in Asia in and other parts of the world, and on its contribution to anaemia.

Given the high prevalence of VAD in Asia and other regions and the potentially high prevalence of deficiencies of other micronutrients that are required for Hb synthesis and other functions, it is logical to assume that supplementation with multiple micronutrients, rather than just iron or iron plus folate, is a rational public health strategy. The development and testing of such supplements, encouraged by UNICEF, WHO and other agencies, is ongoing in several countries including Bangladesh, Peru, and the Republic of South Africa.

## Dietary Interventions to Reduce and Prevent Iron Deficiency

Iron absorption can be improved by changing the foods consumed or their composition. However, this has been demonstrated almost exclusively in small trials with single meals. Neither efficacy nor effectiveness has been adequately tested.

One way to improve the absorption of iron from food is to increase the intake of vitamin C. This enhances the absorption of non-haem iron if the two nutrients are consumed within an hour of each other[211, 340]. The efficacy of vitamin C in vitamin C-rich foods is the same as that of the synthetic form[340]. However, there are few data on the feasibility, and effect on iron status, of increasing intake of vitamin C from locally available foods.

To examine this question, trials were conducted in an area of rural Mexico where traditional maize and legume diets are high in non-haem iron but have poor iron bioavailability due to phytates. It was established, through isotope studies, that consumption of 25 mg of vitamin C was needed twice a day with meals, in order to double iron absorption. The only practical local source of this quantity of vitamin C was a lime-based drink. Iron deficient, nonanaemic women consumed this drink to obtain 25 mg vitamin C, twice a day with meals, for 8 months. At the end of the intervention, there was no improvement in any indicators of iron or Hb status[341].

In many locations, it may be difficult to find suitable, locally appropriate and affordable foods that can supply even 25 mg vitamin C per meal. Moreover,

the improvement in iron absorption produced may not be sufficient to improve iron stores in iron deficient individuals. Vitamin C supplements (100 mg twice a day, with lunch and with dinner, for two months, vs a placebo group) did improve iron status in 27 anaemic preschool children[342]. The supplemented children showed a significant improvement in Hb and red cell morphology, whereas the controls had no change. Perhaps the difference in result compared to the Mexico trial[341] was the larger amount of vitamin C given in India. This amount would be almost impossible to obtain consistently from foods. Moreover, it is unlikely that vitamin C alone would be used as a supplement for iron deficient children.

Vitamin C is probably most effective for improving the absorption of fortificant iron added to foods. For example, the addition of vitamin C to iron-fortified dry milk in Chile reduced anaemia in preschool children more than the milk fortified with iron alone[343].

The addition of meat or fish to a meal provides not only more absorbable iron, but also increases the absorption of non-haem iron, including fortificant iron. For example, when fish was added to a typical plant-based, South-East Asian meal that had been fortified with 5 mg iron (as ferrous sulphate), the amount of iron absorbed from the fortificant was doubled[344]. Interestingly, there have been almost no trials of the effect of increasing meat intake on the iron status of humans. An efficacy trial funded by the Global Livestock Collaborative Research Support Programme (CRSP) is currently underway in Kenya, where school children are being given a meat supplement to their usual school lunch for one year. The promotion of animal products, to improve iron status and intakes of other micronutrients, has not been sufficiently explored. Although cultural, socioeconomic and environmental constraints exist, small amounts of animal products can often be targeted to the most needy (e.g., young children and women), and home production of chickens, small livestock, and fish can generate income as well as improving the nutrition status of the household.

A review of food-based programmes[345] examined what was known about the impact of recent efforts to improve iron status by increasing the intake of animal products. These efforts have included promotion of fishponds and animal production in Viet Nam[346], increased availability and promotion of liver and other organ meats in Peru[347], fishpond promotion in Bangladesh[348] and fishponds and chicken in Thailand[349]. In Viet Nam, the iron intake of children was increased but iron status not evaluated. In Peru, haem iron intake was improved and the prevalence of anaemia reduced. Analysis of the first stage of the

Bangladesh project show that it failed to increase fish or vegetable intake and there was no impact on iron status. In Thailand, both iron and vitamin C intakes were increased as intended, as well as serum ferritin in school girls, although they also received iron supplements and better school lunches.

There are opportunities on the horizon to improve iron status through genetic enhancement of plants. A maize variety that is low in phytate has been produced in relatively small amounts. The single efficacy trial of iron absorption from this source showed that iron absorption was improved from 5% in control maize to 8% in the low phytate maize[350]. Genetic modification to insert ferritin synthesizing genes into rice and other cereals is also being evaluated[351, 352].

## Iron Fortification of Foods

Of all of the strategies used to deliver additional iron to humans, food fortification has the greatest potential to improve the iron status of the largest number of people. Refined cereals are iron-fortified in many developed countries. The characteristics of suitable food vehicles and approaches to fortification have been described[2]. Unfortunately, progress in iron fortification has been hindered not only by the usual constraints to fortification (such as the need for central processing) but also by the lack of useful iron fortificants. When added to refined cereals, iron salts such as ferrous sulphate and fumarate are reasonably well absorbed and are suitable, when storage is not expected to be long term. However, most soluble forms of iron cause oxidation and rancidity of fats and color changes in foods over time. For longer shelf lives, reduced iron is preferred, but this will not be well absorbed unless the size of the particles is very small.

NaFeEDTA has the potential to be a widely used iron fortificant. When consumed with cereals and legumes, its absorption is 2 to 3 times higher than ferrous sulphate. Its structure affords some protection against phytate inhibition of iron absorption. It is about one third as well absorbed as ferrous sulphate from sugar, but has the advantages of greater stability and of increasing the absorption of native non-haem iron and zinc in food. However, changes in the colour of wheat and maize can occur when NaFeEDTA is added. Food-grade EDTA has been difficult to obtain but this situation might soon improve; for example, facilities in the PRC may start to produce NaFeEDTA for use in fortification.

The absorption of iron from iron-amino acid chelates (ferrous bisglycinate or "Ferrochel") is substantially more protected from inhibition by phytate than that from ferrous sulphate. One radioisotope study showed that iron absorption from ferrous bisglycinate was six-fold higher than absorption from ferrous sulphate, when these iron compounds were added as fortificants to whole (high phytate) maize porridge[353]. Iron absorption from the chelate was normally down-regulated by higher iron stores. Absorption from the less soluble ferric trisglycinate in maize was poor. Better absorption of ferrous bisglycinate iron, compared to iron from ferrous sulphate or FeEDTA added to maize or white wheat flour, has also been reported[354]. The potential limitations of ferrous bisglycinate as a fortificant include its promotion of rancidity in whole maize meal, although this is readily inhibited by the addition of an antioxidant such as butylated hydroxyanisole (BHA) and did not affect the acceptability of fortified porridge to infants, preschool children or their parents[355]. Ferrous bisglycinate is added as a fortificant to dairy products and other foods in some countries, such as Argentina, Brazil, Chile, Italy and the Republic of South Africa.

## Efficacy Trials

There are many examples of iron fortification programmes and iron-fortified products. The following section considers only those that have been tested in efficacy or effectiveness trials. Ideally, once the compatibility of the fortificant with the food vehicle has been tested, this should be followed by bioavailability trials, then by efficacy trials to measure impact on Hb and iron status, and finally by large scale effectiveness trials at the community or national level. Although there is a considerable amount of information on the compatibility of fortificants and on their bioavailability, there have been very few trials of either efficacy or effectiveness for improving iron status.

In an efficacy trial in the PRC, 5 mg of iron sodium EDTA (NaFeEDTA) per day was consumed as a soy sauce fortificant. It significantly improved Hb status (A. Malaspina, unpublished data). Double-fortified salt, fortified with both iron and iodine, has been developed in Canada. The potassium iodide is encapsulated with dextrin to prevent it from interacting with the ferrous fumarate. The iron and iodine in the salt are both well absorbed[356]. Efficacy trials are ongoing. The National Institute of Nutrition in India has also developed iron- and iodine-fortified salt. The effectiveness of the salt was tested in school children and increases in Hb and urinary iodine excretion were observed[357].

In an efficacy trial in Ghana[220] iron and other micronutrients were added to "Weanimix" (a cereal-legume blend) promoted by the government and by UNICEF. Infants, almost all of whom were partially breastfed, were given the foods between 6 and 12 months of age. Two levels of electrolytic iron were added (about 300 mg/kg and 120 mg/kg) to cover the needs of those consuming smaller and larger amounts of the food respectively. Unfortified Weanimix was used as a control. The foods were supplied weekly to the mothers, free of charge, and feeding three times per day was encouraged. Many other vitamins and minerals were added, including vitamin C (at 780 or 390 mg/kg). The prevalence of low ferritin concentrations increased from 19% at 6 months to 55% at 12 months in the unfortified group, but fell during this time from 18% to 11% for those receiving the fortified Weanimix.

## Effectiveness Trials

### Maize and Wheat Flour Fortification

In the 1980s, Venezuela underwent an economic crisis that adversely affected the quality and quantity of food consumed by the lower socioeconomic classes. This caused a deterioration in the iron status of the population. In 1993, the government started a national fortification programme in which precooked maize and wheat flours, which together provided 45% of the daily energy of the low income population, were enriched with 20 and 50 mg iron per kg respectively. Both flours contained added thiamine, riboflavin, and niacin, and the maize flour was also enriched with vitamin A. By 1994, the prevalence of anaemia in children age 7 to 15 years in Caracas had dropped from 19 to 9%, and iron deficiency from 37 to 16%[358]. There was no control group.

Other examples of national iron fortification programmes include: wheat and maize flour fortification in Chile[343, 359]; wheat fortification in Sri Lanka; iron fortification of noodles in Thailand and Indonesia; and a national programme of fortification of maize flour with iron and zinc in Mexico[359], which is seen as an appropriate strategy now that a larger proportion of the population lives in urban areas and purchases commercially produced tortillas and flour.

### Condiment Fortification

Sugar can be fortified at the point of production. In Guatemala, NaFeEDTA was added to sugar at a concentration of 1 g /kg, i.e., 13 mg iron/100 g. Average sugar consumption was 40 g/day[360]. On average, iron intake increased by more than 3 mg/day. In the three communities that consumed iron-fortified sugar, iron stores increased significantly within 8 months compared to control communities, and further increases were still occurring at 32 months. Mean iron absorption was about 6%. There were no observable adverse effects of the intervention.

Fortification of salt has been problematic, due to: the relatively high ratio of fortificant to salt required; the need for the salt to have a minimum purity of 99% and a maximum moisture content of 2%; and the fact that iron will oxidize potassium iodate, added as a source of iodine. In India, 3.5 g ferrous sulphate was added per kg salt, where the average salt intake is 15 g/day. Bioavailability was assumed to be 5%. Fortification caused a significant improvement in Hb and a reduction in anaemia, especially among population groups with the highest prevalence of anaemia[357]. Iron fortification of salt is also being tested in Thailand and Indonesia.

In Thailand, fish sauce has been fortified with 1 mg/mL iron (as NaFeEDTA), to increase iron intake by 10 mg/day[361]. Absorption was 8% when the iron compound was added to meals. The sauce was produced in Bangkok and transported every two months to a rural village. The village head man distributed the bottles on request. The villagers were told that the sauce contained something which might make their blood more strong. Compared to a control village where there was no fortification, average haematocrits were significantly higher, by about 1.5%. In the control village 16% of the subjects became anaemic and 20% recovered. In the intervention village, 9% became anaemic and 35% recovered. Thus 25 to 35% of the recipients benefited from the iron. A study on a small subsample of the men suggested that their submaximal working capacity might have improved during the year of supplementation. The large number of producers of fish sauce may be a constraint to wider fortification.

In the Republic of South Africa, NaFeEDTA also improved Hb concentrations within two years, when incorporated into curry powder targeted to the population of South Asian descent[362]. The greatest increase in Hb occurred in the most anaemic individuals. The powder was fortified with 1.4 mg/g and the iron was 10% available. The average intake of absorbable iron increased by 0.8 mg/day.

Major efforts are underway to test the effectiveness of adding NaFeEDTA to soy sauce in the PRC and in Viet Nam, with the intention of reaching 75% of the population (A. Malaspina, personal communication). In soy sauce, iron from NaFeEDTA was twice as well absorbed as that from ferrous sulphate and, as stated above, improved Hb in a small efficacy trial in children. Community-based trials are in progress.

### Fortification of Foods for Infants and Children

Ferrous fumarate, ferrous succinate and small particle size iron are suitable iron fortificants for infant cereals[363]. They are bioavailable yet, unlike ferrous sulphate, they do not cause fat oxidation or discolouration. Infant cereals are widely fortified in developed countries and this has led to a definite reduction in anaemia[364].

Chile supplies low fat milk to low income households as part of a National Supplementary Feeding Programme. The milk is distributed to mothers when they attend health clinics for routine immunization and growth monitoring. Milk powder was fortified to contain 15 mg/L ferrous sulphate (3 mg/L iron) when reconstituted. The prevalence of anaemia fell from 27% to 10% among children aged 3 to 15 months. The remaining anaemia was thought to be caused by the inhibitory effect of milk calcium on iron absorption. To improve absorption of the fortificant iron, vitamin C was added at 100 mg/L. Anaemia virtually disappeared[343]. The limitations of this approach are the additional cost of the vitamin C, and the need to prevent its oxidation, either by appropriate containers or coating.

Peru implemented a national school breakfast programme in which children were provided with an iron-fortified biscuit and milk. After one year, the prevalence of anaemia fell from 66 to 14% (G. de Romana, unpublished data). National programmemes have just been started in Mexico and in Indonesia to distribute fortified foods to low income pregnant women and young children.

### Safety of Iron Fortification Programmes

Iron fortification poses no risk for the normal individual. Iron absorption falls, as iron stores increase, to protect against excessive iron accumulation. However, a small proportion of the population is susceptible to iron overload. This has been reviewed elsewhere[212, 293, 365, 366]. The conclusions are that iron fortification poses little, if any, risk to individuals with thalassaemia minor or other haemoglobinopathies, and that the impact of iron fortification in malarial areas should be monitored. Food fortification with iron has not significantly increased the prevalence of iron overload in the USA[367] or in Sweden[368]. Overall, it is true that: *"the potential benefit of an iron intervention to a predominantly iron-deficient population is likely to vastly outweigh any risk this may pose for a few individuals"* [212].

Oral iron supplements have not increased the risk of infection in any age group in nonmalarial countries. In malarial areas, the effects of iron supplements on clinical malaria attacks, lower respiratory tract infection, and nonmalarial, infectious diseases, have been inconsistent among studies. There remains concern that high dose iron supplementation, during the peak malaria transmission season, may increase the risk of clinical malaria[369]. However, prevention of iron deficiency anaemia and malaria in malarial areas reduces the risk of child mortality from malaria[283].

## Complementary Parasite Control Strategies for Prevention of Anaemia

For areas with endemic parasitic infections that can affect Hb or iron status, the INACG, WHO, and UNICEF recommended the following complementary control measures[279]. Where hookworm is endemic (i.e., prevalence 20-30% or greater) adults and children over 5 years should be treated with at least an annual dose of albendazole, mebendazole, Levamisole or Pyrantel. For pregnant women treatment should be given after the first trimester. Where urinary schistosomiasis is endemic, annual treatment with Praziquantel should be given to school children who report having blood in their urine. If *Plasmodium falciparum* malaria is endemic and transmission of infection high, women in their first or second pregnancies should be given curative antimalarials at their first prenatal visit followed by locally recommended antimalarial prophylaxis. Insecticide-impregnated bed nets in communities decrease the prevalence of severe anaemia in young children. Other primary health care measures such as hand washing and the wearing of shoes in hookworm areas, can have a major impact on the prevalence of anaemia.

## Summary and Conclusions

Asia has the highest prevalence of anaemia in the world. About half of all anaemic women live in the Indian subcontinent where 88% of them develop anaemia during pregnancy. Vast numbers of infants and children are also affected. Low intakes of absorbable iron, malaria, and hookworm are the main causes of anaemia. Intervention trials have demonstrated the benefits from improving iron status and reducing anaemia. The greatest benefits are to be anticipated in the most severely anaemic individuals.

- Randomized, controlled clinical trials show that iron supplementation of pregnant women improves haemoglobin and iron status, even in industrialized countries. Efficacy increases with iron doses up to 60 mg/day. Where iron supplementation has not been effective this has been due predominantly to programmatic constraints such as lack of available supplements, lack of information, education and communication campaigns, and poor counselling by health providers, resulting in poor compliance.

- No conclusions can be made about the benefits of iron supplementation during pregnancy on maternal or foetal health, function or survival. Most trials have been conducted on relatively small numbers of women in industrialized countries. Severe anaemia during pregnancy is thought to increase the risk of maternal mortality but there have been no controlled intervention trials on this question. An association between anaemia and preterm delivery has been reported in several large studies but most placebo controlled trials have been unable to confirm that anaemia causes prematurity.

- Maternal iron supplementation during pregnancy can improve both maternal and infant iron status for up to about six months postpartum.

- A recent meta-analysis comparing the efficacy of daily and weekly randomized controlled iron supplementation trials concluded that daily supplementation is most effective for preventing anaemia—and especially severe anaemia—during pregnancy. The total amount of iron consumed is the most important predictor of pregnant women's haemoglobin response. Antimalarial prophylaxis combined with iron supplementation is particularly important for preventing maternal anaemia and LBW in malaria-endemic areas.

- LBW infants are born with very low iron stores, which are depleted by 2 to 3 months postpartum. Because breastmilk cannot meet their iron requirements they should be supplemented with iron starting at 2 months of age.

- Anaemia during infancy could result in long term or permanent impairment of psychomotor function, although more studies are needed on this question. Iron supplementation of anaemic preschool children improves their cognitive and physical development. Improved growth of iron-supplemented preschool and school children was observed in some studies but not in others.

- Anaemia is associated with lower productivity, even in tasks requiring moderate effort such as factory work and housework. Iron deficiency that has not yet progressed to anaemia may also reduce work capacity. Efficacy trials have shown iron supplements to improve work performance of anaemic individuals.

- Except for iron fortification, there have been few attempts to assess the effectiveness of food-based strategies to improve iron status. Increasing ascorbic acid intake through local foods is probably an inadequate strategy to improve iron status where iron deficiency is prevalent. Targeting animal products to those with highest iron requirements, and supporting the production of small animals and fish, would increase the intake of absorbable iron and other micronutrients. There are strategies available to increase iron absorption through plant breeding but the efficacy and effectiveness of this approach have not been evaluated.

- Fortification of foods with iron has produced improvements in iron status in several countries. Iron fortification of maize and wheat in Venezuela is one such example. Electrolytic iron reduced anaemia and iron deficiency when added to a complementary food in Ghana. Double fortification of salt with iodine and iron has the potential to prevent both iron and iodine deficiencies and has been effective for improving Hb concentrations in India. Fortification of nationally distributed dry milk with ferrous sulphate and ascorbic acid in Chile lowered the prevalence of anaemia in infants from about 27% to close to zero.

- The search for better fortificants continues, and NaFeEDTA has good potential. When added to sugar it increased haemoglobin and ferritin concentrations in a community trial in Guatemala. Iron added to soy sauce as NaFeEDTA appears to be well absorbed and is being tested in large scale production and fortification trials in the PRC.

- Weekly delivery of iron supplements does improve iron status, almost as well as daily delivery in the case of children and adolescents. This programmatic approach may be a cheaper, more effective way to prevent iron deficiency. Ways should be sought to deliver weekly iron through schools, community-based programmes and other situations. However, daily supplements are still more effective for pregnant women because of their high iron requirements and the limited window of time available for supplementation.

- Supplements containing multiple vitamins and minerals could be more effective for improving Hb response than iron alone; multiple micronutrient deficiencies often occur simultaneously and should be prevented and treated, and several nutrients are required for Hb synthesis. Multiple micronutrient supplements are now being formulated and tested by international organizations.

# PREVENTING AND TREATING IODINE DEFICIENCY

## Prevalence of Iodine Deficiency

Iodine Deficiency Disorders (IDD) have multiple and serious adverse effects including cretinism, goitre, impaired cognitive function, impaired growth, infant mortality, LBW, and stillbirths in a large proportion of the world's population. The degree of impairment in function is related to the severity of iodine deficiency. Even marginal degrees of iodine deficiency have a measurable impact on human development. There has been great progress in prevention and treatment of IDD in the last decade. The obvious need for interventions probably explains why there have been relatively few randomized, placebo-controlled trials of the efficacy of iodine supplementation on different aspects of human function.

The most commonly used indicators (Table 9) are: enlarged thyroid volume: prevalence of goitre, or total goitre rate (TGR); enlarged thyroid gland; urinary iodine; and elevated neonatal serum levels of thyroid stimulating hormone (TSH). Iodine deficiency is defined as endemic when it affects more than 10% of the population.

In 1993, the estimated TGR in school children in some Asian countries was, in descending order of prevalence: Nepal, 44%; Indonesia, 28%; Bhutan,

25%; Myanmar, 18%; Republic of Korea, 15%; Sri Lanka, 14%; Thailand, 12%; Bangladesh, 11%; India, 9%; and Mongolia, 7%[370].

In 1999, WHO, UNICEF and the International Coordinating Committee on Iodine Deficiency Disorders (ICCIDD) classified 130 out of 191 countries as having IDD problems, 20 as having eliminated IDD problems and the remainder as having an unknown level of IDD problems[11]. About 172 million people, or 12% in South-East Asia, are affected by goitre and 41% are at risk of goitre, and have probably been affected by marginal iodine status. There has been little change in this situation in the past decade although improvement is anticipated now that 70% of households in South-East Asia consume iodized salt[11].

## Causes of Iodine Deficiency

The main cause of iodine deficiency in soils is leaching by glaciation, floods or high rainfall. Mountainous regions including the Andes and the Himalayas therefore have some of the highest prevalences of iodine deficiency. Iodine deficiency also occurs due to flooding; for example, in Bangladesh and in India around the Ganges. In areas of endemic iodine deficiency, the water and foods (plants and animals grown there) have low iodine content.

TABLE 9: Indicators for prevalence of iodine deficiency disorders (IDD) as public health problems

| Indicator | Normal | Mild IDD | Moderate IDD | Severe IDD |
|---|---|---|---|---|
| % Goitre in school children | <5 | 5-19.9 | 20-29.9 | >30 |
| % Thyroid volume in school children >97th percentile | <5 | 5-19.9 | 20-29.9 | >30 |
| Median urine iodine ($\mu g/L$) | 100-200 | 50-99 | 20-49 | <20 |
| % Neonatal thyroid stimulating hormone (TSH) >5 $\mu U/mL$ blood | <3 | 3-19.9 | 20-39.9 | >40 |

Source: Delange F (1999) Neonatal thyroid screening as a monitoring tool for the control of iodine deficiency. *Acta Paediatrica*, Supplement 88 (432): 21 – 24.

Many staple foods consumed in developing countries contain cyanogenic glucosides that can liberate cyanide. Cyanide is converted to thiocyanate in the body. , This is a goitrogen, as it blocks the uptake of iodine by the thyroid. With the exception of cassava, cyanogenic glucosides are located in the inedible portion of plants. Cassava, however, must be soaked before consumption to remove the goitrogens. Consumption of cassava was associated with endemic goitre and cretinism in Sarawak, Malaysia[371]. The adverse effects can also be overcome by increasing iodine intake.

Selenium is an essential component of the enzyme, type I deiodinase, which catalyzes the conversion of thyroxine ($T_4$) to triiodothyronine ($T_3$) [372]. Combined iodine and selenium deficiencies are thought to cause the myxoedematous form of goitre, which is found in central D.R. of Congo and other locations[373]. Low selenium areas include parts of Australia, the PRC, Egypt and New Zealand. High selenium intakes, such as encountered in some regions of Venezuela, also affect thyroid function by reducing the production of $T_3$ from $T_4$[374].

Iron deficiency impairs thyroid hormone metabolism because the two first steps in thyroid hormone synthesis are catalyzed by thyroperoxidases, which are iron requiring enzymes. Iron deficiency lowers plasma $T_3$ and $T_4$ concentrations, reduces the rate of conversion of $T_4$ to $T_3$, and increases thyrotropin concentrations. Because of these impairments in iodine metabolism, goitre in anaemic individuals may be less responsive to iodine treatment. At 30 weeks after the administration of oral iodine to children in Côte d'Ivoire, the prevalence of goitre was 64% in anaemic, iron deficient individuals and 12% in those with adequate iron status[375]. The inclusion of an iron supplemented group would have made the conclusions more definite, but these results indicate that combining iodine with iron supplements might reduce goitre more rapidly than iodine alone.

# Consequences of Iodine Deficiency Disorders

## Cretinism

Cretinism is the result of iodine deficiency during pregnancy, which adversely affects foetal thyroid function. Normal concentrations of thyroid hormone are needed for normal foetal brain development. The foetal brain is probably damaged when there is iodine deficiency during the first trimester. Neurological cretinism is characterized by poor cognitive ability, deaf mutism, speech defects, and proximal neuromotor rigidity. It occurs where iodine intake is below about 25 µg/day. It is much more prevalent than myxoedematous cretinism which includes hypothyroidism with dwarfism.

## Goitre

The prevalence of goitre increases with age and it peaks during adolescence. Prevalence is higher in boys than in girls. The rate of goitre in school children aged 8 to 14 years is a convenient way to assess the iodine status of a community (Table 9). Goitre itself is unsightly but usually harmless. Importantly, its presence indicates that other damaging effects of iodine deficiency are already present.

## Impaired Cognitive Function

Iodine deficiency is the leading cause of preventable mental retardation and brain damage worldwide. Differences in psychomotor development of iodine deficient children become apparent after the age of about 2.5 years. A comparison of learning ability and motivation was carried out among children, aged 9 to 15 years, in severely and mildly iodine deficient communities in Uttar Pradesh, India[376]. Children from the severely iodine deficient villages learned more slowly and were less motivated to achieve. In rural Bangladesh, children with low $T_4$ levels performed less well than those with normal levels, in tests of reading, spelling and general cognitive ability, after a number of other factors that affected performance were statistically controlled[377]. Even lesser degrees of iodine deficiency, which affect many more individuals, can impair mental and motor function. Problems range from small neurological changes, to impaired learning ability and performance in school, and poor performance on formal tests of psychomotor function[378]. A meta-analysis of 18 studies, on a total of 2,214 subjects, showed that mean cognitive and psychomotor performance scores were 13.5 IQ points lower in iodine deficient individuals[379]. The problem of retarded neurological development is exacerbated by the many individuals in the affected child's social environment who will also be dull, apathetic and unmotivated as a result of iodine deficiency.

## Increased Perinatal Morbidity and Mortality

Maternal iodine deficiency during pregnancy is associated with a higher incidence of stillbirths, abortions and congenital abnormalities. These can be reduced by maternal iodine supplementation before or during pregnancy. In Papua New Guinea in 1976, the rate of perinatal deaths for mothers with very low serum $T_4$ concentrations was twice that of those with higher concentrations[380], perhaps because thyroid hormones have a strong modulating effect on the immune system.

## Iodine Efficacy Trials

Approaches to reduce iodine deficiency have been reviewed in detail[2]. The most widely used method is salt iodization. Universal salt iodization (USI), where 80% of the population must have access to iodized salt, has been adopted by India and many other countries. Another strategy is injection of iodized oil. This is particularly appropriate for isolated regions and where salt is not iodized. A dose (480 mg iodine in 1 mL of poppy seed oil) lasts about 4 years. It should be given to all females up to age 40 years and to all males up to age 20 years. Repeat injections are needed after 3 to 5 years. Alternative strategies, such as adding iodine to drinking water (Thailand and Malaysia)[381] or to irrigation water in the PRC[382], show promise. The latter strategy has the advantage that it can improve also the growth of plants and animals in areas of endemic iodine deficiency.

### Effects on Goitre Reduction

Salt iodization programmes do not always have an immediate impact on the prevalence of goitre. For example, in the Republic of South Africa, the prevalence of goitre in children did not decline after 12 months of mandatory salt iodization[383]. However, in this and many other similar situations, noniodized salt was still being consumed by some of the households. In contrast, after iodized salt was introduced into the northern village of Jixian in the PRC in 1978, the prevalence of goitre fell from about 65% to 4% in the next 4 years, and no cretins were born during that period[384]. Groups of school children in the PRC were supplied with iodized salt (25 ppm iodine which is equivalent to 42.25 g potassium iodate per kg of salt), iodized salt purchased in the market, or a 400 mg iodine dose in oil. Goitre prevalence was 18% at baseline. It fell to 5% within 12 months in the children supplied with iodized salt or oil, and to 9% in 18 months in the group who purchased iodized salt in the market[385].

School children aged 6 to 11 years in the Republic of South Africa were provided with biscuits fortified with iodine, as well as iron and beta-carotene, for 43 weeks. The biscuits supplied 60 µg iodine per day. The prevalence of low urinary iodine concentrations fell from 97 to 5%. However, there was no reduction in the prevalence of goitre, which was about 20% at

the beginning and at the end of the study[386]. These authors concluded that iodine status had improved but that more time was needed to reduce goitre size. The implication from these observations is that urinary iodine concentration is a more sensitive indicator for monitoring the effectiveness of programmes intended to lower the risk of iodine deficiency in a population group.

### Effects on Pregnancy Outcome

The injection of iodized oil before pregnancy can prevent endemic cretinism. This has been confirmed in: Papua New Guinea[387]; the D.R. Congo[388]; and Peru[389]. Programmes to inject iodized oil prevented endemic cretinism in the PRC[390] and Indonesia[391]. An analysis of clinical outcomes in maternal iodine supplementation trials[97] included three studies on a total of 1,551 women[98, 99, 392]. In two of these, in the D.R. Congo and in Papua New Guinea, there was a significant reduction in the mortality of infants and young children. Iodine supplementation also lowered the prevalence of endemic cretinism at the age of four years, and the supplemented children had better psychomotor function between 4 and 25 months of age.

Iodized oil given in the first and second trimester of pregnancy protects against cretinism, but has little effect when given in the third trimester. This was studied in a severely iodine deficient area in Xinjiang, PRC[393]. Iodine was delivered systematically to women, in each trimester of pregnancy, and to groups of children from birth to age 3 years. For the 120 infants whose mothers were given iodine in the first or second trimester, the prevalence of moderate or severe neurologic abnormalities was 2%, compared to 9% in the 752 who received iodine through their mother in the third trimester, or postnatally. Outcomes were best when treatment was given during the first trimester. However, treatment in late pregnancy or postnatally improved brain growth and developmental quotients slightly, but not neurologic status compared to untreated children.

Belgian women with mild iodine deficiency, selected at the end of their first trimester of pregnancy if they had biochemical evidence of excessive thyroid stimulation, responded to daily iodine doses with markedly suppressed thyroid hormone levels and less increase in thyroid volume compared to a placebo group[392]. The thyroid volume of their newborn infants was also smaller. Given the critical nature of iodine status and normal thyroid hormone levels during pregnancy, it is evident that monitoring of maternal iodine status is worthwhile, even in areas of mild iodine deficiency.

## Effects on Infant Mortality

Iodine supplementation during pregnancy results in a substantial reduction in foetal and neonatal deaths. In the D.R. Congo, injection of iodized oil in the last half of pregnancy reduced perinatal and infant mortality and improved birthweight[388]. Moreover, in Papua New Guinea, children born to pregnant mothers who received iodine were significantly faster and more accurate in tests of manual function, when evaluated and compared to controls 12 years later[394].

A randomized, placebo-controlled, clinical trial of oral iodized oil in West Java, Indonesia was designed to determine the effect of giving iodine (100 mg), at about 6 weeks of age, on infant mortality up to 6 months of age[395]. There was a 72% reduction in risk of mortality in the iodized oil group compared to the placebo group, during the first 2 months, and a delay in the mean time to death: 48 days compared to 17 days. The effect on mortality was strongest in male infants. These results illustrate the importance of correcting iodine deficiency, *in utero* and in early life. The WHO estimates that giving a 240 mg dose of iodine once in the first year of life can prevent iodine deficiency for as long as two years. The EPI might offer one opportunity to provide this dose.

The prevalence of elevated serum TSH concentrations (>5 mU/L blood) in cord blood is a sensitive index of iodine deficiency at the population level[396] and can also serve to detect iodine deficient infants at birth. In the late 1990s, the prevalence of elevated neonatal TSH was <4% in areas with adequate iodine nutrition, compared to close to 30% in moderate IDD regions (e.g., 32% in Manila) and 39 to 80% where IDD is severe (including the PRC, Georgia, the Kyrgyz Republic, Malaysia, Thailand, and Pakistan)[396].

## Effect on Child Growth

There have relatively few trials of the impact of iodine supplementation on the growth of iodine deficient children, although such children are often small. In Bolivia, supplementation of 100 goitrous school children, aged 5.5 to 12 years, with a 475 mg oral dose of iodine in oil, showed no impact on growth during the subsequent 22 months compared to controls[270].

## Effects on Children's Cognitive Function

There have been few randomized, placebo-controlled trials of the effects of iodine supplementation on cognitive function in children. Improvement in the IQ score of goitrous school children in Colombia was correlated with goitre reduction and urinary iodine, although this was independent of oral iodine supplementation: not only iodine supplementation groups but also the control group received iodine from some sources during the 22-month study[270]. In Ecuador, 51 children, aged 6 to 10 years, from an iodine deficient community were injected with iodized oil and followed up 2 years later. Compared with a nonintervention group in a different village (there was no placebo control), treated girls, but not boys, performed better on intelligence tests[397]. In Malawi, a double-blind, placebo-controlled study found no effect on motor or mental development when 6 to 8-year-olds were supplemented in an area of endemic goitre[398]. This study has been criticized however, because there was a 25% dropout of participants. A joint Pan America Health Organization (PAHO) World Bank review of this question concluded that: *"the data from childhood supplementation studies are less clear than those from maternal supplementation studies, probably because so few studies have been undertaken with this design.*[a] Clearly additional studies are needed on the benefits of iodine supplementation during childhood on psychomotor performance.

## Potential for Iodine Toxicity

Biochemical and even clinical signs of hyperthyroidism have been reported in two severely iodine deficient African countries, Zimbabwe and the D.R. Congo , soon after the introduction of iodized salt. These two countries also had access to iodized salt imported from other countries[399]. Elderly persons, with long standing nodular goitre, appear to be the most susceptible to iodine-induced hyperthyroidism[400]. Clearly, careful monitoring of the iodine content in commerical salt is necessary, accompanied by reporting of cases of thyrotoxicosis, especially after the recent iodization of salt. The public health benefits of salt iodization, however, far outweigh risks from toxicity.

---

[a] Bank PW (1999) *Nutrition, Health and Child Development. Research Advances and Policy Recommendations.* Washington DC: Pan-American Health Organization.

## Summary and Conclusions

Iodine deficiency is a serious problem in Asia, with the prevalence in South-East Asia exceeding that in all other regions of the world. The need to eliminate iodine deficiency is very clear based on the widespread damaging effects and the large number of people affected. This may explain why there are so few randomized, placebo-controlled trials of the effects of iodine supplementation on the function of population groups. The following conclusions are justified based on existing trials.

- Salt iodization is by far the most important population-based intervention for IDD control and has been shown to be efficacious in alleviating IDD assuming iodine concentrations in the salt are at appropriate levels at the time of consumption.
- Efforts toward establishing and sustaining national salt iodization programmes have accelerated over recent years. Effective partnerships have been forged between relevant UN agencies, national and international NGOs, and the salt industry. Globally, 68% of households in countries with IDD consume iodized salt. Iodization rates are 70% in South-East Asia and 76% in the Western Pacific (WHO regions). These figures reflect household survey data where this is available; otherwise production level data are used as a proxy.
- Cretinism results from maternal iodine deficiency during pregnancy. It can be prevented by supplementing the mother during pregnancy, preferably during the first trimester but no later than the second trimester. Supplementation in late pregnancy, if that is the first time the mother can be reached, may provide some small benefits for infant function.
- Iodine deficiency during early life adversely affects learning ability, motivation, school performance and general cognitive function. It is not yet clear whether iodine supplementation benefits cognitive function if started during childhood. More studies are needed on this question. Neither is it clear whether supplementation improves growth of children.
- In an iodine deficient region, iodine supplementation even in the last half of pregnancy substantially reduced infant mortality and improved birthweight.
- Giving iodized oil to 6-week old infants caused a 72% reduction in mortality in the first two months. This suggests that it may be useful to administer iodized oil to young infants in areas where iodine deficiency is prevalent, although more studies of this question are needed.

# PREVENTING AND TREATING VITAMIN A DEFICIENCY (VAD)

## Prevalence of Vitamin A Deficiency

Vitamin A is required for maintaining normal visual functions and the integrity of several ocular tissues. The clinical signs of VAD include night blindness, Bitot's spots, corneal xerosis and corneal scars or ulcers. The prevalence of clinical deficiency is estimated by combining night blindness and eye changes, primarily Bitot's spots, to form a "total xerophthalmia" prevalence[401]. The prevalence of these clinical signs in Asia is quite low. For the last years in which information is available on children in Asia, it ranged from 0.5% in Sri Lanka to 4.6% in Bangladesh (Table 10) [402]. Other age groups are affected, especially pregnant and lactating women. A prevalence of >1% indicates a public health problem.

Subclinical VAD is much more common. It is defined as the prevalence of serum retinol concentrations below 0.70 µmol/L minus the percentage of individuals with clinical VAD. The prevalence of subclinical VAD is uncertain because there is a paucity of reliable values for serum retinol and few national surveys[403]. In the Fourth Report on the World Nutrition Situation[11], the only national surveys of prevalences of subclinical VAD in Asian countries are for: the PRC, 18%; Pakistan, 50%; and the Philippines, 10%. Again these are only estimates for preschool children. It is highly likely that prevalences are now less than these estimates where there are national supplementation programmes.

## Causes of Vitamin A Deficiency

The main cause of VAD is a low intake of animal products, which contain high amounts of absorbable retinol. Liver and kidneys are a concentrated source of vitamin A. Beta-carotene is the main provitamin in plant sources of vitamin A, and some plants are very high in beta-carotene. However, this is generally less

TABLE 10: Prevalence of clinical vitamin A deficiency (VAD) in Asian countries

| Country | Year | Age (months) | Sample size | Prevalence of clinical signs |
|---------|------|--------------|-------------|------------------------------|
| Bangladesh | 1983 | 4-72 | 22,355 | 4.6 |
| India | 1988 | 0-60 | na | 1.4 [a] |
| Indonesia | 1992 | 6-72 | 18,435 | 0.3 |
| Myanmar | 1994 | 6-60 | 14,059 | 0.8 |
| Nepal | 1996 | 6-35 | 3,386 | 1.5 |
| Philippines | 1993 | 6-60 | 5,049 | 0.4 |
| Sri Lanka | 1987 | 0-48 | 32,643 | 0.5 |
| Viet Nam | 1988 | 0-60 | 23,782 | 0.6 |

Source: MI/UNICEF/Tulane University (1998) *Progress in Controlling Vitamin A Deficiency*. Ottawa: The Micronutrient Initiative, UNICEF.

[a] In 1996, the prevalence of Bitot spots in preschool children in India (from a rural population, which would be expected to have a prevalence of VAD greater than the national figure), was of 1.1% - according to NNMB (1996) Nutritional Status of Rural Populations, Report of National Nutrition Monitoring Bureaus Surveys, Hyderabad, India: National Institute of Nutrition. Another countrywide survey done by the Department of Women and Child Development and published as Nutrition Profile of India gave an overall prevalence figure of 0.21% - Government of India (1998) *Nutrition Profile of India*. New Delhi, India: Ministry of Human Resource Development Government of India. Unpublished data from an Indian Council of Medical Research District Nutrition Project in which over 12,000 children under five are being surveyed per district is in agreement with this lower value, except for two Districts in Bihar.

well absorbed than retinol. Beta-carotene from fruit and from some yellow and orange tubers, including sweet potatoes, is substantially better absorbed than that from leaves and from vegetables in general.

Populations with the highest prevalence of VAD consume low amounts of animal products and fruit rich in beta-carotene. In rural Nepal, for example, risk factors for night blindness in women were reported as: less frequent consumption of preformed vitamin A (in animal products), and of provitamin A (in mangoes and dark green leaves); urinary or reproductive tract infections; vomiting and poor appetite; and a poor diet in general[93]. Breastmilk is the main source of vitamin A for infants. Clinical symptoms of VAD are rare in breastfeeding infants during the first year of life, even where the prevalence of VAD is high[404]. Poor maternal vitamin A status, and subsequently low breastmilk retinol content, is a risk factor for the earlier onset of VAD in infants, as is early cessation of breastfeeding[405].

Infection with the nematode roundworm parasite *Ascaris lumbricoides* lowers serum retinol concentrations. Deworming has improved values[406]. However, in West Java, Indonesia, deworming with albendazole one week before a large oral vitamin A supplement, did not improve retinol concentrations or vitamin A status compared to a placebo control[407]. Poor absorption of vitamin A may also occur in some types of diarrhoea and fever, during which there is a higher rate of utilization and disposal of the vitamin. In severe protein-energy malnutrition, retinol-binding protein synthesis is impaired. Zinc and iron deficiencies also interfere with the utilization and transport of stored retinol.

## Consequences of Vitamin A Deficiency

The clinical symptoms of VAD are described above. There is evidence from intervention trials in vitamin A deficient populations, that VAD has other serious consequences. The results of these trials are discussed below. They indicate that VAD causes: increased morbidity and mortality of infants, children and pregnant women; poor growth of children; and possibly increased mortality and morbidity of infants infected with HIV. It also contributes to anaemia, by interfering with iron transport and utilization for Hb synthesis.

## Efficacy Trials to Improve Vitamin A Status

### Effect on Pregnancy Outcome

Maternal serum retinol concentrations fall during pregnancy, even in well nourished women. This is due to haemodilution and changes in proteins in serum, and not to a high foetal uptake of the vitamin. In fact, infant stores of retinol at birth are low and are relatively little influenced by the vitamin A status of the mother[408].

There has been renewed interest, in areas where the prevalence of VAD is high, in the value of maternal vitamin A supplementation during pregnancy. It is now recognized that there are several benefits of supplementation. First, the prevalence of night blindness normally increases substantially as pregnancy progresses. Relatively recent surveys report VAD prevalences in pregnancy as follows: 8 to 16% in rural Nepal[410]; 0.6 to 2.8% in Sri Lanka[411]; and 1% in a national vitamin A survey in Bangladesh[412]. Night blindness is also associated with a higher risk of maternal mortality and morbidity. For example, in Nepal, the death rate was about 26/1,000 for those pregnant women who reported night blindness, compared to 3/1,000 for those who did not[93].

A double-blind, randomized, placebo-controlled trial in rural Nepal revealed that vitamin A supplementation of VAD populations during pregnancy can have a major impact on maternal mortality[94]. In this study, over 20,000 pregnant women were randomly assigned to three groups prior to conception. They received weekly an oral supplement containing either 7,000 µg RE of vitamin A, or 4,000 µg RE as beta-carotene, or a placebo. Maternal deaths from pregnancy-related causes per 100,000 pregnancies were 704 in the placebo group, 426 in the vitamin A group, and 361 in the beta-carotene group: equivalent to reduced risks of maternal mortality of 40% and 49% in the vitamin A and beta-carotene groups respectively. Limitations of this study include the limited biological plausibility for a vitamin A effect on some causes of mortality, and that the intervention was started preconception or very early in pregnancy; i.e., before most women enter prenatal care. The conclusions drawn from this Nepal study have been quite controversial[413]. This study was conducted in a region with a high prevalence of severe VAD. It is currently being replicated in Bangladesh and Ghana, where the prevalences of VAD are lower.

The current WHO recommendation for women of fertile age, whether pregnant or not, is that their vitamin A intake should not exceed 10,000 IU per day or up to 25,000 IU per week, and that giving a single dose greater than 25,000 IU is not advisable. This recommendation is based on concern about toxicity. High doses of vitamin A cause birth defects. The foetus is most vulnerable in the first two months of pregnancy but it is not certain that higher doses later in pregnancy are safe. Beta-carotene is the safest way to supplement pregnant women, because it is not teratogenic.

## Impact on Morbidity and Mortality of Infants and Children

High dose vitamin A has been given to newborns in only one trial[414]. On their day of birth, 2,067 Indonesian neonates were given either 50,000 IU of vitamin A or a placebo. During the subsequent 12 months, there were 19 deaths in the placebo group and 7 in the vitamin A group: a 64% reduction in mortality. All of the impact on survival occurred in the first 4 months of life. This is not surprising, given that the additional stores provided by the supplement are likely to have become depleted by then. The investigators in this trial believe that the fact that the supplement was given on the day of birth may have contributed to the observed reduction in mortality, possibly because of differences in the absorption or function of the vitamin in this early period (J. H. Humphrey, personal communication). A modified form of this study is being repeated in Zimbabwe.

There is no consistent evidence that high dose vitamin A supplements reduce mortality or morbidity later in infancy. The Vitamin A and Pneumonia Working Group[409] performed a meta-analysis of five trials, which included an evaluation of the impact of vitamin A on infant morbidity and mortality in the first year of life. No effect of high dose vitamin A on mortality was seen in the first 5 months of life, but there was a 31% lower mortality in the second six months for the vitamin A supplemented group. These results reflect substantially those of two larger studies, both conducted in rural Nepal[415, 416]. Taken together, the studies show that there is an impact on subsequent mortality when the doses are given at or later than six months of life.

High dose vitamin A also reduces the mortality of older children in countries where the prevalence of subclinical VAD is high. A meta-analysis revealed that mortality was reduced on average by 23%, for infants and children aged 6 months to 5 years[254]. The reduction in mortality was also 23% for infants under 6 months, but was not statistically significant, possibly due to the small sample size. The mortality effect was strongest for diarrhoeal disease and was also demonstrable for deaths due to measles.

### Prevention of Childhood Illness

A review of the benefits and safety of high dose vitamin A for the treatment of common illnesses in children[417] is helpful in identifying randomized, placebo-controlled trials. Only 24 out of almost 1,500 trials were designed adequately.

There is substantial evidence that high dose vitamin A supplements reduce mortality from measles.

In the Republic of South Africa[418], and in Tanzania[419], providing 200,000 IU on two consecutive days significantly reduced morbidity and mortality in children hospitalized for measles, compared to a placebo group. A review of a large body of data from the Republic of South Africa revealed that high dose vitamin A, provided to children with measles reduced mortality to 1.6%, compared to 5% in untreated children[420]. It is now standard practice to provide high dose vitamin A during the treatment of measles. A placebo-controlled study, in South African children less severely affected with measles, showed no benefits of high dose vitamin A in reduction of respiratory symptoms[421].

High dose vitamin A does not seem to be useful for the treatment of acute, watery diarrhoea, according to three placebo-controlled trials: two in Bangladesh[422, 423], and one in India[424]. However, children with acute shigellosis in Bangladesh were cured more rapidly if given 200,000 IU of vitamin A[425], and low dose (but not high dose) vitamin A significantly reduced the incidence of severe diarrhoea in severely malnourished children in the D.R.Congo[426].

Most efficacy trials found no effect of high dose vitamin A on recovery from acute lower respiratory tract infections: e.g., in Brazil[427]; the D.R. of Congo[426]; Guatemala City[428]; Tanzania[429]; and Viet Nam[430]. Doses ranged from 200,000 to 400,000 IU. Based on the results of some studies it has been suggested that low dose weekly supplementation may be more effective for reducing morbidity than high doses given months apart[426]. However, no meta-analysis on this question has been done.

## Benefits of Providing Vitamin A to Infants in the Expanded Programme in Immunization

Based on the observation, in at least one study, that vitamin A supplementation at birth reduced infant mortality, and on concern that vitamin A stores become depleted at around six months of age in some developing countries, a multicentre trial was conducted to evaluate the benefits of providing vitamin A supplements to lactating mothers and young infants. The double-blind, randomized, placebo-controlled trial was conducted in Ghana, India and Peru and included 9,424 mother-infant pairs[255]. Half of the mothers received 200,000 IU of vitamin A, and their infants 25,000 IU, with each of their first three doses of DPT/poliomyelitis vaccine at 6, 10 and 14 weeks of age. The control group received a placebo at the same times. At 9 months, along with a measles vaccine, the infants in the vitamin A group were given an additional 25,000 IU of vitamin

A and those in the control group, 100,000 IU. During the 12 months of the study, there were no differences between the groups in rates of acute lower respiratory infection, diarrhoea, mortality or infant growth. The vitamin A status of the supplemented infants was slightly superior only at 6 months. In a recent consultation to discuss whether or not vitamin A should be provided in the EPI, it emerged that the most likely reason for the lack of efficacy of vitamin A was that the dose was too small to improve infant status[256].

## Improved Growth

VAD has been widely associated with stunting. In Java, Indonesia, rural children aged 6 to 40 months were provided with 206,000 IU, or with half of this amount if they were less than 12 months old, or with a placebo, every 4 months[263]. Within 4 months, the high dose vitamin A supplement had improved linear growth, although only by 0.10 to 0.22 cm in the group as a whole. This effect was stronger in children who had very low serum retinol concentrations (<0.35 μmol/L) at baseline, but still they grew only 0.39 cm taller than the control group. Surprisingly, the effect was significant only in children aged >24 months. Thus it appears that if there is any growth response to vitamin A, it is small and benefits only the most severely deficient children after two years of age.

## Impact on HIV Infection

Low serum retinol concentrations are very common in HIV infection, and are often associated with viral load, increased progression to disease and mortality, and a higher risk of mother to child transmission of HIV[431]. The low serum retinol is probably a result of acute infection, rather than an indication that risk of HIV is increased by VAD or that retinol stores are low in women with HIV[432].

Some randomized, placebo-controlled trials in pregnant women show that pregnancy outcomes may be improved in HIV women if they receive high dose vitamin A. In the Republic of South Africa, 728 HIV-infected pregnant women were randomly assigned to a treatment group that received daily 5,000 IU vitamin A and 30 mg beta-carotene during the third trimester followed by 200,000 IU vitamin A at delivery, or to a placebo group. The vitamin A reduced the incidence of preterm deliveries from 17 to 11%[433]. In Tanzania, vitamin A alone had no effect on perinatal outcomes in HIV-infected women[101]. In Malawi, however, there was a lower incidence of LBW among HIV-infected women who were given 10,000 IU vitamin A in the third trimester, compared to the placebo group[434].

Vitamin A supplementation may be effective at improving the health of children born to HIV-infected women. In the Republic of South Africa, 118 infants, born to HIV-infected women received 50,000 IU of vitamin A at 1 to 3 months of age, 100,000 IU at 6 to 9 months and 200,000 IU at 12 and 15 months, or a placebo at all three time points. The supplemented group had an almost 40% reduction in morbidity, mostly due to lower diarrhoeal morbidity[435]. In Tanzania, 9% of a subgroup of children, aged 6 months to 5 years, who had been admitted to hospital with pneumonia, were HIV-infected. Vitamin A supplementation (400,000 IU on entry and at 4 and 8 months later, or half these amounts for infants) resulted in a 63% reduction in all-cause mortality in HIV-infected infants: significantly greater than the 49% reduction among all children[101]. Vitamin A may be improving the mucosal immunity of these children. HIV-infected infants born to mothers who were given vitamin A supplements in the last trimester had better integrity of the intestinal mucosa when tested at 1 to 14 weeks of age: an effect not seen in noninfected infants[436].

## The Efficacy of Food-Based Strategies to Improve Vitamin A Status

A major immediate cause of undernutrition is the habitual consumption of poor quality diets. "Poor quality" refers primarily to a low content of absorbable micronutrients. In addition, some people also have a low energy intake. Where low energy intake is due to lack of food availability, it is almost certain that the quality of the diet is also poor.

Typically, poverty is associated with a low intake of animal products, and subsequently low intakes of riboflavin, vitamin $B_{12}$, absorbable iron and zinc, calcium, and preformed vitamin A. Intake of fruit and some vegetables may also be low, and associated with inadequate intakes of vitamin C and folic acid.

Thus a food-based strategy is important. It can increase the availability and intake not only of vitamin A and iron, but also of many other micronutrients. Other advantages of a food-based approach are the reasonable likelihood that the strategy can be sustained, and the potential for households to benefit economically from increased production of high value foods.

A review of food-based strategies[345] recognized three main types: increase production of micronutrient-rich foods, from either commercial or home gardening, small livestock or aquaculture; increase intake of micronutrient-rich foods through nutrition education, mass media and other programmes intended to change food selection; and improve nutrient bioavailability, by food processing or the simultaneous consumption of enhancing foods. Plant breeding technologies are discussed as an additional category but are essentially another approach to increase both the intake and the bioavailability of micronutrients. Most food-based strategies use elements of several of these strategies.

There is usually substantial potential for increasing vitamin A intake from the diet, because some foods with high content of this vitamin may not be currently available or selected for consumption. For example, squash, orange sweet potatoes and yams, carrots, some fruit (such as mangoes) and red palm oil have high provitamin A content. These are foods that can often be grown in home gardens. They have the added advantage of being storable and therefore available in the off-season. Provitamin A in dark green leafy vegetables is probably relatively poorly absorbed compared to that in fruit and vegetables such as squash. Some animal products, including liver and eggs, are excellent sources of preformed vitamin A.

Unlike iron, many foods that are rich sources of vitamin A are relatively affordable, easy to produce at home and do not deteriorate rapidly. For this reason, a number of programmes have attempted to increase their production and consumption. Few, however, have been appropriately evaluated, and there is little information on the efficacy or effectiveness of such food-based approaches for improving micronutrient status.

There are many examples of food-based programmes that were intended to improve vitamin A status. Forty publications on this topic were reviewed as part of the VITAL Vitamin A Support Project[437]. Work published between 1989 and 1993 has been reviewed[438] and subsequently updated with 10 additional projects in a further review[345]. The following discussion is limited to what is known about the impact of programmes on vitamin A intake and status and draws heavily from the abovementioned review[345].

Many earlier programmes did not attempt to integrate behaviour change with home gardening or other strategies. Moreover, some of these programmes were implemented before it became known that the bioavailability of provitamin A (mostly beta-carotene) in some fruit and vegetables is about 50% lower on average than was previously assumed[439]. Some plant sources, however, including yellow and orange squash, fruit and red palm oil, contain large amounts of well absorbed carotenoids. In two such programmes, in which impact on intake and nutrition status were evaluated, there was no impact. In later

programmes that addressed behaviour change, there are some examples of increased intake of vitamin A; e.g., an increase in consumption of dark green, leafy vegetables, and high dose vitamin A capsules in Indonesia[440] and increased intake of ivy gourd and fat in Thailand[349]. A social marketing programme in Indonesia improved dark green, leafy vegetable intake[441]. Home gardening programmes increased the intake of: dark green, leafy vegetables in Bangladesh[442], beta-carotene-rich sweet potatoes in Kenya[443] and vitamin A-rich foods in Ethiopia[444].

The important question is whether any of the food-based vitamin A programmes improved vitamin A status. Although few were evaluated, the authors of reviews of these programmes generally concluded that there was a significant impact on nutrition status[345, 438]. Positive outcomes included: reduced clinical eye signs of deficiency in the Philippines[445]; a small reduction in night blindness in young children[446]; higher serum retinol in young children in Bangladesh[441]; higher serum retinol in Thai school children[349]; and a lower prevalence of Bitot's spots and night blindness in Ethiopia[444]. In the PRC, a programme was instigated to increase the fruit and vegetable intake of children in a kindergarten[447]. For 5 days per week, for 10 weeks, 22 children were provided with 238 g per day of green and yellow vegetables. This maintained serum retinol concentrations in the season of usual low intake, while those in a control group fell.

Red palm oil is extremely rich in carotene (500-500 µg/g) and has attracted considerable attention as a potential food for improving vitamin A status. Other benefits of this food are its high content of vitamin E and the fact that it can increase the energy density of the diet. The more palatable refined oil retains most of its carotene content even when cooked[448]. A small efficacy trial in India showed that 2,400 µg of carotene in red palm oil raised serum retinol and liver stores to the same extent as 600 µg retinol[449]. Feeding 8 g red palm oil per day increased the serum retinol of Indian children (number not stated) for at least 3 months and substantially reduced the number with serum retinol concentrations <20 µg/dL[450]. When the oil was distributed to children in feeding programmes it had a small impact in reducing the prevalence of clinical VAD. However, the 6 month trial was probably too short to expect a major impact on this. A long term trial is planned. In Honduras, red palm oil (90 mg beta-carotene) increased maternal serum and milk retinol approximately 3-fold, as well as infant serum retinol[451]. A similar improvement in breastmilk retinol was seen when red palm oil was given to Tanzanian women late in pregnancy[452].

## Summary and Conclusions

There is little doubt therefore that food-based approaches can improve vitamin A status in some situations. Rigorous evaluation of well designed trials would be very useful to stimulate more support for this approach. The following conclusions are drawn from this review.

- The prevalence of clinical VAD is quite low; for the last years in which information is available on children in Asia it ranged from 0.5% in Sri Lanka to 4.5% in Bangladesh[11]. Other age groups are affected as well, especially pregnant and lactating women. A prevalence of >1% indicates a public health problem.

- Subclinical VAD is much more common, though the actual prevalence is uncertain owing to a paucity of reliable national level data. The only national survey prevalences of subclinical deficiency in Asian countries are 18% for PRC, 50% for Pakistan and 10% for the Philippines[11]. Again these are only estimates for preschool children, and it is highly likely that the prevalence is now less than these estimates where there are national supplementation programmes.

- VAD causes increased morbidity and mortality of infants, children and pregnant women; poor growth of children, and possibly increased mortality and morbidity of infants infected with HIV. It also contributes to anaemia by interfering with iron transport and utilization for Hb synthesis.

- The main cause of VAD is a low intake of animal products, many of which contain a large amount of retinol. Beta-carotene is the main provitamin A in plant sources of the vitamin, and although some plants are very high in beta-carotene, it is generally less well absorbed than retinol. Beta-carotene in fruit, including squashes, is substantially better absorbed than that in leaves and vegetables in general. Populations with the highest prevalence of VAD consume low amounts of animal products and fruit rich in beta-carotene. Breastmilk is the main source of vitamin A for infants. Clinical symptoms of VAD are rare in breastfeeding infants during the first year of life even where the prevalence of VAD is high[404]. Poor maternal vitamin A status, and subsequently low breastmilk retinol content is a risk factor for the earlier onset of VAD in infants, as is early cessation of breastfeeding[405].

- Infection with *Ascaris* lowers serum retinol concentrations and deworming has improved the values. Poor absorption of vitamin A may also occur in some types of diarrhoea and fever, during which there is also a higher rate of utilization and disposal of the vitamin. In severe protein-energy malnutrition, retinol binding protein synthesis is impaired. Zinc and iron deficiencies also interfere with the utilization and transport of stored retinol.

- The great majority of countries where VAD is known to be a major public health problem have policies supporting the regular supplementation of children, an approach of known large scale effectiveness that can reach the subpopulations affected by, or at risk of being affected by, VAD.

- Supplementation of women during pregnancy reduces the higher prevalence of night blindness that occurs in such women in areas of endemic VAD. Night blindness carries a higher risk of maternal morbidity and mortality. Maternal mortality from pregnancy-related causes was reduced by 40% with weekly vitamin A supplements and 49% with weekly B-carotene supplements, in one study conducted in a region with a high prevalence of VAD in rural Nepal. While these results are exciting they need to be confirmed by the two ongoing studies of this question. High dose vitamin A supplements cannot be given safely to pregnant women.

- A high dose supplement given on the day of birth lowered total infant mortality during the subsequent 4 months, but a multicentre trial of the efficacy of high dose vitamin A, given in the EPI programme failed to find an impact on mortality or morbidity during the first year of life. It is likely that the dose given was too low to improve infant vitamin A status for long. Maternal supplementation postpartum can improve both maternal and infant vitamin A status, the latter through higher breastmilk content of the vitamin.

- A meta-analysis revealed that high dose vitamin A supplementation reduced mortality from diarrhoea and measles by 23% for infants and children age 6 months to 5 years. Severe diarrhoea was reduced by low-dose vitamin A in one study of severely malnourished children, but the reported benefits of high dose vitamin A on diarrhoea-related outcomes have been variable. Little impact on recovery from acute lower respiratory tract infections has been found.

- Ongoing research will clarify the benefits of vitamin A supplementation in HIV-infected populations. Evidence to date suggests that supplementation of HIV positive women may improve pregnancy outcome and that supplementation of infected infants and children can reduce mortality.

- Food-based strategies have good potential for preventing VAD. A number of food-based interventions have been implemented on a large scale but few have been evaluated adequately. Significant progress has been made in understanding how to effect behaviour change in such programmes, and about which food-based strategies are likely to be effective for improving vitamin A status. Food-based approaches need to be pursued more vigorously so that they become a larger part of the longer term global strategy for alleviating VAD.

- The recent finding that the bioconversion of provitamin A in dark green leafy vegetables is less than one quarter of that previously thought[439] has however raised doubts about the degree of efficacy of certain diet modification approaches in improving vitamin A status.

- Innovations include the promotion of egg consumption by small children in Bangladesh, which has shown promising results.

- Breastfeeding promotion, protection, and support remain an essential component of control programmes for young children, as does infectious disease control, not only through immunization, but also via complementary hygiene and sanitation interventions.

- There is urgent need to expand efforts in fortification where foods reaching the target population groups are processed or where local fortification is feasible. Oil fortification with vitamin A is mandatory throughout most of South Asia, although not often enforced.

- Approaches based on improved availability of vitamin A rich foods and possibly genetic modification of staple foods to enhance vitamin A availability, as with iron, have been slower to develop and more difficult to implement, but progress is being made.

# EFFECTIVENESS OF LARGE SCALE NUTRITION INTERVENTIONS

As described above, many interventions work under certain controlled conditions, but are they effective on a large scale? Do they have an impact at national or subnational level? Many large scale nutrition interventions have been studied, [453, 454, 455] including recent studies in Asia[4, 5, 6]. Summary profiles of community-based nutrition programmes in this region are provided in Appendix I.

There are few published examples of well designed evaluations of community-based nutrition interventions. A recent review of attempts to improve complementary feeding[168] stated that even in the very few large scale programmes that have been adequately evaluated in terms of nutrition impact, it is difficult to isolate the effects of the complementary feeding components. This is a common finding. Most of the efficacy findings discussed above relate to single interventions, whereas many large scale programmes are implemented as multicomponent, integrated programmes. It is rare to find a rigorous evaluation which has demonstrated plausibly the net effects that are clearly attributable to a community-based nutrition intervention. The first Tamil Nadu Integrated Nutrition Project (TINP-I) is one well known example[456]. Regional evaluations, in which the relative effects of the various programme components are differentiated and quantified, are even rarer.

Whether an evaluation is complex or simple, it should be rigorous in relating evaluation design to decisions. A useful matrix for deciding on an appropriate design has been proposed[457]. This relates indicators of interest (provision or utilization of services, coverage or impact measures) to the types of inference to be made (adequacy, plausibility or probability), and considers the degrees of confidence that are required by decision makers, as to whether observed effects (in terms of performance and impact) are due to an intervention. Other factors that affect the choice of an evaluation design include intervention efficacy, the adequacy of knowledge, timing, and costs. Evaluation design has been thoroughly discussed elsewhere[7].

Anthropometry is one of the main indicators used in evaluations, yet it does not capture benefits of improved nutrition such as the increased activity, exploration and cognitive skills of children. Severely underweight children are most likely to respond to nutrition interventions with improved growth, but moderately underweight children are more likely to respond with increased activity, greater disease resistance and possibly improved cognitive development. These outcomes are important, albeit very difficult to measure. Nevertheless, following the principle of "plausible inference", it is well known that, for a given anthropometric improvement, other beneficial outcomes are likely; for example, those relating to cognitive development, productivity, and mortality, among others. These have already been demonstrated in longitudinal studies. One well known example is the meta-analysis that conclusively established the contribution of child undernutrition to child mortality[171].

Programmes that are regarded as "nutrition programmes" are broadly similar, across countries and indeed continents. They generally involve one or a mix of the following interventions: growth monitoring and promotion; promotion of breastfeeding and appropriate complementary feeding; communications for behavioural change (nutrition IEC or nutrition education); supplementary feeding; health-related services (including the Integrated Management of Childhood Illness (IMCI)), and micronutrient supplementation[455]. One distinct variation, with important resource implications, is whether or not supplementary feeding is included.

Most of these interventions can potentially affect most of the problems discussed above: low birth weight, growth failure in young children; and the three main micronutrient deficiencies (iodine, iron, and vitamin A). The following guidelines for improving the effectiveness and ultimate impact of interventions are derived from lessons learned through large scale programmes and from programme design manuals; e.g., [458, 459, 460, 461, 462, 463, 464, 465, 466].

The key strategies, for which descriptions follow here are: growth monitoring and promotion, integrated care and nutrition, communications for behavioural change (CBC), supplementary feeding for women and young children, feeding at schools, health-related services, micronutrient supplementation and food-based strategies. Fortification is described in a separate paper[2].

## Growth Monitoring and Promotion

Sustainable improvements in child health and nutrition depend on families and communities being motivated to take timely and appropriate actions and being able to see benefits from these actions. An effective programme design for growth promotion begins with clarity on its purposes, its scope, and the circumstances in which it functions well. The full impact of growth promotion can be realized when it is employed to make decisions about three types of action: i) recommendations for individual children's care, particularly related to illness and feeding, but also to cognitive and motor development; ii) activity plans for the community that aim to make it easier for families to maintain the growth of their children by, for example, addressing problems of food shortages, poor water conditions, or collective child care needs that extend beyond a single household; and iii) programme activities to bolster community actions that affect households with special needs, such as income generating or transfer schemes. Guidance is needed on the selection of appropriate actions and the content of counselling to improve child health and nutrition.

Based on lessons from multiple experiences that achieved significant impacts on child nutrition, the following technical elements of growth promotion are essential for designing new programmes and for assessing existing operations: programmes should be community- or neighbourhood-based, and aimed at universal coverage; monitoring individual weight begun at birth and done frequently (monthly) for the first 18-24 months; child caretakers involved in monitoring; adequate growth (weight gain), rather than nutrition status, as the indicator of action, either alone or combined with other easily obtained information on the child's condition; growth charts to record the growth progress of individual children, to make growth status visible to the caretakers; analysis of the causes of inadequate growth is required, leading to clear and feasible options for action; negotiation with families, guided by tailored recommendations for what they will do to improve their children's growth; and follow-up.

Growth charts should be of adequate size and should have adequate spaces for clear recording of weights and months etc. All charts should be pretested

with workers. Culturally relevant details should be included. Nutrition status categories should be replaced with growth trajectories or channels indicated with thin lines or shading. There should be reminders of key behaviour for particular ages. On one panel of the chart, it is helpful to have key counselling points or cues for the worker about what caretakers should be feeding a child of a particular age, to aid in problem diagnosis.

Good management principles are as important for effective growth promotion[6]. Programmes should have community-based workers, who are assigned limited and well-defined tasks (Box 1).

Detailed, area-specific plans should be made, but with room for local innovation. Training should be task-oriented and hands-on, covering the entire growth promotion process, with an emphasis on problem solving. Supervision needs to be supportive, continuing the training of the workers and addressing directly problems that they confront. Commitment to programme goals should be evident at all levels.

Continual monitoring is essential, to alert all administrative levels to developing problems. One example of a good monitoring tool comes from Indonesia, comprising four key indicators: total number of children under age 2 in the community; total number enrolled in growth promotion; total number that attended growth promotion for the current month; and total number who are growing adequately. The ratio between the first and each subsequent indicator should approach 100% as the programme progresses.

Table 11 provides a guide for the evaluation of growth promotion programmes from the World Bank's Nutrition Toolkit[463]: a checklist for assessing their implementation, based on current knowledge for optimizing decision making in response to growth failure. The scale ranges from negligible to excellent use of a concept. A project with a higher score will be more effective, all other things being equal.

## Integrated Care and Nutrition Interventions

Adequate care is of fundamental importance to the nutrition status of women and children. Psychosocial stimulation is but one of several caring practices that have been increasingly recognized as key child development strategies (Figure 4).

Large scale programmes that include both nutrition and psychosocial components have been implemented throughout the world and continue to increase. A recent state-of-the-art review[467] concluded that, although only seven combined programmes have been evaluated, such programmes are generally

BOX 1

## Example of a Job Description for a Community Growth Promoter

- Maintain a roster of all children under two in the community - enrolling children at birth.
- Organize a monthly weighing of all under-2s in a community, ensuring 100% participation.
- Assist each mother in weighing her child and plotting the weight on the growth chart.
- Help the mother to interpret the growth pattern and diagnose the problem, if there is one.
- Depending on the result and a discussion with the mother about causes, refer her to the appropriate programme activities, including health consultation and supplementary food.
- Counsel her on one or two activities that she can do at home to help her child.

- Make home visits to children not growing well to provide more encouragement to the mother.
- Organize and participate in community meetings to analyze the growth of the community's children and motivate collective action by the community.
- Help different groups organize specific activities.
- Hold group education sessions on common problems that mothers face in caring for their children.
- For some workers, managing records, food, cases of diarrhoea, or coordinating with the health centre might be part of the job description ■

effective. The following conditions tend to maximize their impact: interventions targeted to early life, prenatally, or infancy and early childhood; targeting children in the poorest households, with parents lacking relevant knowledge; employing several types of intervention, and more than one delivery channel; long duration and higher intensity; and high parental interest and involvement.

Combined interventions are likely to be more efficient than separate interventions, because they are intended for the same population and make use of the same facilities, transportation and client contacts. From an economic standpoint, the marginal costs of integrated programmes, that combine interventions are expected to be low, relative to impact.

From the perspective of the family, a combined approach increases access to services. It may also increase overall effectiveness, because families who need early intervention often have a variety of risk factors (e.g., lack of maternal education, LBW, poverty), several of which may need to be addressed.

The WHO review[467] gives the following examples of combined nutrition and care interventions: incorporation of child psychological development into primary health care through the use of development milestones on health cards and the inclusion of simple messages for parents on how to facilitate psychological development; promotion and support of home-based, group child care, combined with supplementary feeding for children of working mothers, sometimes with a micro-credit programme; a child-to-child strategy in which older siblings learn skills to help

improve the psychological development, health and nutrition of preschool children; community development projects that use home visiting and preschool programmes as an entry point for other interventions such as income improvements; interventions with high risk children, such as LBW infants, that combine both psychosocial and nutritional care; parent education courses and mothers' groups including breastfeeding support groups; and mass media programmes (radio, television, videos) that target both physical growth and psychological development.

Recommendations of programme type (e.g., home-based, centre-based, or a combination) depend upon the availability of several critical variables including: responsible caregivers in the home; safety of the home; quality of caregiving in the centre; and stability, support, and training of caregivers in the centre. In general, centre-based programmes are not recommended for children from birth to three years of age, except when the child is an orphan, the mother is in fulltime employment, there is no suitable adult caregiver in the home, or there is extreme family disruption, child abuse, or neglect.

Actions taken to facilitate child development should contain, in addition to nutrition and health interventions at least the following: age-appropriate responses of adults; stable relationships with adult caregivers; supporting the child's development of language through labelling, encouraging the child's vocalizations, expanding, explaining, and two-way conversations; providing an environment for the child

TABLE 11: Guide for assessing the quality of implementation of a growth promotion programme

| Implementation Quality Issue | 1. Negligible | 2. Minimal | 3. Fair/Moderate | 4. Good | 5. Excellent |
|---|---|---|---|---|---|
| **Participation of mothers and families** | Mothers attend only if receive some incentive; attend sporadically; not asked to be involved; chart not made for or kept by family. | Most mothers attend <6 times per year and are passive participants; keep child's chart but have little understanding of it. | Mothers attend >6 times per year; participate in weighing and want to know weight; express motivation to change practices so child will gain weight; ask questions; keep chart. | 80% of mothers attend regularly; interpret growth pattern; plan to try specific behaviour; use weight gain to indicate success; growth chart tailored for family. | Mothers help to weigh child, interpret growth pattern; with worker, choose actions to improve growth; offer experiences to other mothers; all materials are developed for mothers. |
| **Guidelines for decision making based on child's progress** | No guidelines for decisions. | Guidelines use only nutrition status; status used for supplementary feeding decisions at service delivery point. | Guidelines combine nutrition status with health or weight gain criteria; interpretation not clear; action plan suggestive, not specific. | Guidelines for decisions by gaining, not gaining, or losing weight, but are developed for only one aspect of programme, (e.g., food) or for one level (e.g., community). | Criteria for adequate and inadequate growth combined with health status; used at all programme levels, with clear guidelines for decisions and action. |
| **Targeting and integration of programme components** | Children weighed but weights not used for targeting or integration. | Weighing linked only to decisions such as feeding; or frequency of weighing, based on nutrition status. | Targeted referral within health system, based on nutrition status and/or growth. | Use growth for referral to other services in community and some targeting of programme actions, such as health care, but no follow-up. | Close coordination with programme and community services; good targeting and follow-up. |
| **Community awareness and decision making** | No community-level use of data (health system only). | Health system provides some feedback to part of community | Community worker compiles nutrition status data periodically and shares results with community, but information does not trigger actions. | Community organization receives and discusses aggregate growth and status information regularly; and analyses causes of problems. | Community compiles, discusses and frequently bases decisions/actions on data; takes pride in having few under-nourished children and in children who grow adequately. |
| **Individual nutrition counselling** | Either no counselling or messages concern only attendance at weighing; | Group nutrition education talks for mothers; topics are generic. | Individual nutrition education for those targeted, but messages are general, not tailored. | Counselling tailored to the individual child who is not growing; counselling more intensive, as needed. | Adequacy of growth determines content and intensity of counselling; nutrition negotiation used; targeted materials used. |
| **Worker and workload** | In a fixed facility; growth promotion is one of many responsibilities; no incentive to give attention to growth promotion tasks. | In fixed facility with occasional outreach has auxiliary assigned responsibility; no incentive to give attention to growth promotion except to food distribution. | In community, extension of health centre, multipurpose; overworked; few incentives. | Community worker with responsibility for nutrition, may work with multipurpose worker; not overworked; some performance-based incentives. | Community worker has help and will make home visits; percent of children gaining weight is part of job performance. |

TABLE 11 continued

| Implementation Quality Issue | 1. Negligible | 2. Minimal | 3. Fair/Moderate | 4. Good | 5. Excellent |
|---|---|---|---|---|---|
| **Training of workers** | Emphasis on weighing and charting; one-time occurrence; didactic, theoretical. | Emphasis on weighing and charting, plus nutrition education and rehabilitation are discussed, but low priority and are nonspecific; still theoretical, but divided into shorter sessions. | Emphasis on weighing and charting, plus analysis of causes and how to target feeding, general nutrition advice, recipes, etc.; task-oriented; cases presented; short sessions. | Emphasis on weighing and charting plus analysis of causes and how to target and give general nutrition advice and recipes, plus community dynamics, counselling, using materials and giving targeted advice; task-oriented; cases and practices; short sessions with follow-up of training in community. | Previous accomplishments plus teaching how to negotiate with mothers; emphasis on community motivation and counselling; previous characteristics plus methods devoted to practice, self-assessment and community follow-up. |
| **Supervision of nutrition worker and activities** | Check only monthly reporting forms, at best growth charts; visits are at best sporadic. | Check records and frequency of education or receipt of food; visits infrequent; if a problem occurs, blame placed on worker. | Previous accomplishments plus observes growth monitoring session and asks about child nutrition; visits are at least twice a year and attention given to improved performance. | Observe sessions, assess targeting and decisions on actions based on growth data; quarterly visits; work with community; emphasis on improved performance. | Previous accomplishments plus visits to mothers with worker to help solve problems; initial visits monthly; continued training. |
| **Detailed operational planning** | Only a few general norms available. | Norms developed with general guidance but not for all aspects of programme. | Guidelines developed for implementation of all aspects of programme; some response to local needs in purchase of weighing scales, etc. | Full set of operational guidelines and tools available to respond to local needs. | Full set of operational guidelines with options and examples of local initiatives; materials respond to local needs; budget for local innovations. |
| **Programme level monitoring** | Data not compiled, although can be sent through system. | Data compiled, but not used to affect programme. | Compiled only for nutrition status; decisions taken on supplies of commodities only. | Data on growth and nutrition status compiled, presented, and discussed, but not at all levels. | Data on growth used for programme decisions (design, expansion) and advocacy at all levels. |
| **Commitment to sustain programme** | Undernutrition part of dialogue at national level only, among programme personnel. | Commitment to reducing undernutrition seen only in general terms, not in local action. | Commitment at all levels to reducing undernutrition. | Adequate growth is used at household and community levels but does not have commitment outside of programme personnel at other levels to sustain resource allocation. | Adequate growth is a national development objective; commitment to achieving this is seen at all levels; local resource allocation. |

to explore safely; providing interesting play materials and books that reflect the child's everyday experiences; warm, affectionate, sensitive and responsive behaviour to the child's signals; and play activities with peers and adults[468]. Many children with disabilities can respond as productively as children without disabilities to the same developmental interventions, and should therefore be included.

Actions should be taken to strengthen the parent's or caregiver's sense of effectiveness as a promoter of child development. Interventions with parental and nonparental caregivers are needed: to help them to use developmental materials appropriately; to provide challenging activities at the appropriate level of difficulty in which the child can be successful; to become increasingly involved with their children; to respond verbally to the child's vocalizations; to be responsive to the child's emotional needs; and to avoid physical punishment as a standard child rearing practice. Parents or caregivers should be taught how to integrate child development activities into activities as much as possible of daily living. Involving other family members in these activities has the potential to increase their impact.

Systematic and continuous training and supervision, for both professional and paraprofessional staff, and larger-scale studies of effectiveness with careful evaluation of process and impact are two other critical elements of programme expansion[7].

Adaptation of direct (developmental scales and cognitive tests) and indirect (e.g., parent's report) assessments of development in children aged 18 months to 6 years, (focusing on psychomotor, gross motor, reasoning, language, and adaptive tasks, including social and emotional behaviour) can be used to evaluate programme success, when programmes are intended to promote and to enhance these outcomes.

There is need for an investment to develop new instruments and to improve existing instruments for assessing the cognitive and noncognitive development of children below the age of three years. This is particularly true for large scale evaluations of programme interventions. Further research is needed on the use of parental reports and other approaches, including brief observations.

Process measures of developmental interventions are critical for the continuous improvement of programmes and for providing assessment of the strengths and weaknesses of programme practices; e.g., children's and parent's responsiveness to the intervention, children's level of development and change over time, parental level of participation, and factors that inhibit participation. Such process measures can also serve to provide caregivers with information about how to modify their behaviour with their children. Simple checklists, combined with training and supervision, can be used for this purpose.

The importance of care practices and resources, particularly the linkages between health, nutrition, psychosocial care and stimulation, and cognitive development, justify their inclusion within programming. Early nutrition and care interventions with children have long term consequences on later growth, development and functioning[4]. A key element in psychosocial care is the sensitivity or responsivity of the caregiver to the child's emerging abilities. Programmes that include care are likely to be effective in increasing nutrient intake and improving growth and development of children, particularly if they begin prior to 3 years of age. In developed countries, effects on children are most likely to be seen with high intensity interventions that are made directly with children. However, in developing countries with more "collective" cultures, the effectiveness of interventions that are made directly with caregivers is likely to be greater. Although there is a general recognition of the importance of care, much more needs to be learned about the best approaches for improving it. Assessment instruments and outcome indicators are being developed and will require careful efforts to become accepted. One of the main strategies for improving caring practices is 'communications for behavioural change' (CBC), as discussed below.

The evolution of the Tamil Nadu Integrated Nutrition Project (TINP) provides an interesting illustration of the need to go beyond supplementary feeding and to focus on improving caring practices within the home, in order to achieve an impact on moderate levels of underweight The TINP-I initiated in 1980 and a forerunner of the Bangladesh Integrated Nutrition Project (BINP) became well known in international nutrition circles during the 1980s as a success story, having achieved a highly significant reduction in severe early childhood undernutrition. Evaluations indicated a decrease in underweight prevalence of about 1.5 percentage points per year in participating districts, twice the rate of nonparticipating ones[469]. The success of the TINP-I was founded on several factors including: selective feeding, careful focus on supplementing the dietary intake of young children when their growth faltered and until their growth resumed; favourable worker-supervisor ratios; clear job descriptions; and a well-focused monitoring system. The second Tamil Nadu Integrated Nutrition Project (TINP-II) was launched in 1991, in 318 of Tamil Nadu's 385 rural blocks. It sought to move beyond reducing severe undernutrition to make a significant reduction in the high prevalence of children suffering from moderate undernutrition, i.e., shifting towards a more preventative focus. The core strategies were: regular growth monitoring and promotion; nutrition education and health checks for all children; and supplementary feeding of moderately/severely underweight and growth-faltering children, and high risk pregnant and lactating women. The Implementation Completion Report[470] of the TINP-II found that: "*While the project was successful in achieving its severe undernutrition and infant mortality rate reduction objectives, moderate undernutrition and low birthweight prevalences were not significantly reduced, although some progress was made*".

The main lesson learned from the TINP-II concerned the need to intensify the focus on localized capacity-building, community mobilization and targeted, interpersonal communications, aimed at improving the home-based care and feeding of 6 to 24 month-old children in order to prevent their becoming malnourished. An overarching recommendation was that supportive counselling of caregivers and high quality service delivery, allied with a concerted move towards social mobilization and participatory planning, should be the pillars of a future nutrition improvement strategy for Tamil Nadu.

Most of these substantive lessons are relevant beyond Tamil Nadu. The TINP-I showed that nutrition interventions that are targeted using nutrition criteria, integrated within a broader health system, and effectively supervised and managed, can significantly reduce severe undernutrition. The TINP-II showed that to attempt to go further so as to prevent children from becoming moderately malnourished is, in many ways, a harder task and one that requires a significant shift in emphasis. Nutrition programming in Tamil Nadu is still evolving towards such an approach: emphasizing human capacity building for home-based action, a proactive integration with the health system, and the mobilization of communities to sustain the process beyond the project[470].

## Communications for Behavioural Change

Communications for behavioural change (CBC) is a self-explanatory strategy. Other terms in the past have included nutrition information-education-communication (IEC) or nutrition education; though the latter has tended to imply a fairly didactic and often top-down approach, that has seldom been effective in the long term.

CBC has drawn from the literature on social marketing to improve its relevance and effectiveness. It operates on the basis that new ideas, services, or products can best be introduced if the intended beneficiaries see them as fulfilling their own aspirations and wellbeing. People will not accept new ideas and technologies designed solely from specialists' concepts. CBC follows a disciplined series of programme development and implementation phases, each with steps designed to learn from the community itself: conducting formative research to formulate the whole programme's strategy; testing those strategies; designing, testing, and improving messages; designing, testing, and producing communication materials; and monitoring and making necessary revisions in programme strategies to better address people who have not tried or who have stopped desired practices. As the programme matures and behavioural changes begin, the design of communication and other programme elements should be revised and adapted to that change.

CBC may be directed to several nutrition-related objectives; e.g., improved feeding or caring practices, or compliance with supplementation regimens, among others. It may be employed as a complementary strategy alongside, for example, supplementary feeding or growth monitoring (as growth promotion).

There is a need, however, to redirect some CBC toward women, particularly wirh regard to eating practices. These are important for the health of the women themselves and for that of their children, particularly in rural areas where women endure the dual burden of moderate to high levels of physical work and frequent pregnancies without noticeable increases in energy and nutrient intakes. Studies show that female discrimination in developing countries may be to a large extent self-inflicted as a result of a "self-sacrificing" role through which they meet their own needs last[471]. For example, increased female wages were associated with improved nutrient intakes of most household members except the women themselves[472]. CBC activities targeted toward women could be specifically designed to reduce, and to ultimately remove, these attitudes.

It is also important to delay childbearing among adolescents. First births can be delayed by postponing the age of marriage and the onset of sexual activity and by using effective methods of family planning. This requires culturally sensitive CBC programmes for changing individual and societal motivations for early childbearing and enhanced opportunities for formal education of girls.

There are few well designed, large scale evaluations of CBC for nutrition in the existing literature. Several large scale programmes aimed at improving complementary feeding through nutrition education or CBC, have been reviewed[168]. Few had been adequately evaluated but this review[168] stated that: "*it is clear that nutrition education can have a large impact on complementary feeding practices*".

...ype of programme, currently implemented in Haiti, Viet Nam and Bangladesh, is the Hearth
r... ...me (Box 2).

**BOX 2**

## The Hearth Model

The Hearth Model is currently being implemented in countries such as Haiti, Vietnam and Bangladesh. It is intended to function as part of a comprehensive programme that includes growth monitoring, deworming, vitamin A and iron supplementation, and treatment for infectious diseases. In this approach, volunteer mothers from the community are trained to conduct feeding sessions (called 'hearths') in their homes, to provide malnourished children with one nutritious meal per day in addition to their normal diet. Mothers attend with their malnourished children each day during the two-week rehabilitation period, to learn how to prepare nutritious foods and observe the improvement in appetite, activity and overall health of their children. The meals fed during the sessions are usually developed using a positive deviance-approach, by determining which foods are fed by low income mothers in the same community whose children are well nourished. This ensures that local, affordable foods are chosen and, through the process of discovery, convinces participants that a solution exists that is within their means. Social learning theories are the basis for the nutrition education component of the model.

The impact of the Hearth model has been formally evaluated in Haiti[a] and Vietnam[b] by collecting data on child weight (though not height). In Haiti, a quasi-experimental longitudinal design was used to compare 192 participants and 185 comparison children from nonprogramme communities who were similar in initial weight-for-age Z-score (approximately -2.7). In multivariate analysis, there was a significant difference between groups in change in Z-scores during a 12-month period, in favour of the hearth programme. The effect was greater among children with higher initial weight-for-age (WA), which was unexpected.

The authors speculated that the Hearth Programme was most effective at preventing further deterioration among moderately malnourished children, but for those who were severely malnourished the local growth monitoring programme may have been more effective because such children were more likely to be referred for medical care. In Vietnam, the Hearth Programme is called the Nutritional Education and Rehabilitation Programme (NERP), and is part of a larger strategy (formerly called Poverty Alleviation and Nutrition Programme and now called Community Empowerment and Nutrition Programme) implemented by Save the Children/US that involves multiple components, including a programme to promote health of mothers and infants, pre- and postnatally. Data collected before and after implementation of the programme in 52 hamlets indicated that within two years, the prevalence of severe underweight (< -3 WAZ) decreased from 23% to 6%, a trend not observed in other parts of the country. Improvements in child weight appeared to be maintained even after NERP sessions were discontinued (which occurred when the number of eligible malnourished children was too low to warrant the sessions), suggesting long term improvement in child feeding and caregiving practices. The scope of the programme in Vietnam (i.e., both pre- and postnatal interventions) makes it difficult to attribute the changes in child weight solely to complementary feeding, but the sustained effectiveness of the overall approach is encouraging ∎

Sources: a Burkhalter BR, Northrup RS (1997) Hearth Programme at the Hôpital Albert Schweitzer in Haiti. In *Hearth Nutrion model: Application in Haiti, Vietnam and Bangladesh*, ed. O. Wollinka et al. Arlington, VA, 1997: 13 – 42.
   b Sternin M, Sternin J, Marsh DL (1997) Rapid, sustained childhood malnutrition alleviation through a positive-deviance approach in rural Vietnam: Preliminary findings. In *Hearth Nutrition Model: Applications in Haiti, Vietnam and Bangladesh*, ed. Wollinka O. Arlington VA: BASICS.

The following process guidelines for CBC on nutrition have been derived from various articles and reviews.

First, focus on behaviour: on understanding existing attitudes, perceptions, and practices; the social context in which these practices exist; the blocks or obstacles that impede uptake of desired practices, such as social, cultural, cost concerns, availability, poor service, lack of appeal; and how these constraints may be overcome.

Second, take a systems approach to managing behavioural change, integrating the technical (or clinical) aspects of the programme with service or product delivery and with motivations for change. To address truly behavioural and development objectives, the social marketing process keeps in mind larger intersectoral processes as well.

Third, appreciate that not all target audiences are the same and that even within one audience (e.g., mothers), there may be important segments (e.g., nursing mothers, mothers with children who "don't want to eat") that need to be identified and addressed differently.

Fourth, enforce rigorous discipline in the message development processes, to ensure that messages always: call for and motivate a desired action; surmount all known obstacles convincingly; offer meaningful benefits; are memorable; and are presented by a convincing authority. Linkages with commercial advertising agencies may enhance this process and the presentation of ideas to identified audiences.

Fifth, base media strategies upon sound research, to ensure that message reach and frequency are sufficient to achieve the required behaviour-change objectives. The choice of communication channels is location-specific and may include: direct counselling from fixed sites or door-to-door; generation of word-of-mouth within the community; traditional drama, singing troops, or puppet shows; promotional events; point-of-sale display material; and innovative use of available mass media.

Sixth, give special attention to service personnel and train them in sound counselling practice to be real motivators of behavioural change.

Seventh, recognize that effective programmes must achieve a balance between centrally managed activities and initiatives that are developed locally, within target communities themselves. This often means that project funds must be allocated in a decentralized fashion.

## Specific Nutrition-Related Recommendations

The following recommendations relate to content:

First, find a balance between food and practices. Unless breastfeeding techniques and complementary feeding practices are both addressed, providing food alone has a minimal impact. For example, just promoting "breast is best" is not useful when almost all mothers of young babies are already breastfeeding but need to do it more frequently and exclusively.

Second, target changes in feeding practices. In any culture, the following appear to be important factors: viscosity of food, frequency of feeding, nutrient density, quantity, hygiene, patience, and persistence. Very specific behavioural recommendations must be developed for each age group of children: an important step that can be achieved only on the basis of thorough qualitative research.

Third, do not ignore the first days of life. Bad practices begin with prelacteal feeding. In addition to traditional and nontraditional prelacteal foods, there is an increasing tendency to introduce foods early to "accustom the child to food" often because the mother must return to work.

Fourth, expect the worst characteristics of the daily feeding pattern during, and immediately following illness. If mothers give only a small amount of food regularly, they typically reduce the quantity even more during illness. What commonly happens is that mothers try to feed a sick child but give up because the child "just won't eat." Rarely does the concept or practice of recuperative feeding (feeding during recovery from illness) exist.

Fifth, recognize the extent to which families can do more for themselves. Poverty and lack of coping skills may be so prevalent that the mother, family, and community cannot change their practices enough to have a significant nutrition impact.

Sixth, define clearly the barriers to change. Both environmental and attitudinal barriers need to be identified. Environmental barriers include the lack of certain foods and feeding utensils, as well as health care professionals' misinformation to mothers about child feeding. A common attitudinal barrier to improved feeding practices is a mother's feeling that she lacks control, which derives from her low social status. The feeling that she exists to serve her family often means that she lacks the confidence to overcome resistance from her child. Also, mothers may feel they lack time to employ new practices.

Seventh, pinpoint motivators or enabling factors. For example, fathers, whose potential contribution is often undervalued, particularly when it comes to purchasing "special" calorie or nutrient dense foods for young children may play important roles, as can food vendors and owners of small food shops or stalls, and individuals who are credible and available sources of information related to food purchases.

## Supplementary Feeding of Young Children and Women

The efficacy of prenatal food supplementation (during pregnancy) and postnatal supplementation to young children has been reviewed above. This section considers whether such approaches work in large scale programmes and whether they represent the best use of resources for nutrition improvement.

The most common purpose of supplementary feeding is to prevent or to alleviate undernutrition, through reducing the gap between an individual's actual consumption and requirements. A secondary objective may be to improve household food security, through a food or income transfer effect, and thus to facilitate the caring capacity of the household.

Prior to any consideration of appropriate nutrition-relevant action, it is essential to ensure the problem of undernutrition has been assessed and its causes analyzed. The essential stages in problem analysis may be broken down into four stages: assessment of the nature, extent, severity and distribution of undernutrition; analysis of the main causes of undernutrition to clarify whether supplementary feeding is a potentially relevant action; analysis of the resources and institutional capacity for action, to reveal whether it is feasible; and cost-effectiveness analysis, as far as data permit, of supplementary feeding and other alternative relevant and feasible interventions aimed at reduction of undernutrition. This will ultimately lead to a decision on whether supplementary feeding is ultimately the most appropriate intervention to initiate, given the existing context.

In order to assess the relevance of supplementary feeding, it is necessary to assess the degree to which the problem of undernutrition is associated with inadequate dietary intake at the individual level. The priority for supplementary feeding will be "food insecure" households, where target individuals do not consume adequate food. In such situations, there will also be a need for household food security actions: particularly if the household is "ultra poor" (or "food poor").

There are risks attached to supplementary feeding (Box 3), which should be borne in mind when considering the relevance of a programme.

Food supplements are costly. In addition to the cost of the food itself (often financed by food aid) there

BOX 3

---

## Common Causes of Failure in Scaling Up Supplementary Feeding Programmes

- Irregular or inefficient supply, delivery and/or distribution of food for various reasons, including corruption.
- Inadequacies in institutional capacity, training, supervision, monitoring, evaluation, community involvement
- Leakages, due to poor targeting
- Irregular participation of the target group
- Inappropriate timing or duration of supplementary feeding
- Leakages, due to intrahousehold sharing of food with the non-needy, or sale of take home rations
- Leakages due to the substitution of a portion of the normal diet by the on-site food consumed by the target individual.

- Inadequate quantity or quality of food basket to close nutrient gaps.
- Insufficient calorie density of foods, rendering it difficult for the target child to consume enough to meet the nutrient gap
- Types of food culturally inappropriate
- Lack of understanding of beliefs and perceptions underlying intrahousehold food distribution practices
- Lack of counselling on the need to actually feed supplementary foods to the targeted child.
- Lack of attention paid to combatting other important causes of undernutrition, including through communications approaches aimed at improving home-based caring practices ■

Source: Gillespie SR (1999) *Supplementary Feeding for Women and Young Children*: Nutrition Toolkit Module No. 5. World Bank Nutrition Toolkit. Washington DC: The World Bank.

are hidden costs: transportation and storage; leakages and corruption; and disincentive effects on local agriculture. Food supplements may also cause dependency: not only from an income substitution point of view, but also from the behavioural point of view. Food supplements may create adverse dietary beliefs; from example, the ubiquitous use of cow's milk gives mothers the false impression that this is necessary for healthy child growth, even though most poor families cannot afford to buy milk and do not own dairy cows. Widespread and long term feeding programmes may have a pernicious effect by disempowering families from resolving their problems and parents from meeting their obligations.

If it appears, from causal and resource analysis, that supplementary feeding is relevant to a given problem and its causes, and that the selected infrastructure appears capable of supporting it, a further question is: is supplementary feeding the most efficient or cost-effective approach in this situation? Cost-effectiveness analysis may be carried out prior to the choice of intervention, if data are available to compare options on the grounds of efficiency. Otherwise (or additionally) it may be carried out as part of the evaluation process.

As discussed earlier, there is evidence for the efficacy of maternal supplementation, mostly from The Gambia. The lower a woman's prepregnancy weight, the greater is the potential increase in birthweight from a given unit of supplemental food. Given the higher prevalence and severity of low prepregnancy weight in South Asia, it may be assumed that the benefits to birthweight there would be at least as high.

In many situations, the choice of "food or no food", of supplementary feeding versus some other intervention, is not one that can be completely determined by the logical process described above. Food is a political issue. Giving food is an effective vote catching device for populist governments. Nevertheless, in such situations, there should be some scope for influencing the actual use of food, so as to improve nutrition outcomes more efficiently, through nutrition logic.

Once a decision has been made to undertake a supplementary feeding programme, an early and critical stage of project design is targeting, to increase efficiency through focusing on the most needy and responsive. The beneficiaries should be those individuals who are at risk of becoming malnourished (or are already malnourished), as a result of factors which can, at least in part, be addressed by supplementary feeding.

Targeting may be: i) geographical, to the most needy areas in a country; ii) functional, to those population subgroups who are most vulnerable, as usually defined by age or physiological status (e.g., 6 to 24-month-old children, pregnant and lactating women; and iii) individual, to those who are becoming malnourished (e.g., children whose growth is faltering). As well as being needs-based, the chosen targeting mechanism must also take account of the available infrastructure, administrative capacity, and any important sociocultural and political considerations which may be antagonistic to the notion of selection.

Transparent and enforceable entry and exit criteria are required for food supplementation. This means that the indicators for screening must be modifiable with food. Growth of children (monthly weight gain) is the best indicator for children. Too frequently, static weight-for-age is used as the indicator despite it being less sensitive for food intake, especially in children older than two years. Unfortunately, the use of children's growth in screening for food supplements is widely believed to be a disincentive for mothers to do whatever they can to improve their child's growth[462]. One solution is to enforce a maximum duration of benefit, and to have growth promotion efforts isolated, in time and place, from food distribution.

The next design stage concerns the strategy adopted to distribute food, which requires consideration of: the nutrient content of the food supplement; the type of foods used; systems of supply and distribution; and the timing, frequency and duration of feeding. Supplementary foods should be culturally acceptable and should permit the preparation of meals which are digestible, palatable, energy dense, and micronutrient rich, without being bulky. Other important prerequisites include: cost-effectiveness in closing the nutrient gaps of recipients; reliability of supply; feasibility of transport, storage and processing; short cooking time; low fuel costs; and adequate shelf life. The choice of local versus external production should be based on such criteria.

Supplementary feeding, if it is considered appropriate, should never be seen as the pivotal intervention in a strategy to combat undernutrition, but rather as an adjunct to approaches designed to optimize the use of existing household level resources, such as CBC. Because growth failure starts between 6 and 24 months of age, it is clear that supplementary feeding alone cannot offer the best means of prevention. At this time the child does not need much food *per se*. The quality of food (including, most importantly, its micronutrient content), how it is prepared and how it is fed to the child that are crucial concerns, along with the protection of the child from disease.

The benefits of supplementary feeding will be enhanced by complementary actions which address the health- and care-related causes of undernutrition, to the extent that these exist. Important nutrition-relevant, complementary actions, aimed at young children, include: growth monitoring and promotion; protection and promotion of breastfeeding and appropriate complementary feeding practices; immunization; disease management, including oral rehydration therapy; micronutrient supplementation; and deworming. For women, high quality and timely ante- and postnatal care is essential, including: tetanus toxoid immunisation; micronutrient supplementation (iron and folic acid tablets for pregnant women; possibly postpartum vitamin A megadosage, where VAD is a problem, and iodised salt consumption); malaria chemoprophylaxis, in endemic areas; and reproductive health education.

Other prerequisites include adequate technical and operational capacities of implementing institutions. Functional administrative support systems are crucial for programme operation, including: effective logistics, supplies, transportation, storage and delivery systems, and efficient funding mechanisms for regular support. Strong managerial capabilities and efficient technical support systems (including staff training, retraining, technical backstopping, supervision, monitoring and evaluation) are also critical, as is the adequate selection and motivation of programme staff. A functional management information system is especially important for the collection, processing, timely analysis, interpretation, and regular feedback of information required for ongoing decision-making and motivation.

## School Feeding

The physical growth of school children aged 6 to 9 years is mainly the result of environmental and genetic factors and their interaction[473]. In population groups that have experienced constraints to economic and social development, most of the factors affecting the physical growth of school children are related to environmental factors experienced before puberty, including poor food consumption patterns, illness, lack of sanitation, and poor health and hygiene practices[474].

Data on the nutrition status of school children are scarce. The ACC/SCN's Fourth Report on the World Nutrition Situation[11] provided data for only the Latin America and Caribbean region. Height census data on school children has been used for planning, evaluation, and advocacy in Central America[475]. This information has allowed governments and other organizations and institutions to detect growth retardation, to screen high risk groups, and to target social interventions for nutrition security and human development.

As discussed earlier, the potential for catch-up growth among stunted school children is thought to be limited after 2 years of age, particularly when such children remain in poor environments[145]. In a study in the Philippines, some catch-up was observed between the ages of 2 to 8.5 years, for children who were not of LBW or severely stunted in infancy[476]. However, stunting at age 2 years, regardless of whether catch-up is achieved or not, has been shown to be significantly associated with later deficits in cognitive ability[152]. This further emphasizes the need to prevent early stunting.

The fact that hunger alleviation in school children improves school performance has been documented in developing and developed countries. Studies in Jamaica, for example, have shown that those children who benefited most from nutrition improvement were wasted, stunted, or previously undernourished[181].

A review of school feeding programmes[477] has highlighted the following, as key concerns, when considering the option of feeding at schools. First, clarify goals. The following are possible goals: alleviate short term hunger (evidence strong); increase enrollment and attendance (evidence strong); improve micronutrient status (evidence available from a few programmes); improve learning outcomes (evidence weak); raise community participation (depends on modality and local circumstances); improve health and nutrition of school children (evidence weak); and improve health and nutrition of children's families (no evidence).

Second, identify and target population sub-groups (e.g., using socio-economic, geographical, gender and/or age indicators) according to goals and which groups need food to achieve those goals. Targeting should be transparent, with clarity on whom is targeted and why.

Third, consider timing, which again depends on goals: a breakfast or morning snack is generally better than lunch, for alleviating hunger and achieving learning objectives.

Fourth, define lowest cost rations to achieve the goals. This requires consideration of: calories (amount to supply 25% to 50% of daily needs); micronutrients, especially iron (to supply up to 100% needs); cost-effectiveness of fortification vs. supplementation; prior preparation (prefabrication) vs. cooking on site (prefabrication can be cheaper and obviates the need for a school kitchen and cooking equipment); on-site vs. take-home feeding (eating at school does not guarantee that food is "supplemental" and food taken home is generally shared and is more like an income transfer); and local vs. imported foods (consider comparative costs, foreign exchange, shifts in dietary habits).

Fifth, estimates the cost per person. These have been found to be in the range US$20 to 200/1,000 kcal/ yr, with a median US$81. It is important also to consider the opportunity cost (i.e., how else might this money be used to achieve the same goals) and other options (including parental education, deworming, micronutrient supplementation and cash transfer) and their costs.

Sixth, assess the complementary services that are necessary to achieve nutrition, health or education goals. These include: a curriculum for the nutrition education of children and their parents; water supply and sanitation at school; health services and first aid at school; parental education; deworming; detection and compensation for learning disabilities (e.g., hearing, vision); and CBC.

Deworming can have a high payoff for school children. Helminth burdens are most intense during the years of schooling[478]. Single and multiple helminthic infections have been shown to be associated with growth retardation[316] and catch-up growth has occurred in preschool children after deworming[479]. Deworming preschool and school children has improved physical growth[480, 481]. Where hookworm is heavily endemic, primary school deworming programmes can also improve iron status and prevent moderate and severe anaemia, but such deworming may be needed at least twice yearly[304]. Iron supplementation and deworming have the lowest cost/DALY in school health programmes[465].

Increasingly, early childhood learning centres (ELCs) are being put in place with World Bank support. Together with primary schools, they facilitate interventions to reach children aged 2-9 years, as well as older children who are still in primary school. But because not all children go to school, child-to-child nutrition-related activities need to be explored further and tested. This may be particularly relevant in situations such as India, where many girls do not go to school.

## Health-Related Services

Health services can benefit nutrition directly with regard to disease prevention and management, health promotion, and delivery of nutrition-relevant services. This includes the enhancement of maternal (and foetal) health and nutrition through antenatal care and micronutrient supplementation; counselling mothers at delivery on early initiation and exclusivity of breastfeeding (vitamin A can also be given as a single high dose at this time); growth monitoring during infancy and early childhood to give timely warning of health and nutrition problems; use of immunization contacts for vitamin A supplementation and for counselling on complementary feeding; periodic deworming with iron supplements; and management of disease, with an emphasis on the importance of continued feeding, including breastfeeding, diet composition (energy density, micronutrient content), and administration of vitamin A in VAD endemic areas.

Maternity care that is effective, affordable, accessible, and acceptable is essential. It should include prenatal health and nutrition services, safe delivery, and postpartum care. The well documented increase in the coverage of prenatal services enables pregnant women to be reached with health and nutrition services, including education, counselling and micronutrient supplements. Many women, however, especially poor and uneducated women who live in rural areas, still lack access to good quality health services during pregnancy and childbirth.

For adolescent girls, the prevention and management of unwanted pregnancies is a priority through improving access to birth spacing information and to counselling, education, and family planning services. Family planning services still need to be fully integrated with other health and nutrition services for women of childbearing age. Family planning IEC strategies need to incorporate women's health and nutrition concerns. Existing service delivery channels for contraceptive products can be used effectively for the provision of iron supplements and other nutrition services for women.

Some of the interventions that are regarded as essential for nutrition (e.g., antenatal care, safe delivery, immunization, disease management) are by their nature normally part of the regular health services, and a "nutrition minimum package" has been proposed[461]. The BASICS project, supported by USAID, has provided a strong justification for a concerted focus on interventions, through the health system, that aim to improve the following six nutrition-related aspects of behaviour: exclusive breastfeeding for about six months; appropriate complementary feeding, starting at about six months, in addition to breastfeeding until 24 months; adequate vitamin A intake for women, infants and young children; appropriate nutrition management during and after illness; sustained consumption of iron/folate tablets taken by all pregnant women; regular use of iodized salt by all families. Such a minimum package of interventions should be integrated in to all primary health care projects, with health workers playing an important supportive role in catalysing improvements in home-based caring practices.

Some nutrition activities within health services are being promoted and codified in the WHO/UNICEF Integrated Management of Childhood Illness (IMCI) programme. The IMCI is a comprehensive programme to improve child health and to reduce deaths from major childhood illnesses (Box 4).

Because undernutrition is a contributory factor in an estimated 54% of child deaths[171], the programme includes extensive guidelines on child feeding, for health care workers and for parents. The ultimate aim is to break the vicious cycle of inadequate dietary intake and disease.

BOX 4

## Integrated Management of Childhood Illness (IMCI) Evaluation

To evaluate the impact of the nutrition counselling component of IMCI, a randomized controlled trial was conducted in Pelotas, Brazil. The 28 government health clinics in the city were stratified by baseline levels of child malnutrition and socioeconomic status of the neighbourhood, and then randomly assigned to intervention and control groups. In the intervention group, all doctors in charge of child health care received a 20-hour course in nutrition counselling using a local adaptation of the IMCI guidelines. In total, 33 doctors were included in the study and 13 patients < 18 months of age were recruited from each doctor's practice. The nutritional advice promoted in the intervention group was specific to the child's age, and included: promotion of exclusive breastfeeding for at least 4 months; frequent breastfeeding; avoidance of bottles; 3 meals per day (or 5 if not breastfed) for children 6-24 months; inclusion of specific foods such as mashed chicken liver, shredded or minced chicken or meat, egg yolk, and mashed fruit; use of dense mixtures of foods; addition of a teaspoon of oil or fat to the food; and stimulation of the child to eat. The study included an evaluation of doctor's knowledge immediately after training and six months later, observations of consultations, and home visits of study children at 8, 45 and 180 days after the initial consultation to assess maternal knowledge and practices and child dietary intake and anthropometric status.

The results indicated that doctors' knowledge of child nutrition and counselling skills improved, although their performance waned six months after the training had been completed. Maternal recall of key messages and satisfaction with consultations were significantly better in the intervention group. There were no significant differences between groups in energy or protein intake of children, but fat intake was higher in the intervention group (34 vs. 31 g/day) (micronutrient intake was not reported). Although there were no significant differences between groups in growth of children under 12 months of age, weight gain (though not length gain) and change in weight-for-height Z-score among children older than 12 months were greater in the intervention group than in the control group. Mean height-for-age Z-scores at the last home visit in children > 12 months were 0.24 in the intervention group and -0.13 in the control group, suggesting relatively little stunting in this population. Thus, it is not surprising that linear growth did not differ between groups, but it is also unclear whether increased weight gain can be considered a beneficial outcome. Parallel studies of the impact of IMCI in other populations are currently underway ∎

Source:    dos Santos I, Victora C (1999) Evaluating the efficacy of the nutritional counselling component of the Integrated Management of Childhood Illness Strategy. Final Report submitted to WHO. Geneva: WHO.

## Complementarities Between Health Service Delivery and Community Nutrition

Community-based programmes are different and complementary to health services in several important respects. They are aimed primarily at preventing undernutrition, although they need to facilitate referral to health services for those that become malnourished. They usually include some developmental activities, e.g., infrastructure (water/sanitation, food storage, buildings), income generation, safety nets, or credit. Community involvement and ownership are crucial, in contrast to the top-down delivery of health care (parts of which, like supplies, equipment, and trained personnel, remain necessary).

Community-based, nutrition programmes have an important role in ensuring wide and timely coverage of key health services, such as immunization. Women's visits to health services, whether for curative or preventive child health care, are excellent opportunities for health workers to provide health and nutrition preventive services to women (e.g., education, counselling, and micronutrient supplements).

Another important connection is that health (and other) services can provide supervision and support for community workers. They are often the crucial link with government and other more central resources[6]. Strengthening nutrition-relevant activities in the health services thus provides a synergistic opportunity for addressing undernutrition. The incremental nature of the costs of strengthening nutrition activities within the health services may also make it an attractive option.

All of this emphasizes the complementarity of community programmes and health services and the fact that each needs the other for combatting undernutrition which in turn benefits health. Some examples of health service-based programmes are given in Appendix I.

## Effectiveness of Supplementation for the Control of Iron and Vitamin A Deficiency

### Iron

In contrast to vitamin A and iodine deficiency control, there remains a significant gap between the efficacy (potential effect) and the effectiveness (actual effect under expected conditions) of programmes aimed at controlling iron deficiency anaemia (IDA) among highly vulnerable subgroups, such as pregnant women and older infants. Most large scale iron supplementation programmes have not been evaluated with respect to impact. The main

operational constraints, identified in a review of six large scale programmes aimed at pregnant women[482], were: inefficient and irregular supply, procurement and distribution of supplements; low accessibility and utilization of antenatal care by pregnant women; inadequate training and motivation of frontline health workers; inadequate counselling of mothers; and low compliance of the intended beneficiaries with the supplementation regimen. Similar problems were found in later assessments[483].

Micronutrient supplementation programmes thus share many of the problems that hinder primary health care and essential drugs programmes in developing countries. Many of these deficiencies can be avoided or rectified in supervised clinical trials but, in the real world, small scale trial efficacy does not readily translate into large scale programmatic effectiveness. Iron tablets are not 'magic bullets' and interventions to combat anaemia in women and children must be seen in the context of overall quality of care. A severely anaemic woman, for example, is at much greater risk during child birth if birth care is not adequate.

Examples of large scale programmes which have not in the past led to a significant decrease in the prevalence of anaemia include those in Indonesia[295, 484]; India[482, 485] and the USA[486].

In many programmes, problems in supply-side factors have been so serious as to render it difficult to know the full extent of poor compliance as an obstacle to success; i e., the tablets have just not been getting to people regularly for them to consume. Recently in Bolivia, one million tablets deteriorated in storage as they were not distributed to peripheral health centres, nor was there a demand for them (E. Schoffelen, personal communication). The reasons for dropout from a supplementation programme are more likely to be related to poor supply and availability of the tablets than to side-effects[482]. For example, in India, the rate of beneficiary dropout from the National Anaemia Control Programme in the mid-1980s, ranged from 9-87% between different states with a mean of 58%[487]. Over 80% cited tablet supply failure as the reason, whereas fewer than 3% cited side-effects from consumption. Similarly, a publication from MotherCare[483] stated that: *"there is little evidence that non-compliance due to gastro-intestinal side effects is an important reason that women are not taking the recommended number of iron-folate pills"*. Nonetheless, there is some evidence that compliance has been a significant problem in current daily regimens[488, 489], possibly related to undesirable side-effects[297, 490] and/ or poor communications[491].

The effectiveness of iron supplementation programmes is likely to primarily depend on the following factors, starting at the community level.

There must be community demand, based on community awareness of the problem, consequences of IDA, and the benefits from supplementation. There must also be motivation to continue taking supplements. To generate such awareness and demand, an explicit communications component is required, aimed at both women and men, Communications need to evolve from an understanding of local terms, perceptions, beliefs, traditions and perceived obstacles to compliance, including side-effects.

Motivated, well trained, approachable and supportive community-based programme functionaries are essential. They must be able to explain the nature of the problem and how it can be tackled successfully, including other diet-based approaches. Supplements should be promoted positively as "health-promoting" rather than negatively as "disease-curing". Adequate supervision and performance monitoring is also required. Community leaders should also be involved as educators.

There must be good population coverage and targeting to groups at risk (e.g., pregnant women, adolescent girls) and areas at risk (e.g., endemic malarial or hookworm infested areas) with early initiation of supplementation during pregnancy. Late initiation cannot be compensated for by higher doses (e.g., 120-240 mg daily) later. These would also lead to more side effects.

Delivery systems should be of good quality, accessible to the target population, and as far as possible, functionally integrated within (but not necessarily limited to) existing channels; e.g., schools, traditional birth attendants (TBAs) and EPI outreach, among others. Supplements can also be made available at retail stores, for free, at-cost, or in exchange for a coupon from the health centre. These delivery systems require in turn an organized procurement process and a regular and timely supply of low cost supplements to delivery outlets, based on appropriate targeting criteria.

The supplements should have good quality, stability, shelf life, colour, smell and should be acceptable to the local population.

There should be simple, but effective, monitoring at all levels of the system from supply of supplements, through coverage and compliance with consumption, to biological impacts.

Operational research is needed to improve understanding of how to implement appropriate interventions effectively on a large scale. Allied to this, more effective advocacy and communication on the national importance of iron deficiency prevention and control is urgently required. Combatting IDA is further hampered by uncertainties that persist over its aetiology in different situations: particularly in

Africa, where causes of anaemia other than iron deficiency may be significant. Working criteria are needed, to distinguish different types of anaemia, in order to define better the target groups as well as the most appropriate actions. A recently developed tool, the life cycle anaemia risk matrix, may help in organizing aetiological assessments, with a view to better determining and prioritizing appropriate control strategies[281].

## Vitamin A

There is both an opportunity and a need for targeting[11] vitamin A deficiency (VAD) control programmes to particular sectors of the population within VAD affected countries. Unlike iodine, VAD is linked much more to the nature of foods available and to feeding practices than to geochemical or other conditions that affect the whole population of geographic areas. Many studies suggest that VAD has, like iron deficiency, strong socioeconomic associations. Indeed, iron and vitamin A deficiencies often coexist in the same subpopulations.

Most countries where VAD is a major public health problem have policies supporting the regular supplementation of children, an effective approach for reaching subpopulations affected by or at risk of VAD. Supplementation coverage has increased significantly in the last few years, spurred on by the linkage of supplementation to immunization. Integrating vitamin A supplementation with immunization services, which contact 80% of the world's children, has been WHO and UNICEF policy since 1994, but progress has been slow and somewhat limited. However, vitamin A supplementation during polio immunization campaigns has been quick to catch on and is proving to be one of the most successful implementation strategies for reaching large numbers of children at risk. National Immunization Days (NIDs) offer a ready made delivery infrastructure and unparalleled reach. In 1997 alone, more than 450 million children were immunized during polio NIDs. In 1998, 88% of the countries where VAD was a severe to moderate public health problem conducted NIDs, and two-thirds included vitamin A, benefiting more than 24 million children at risk from VAD. This success was the result of a coordinated strategic effort between UNICEF, WHO, major international donors, NGOs, and academic institutions[8].

The main limitation of NIDs is that they provide the opportunity for only one dose of vitamin A per year, whereas VAD children need to receive supplements at least twice a year. A minor setback has been the report WHO[366] that coupling vitamin A administration with immunization, while safe, may not have been as effective as had been hoped, at least in terms of mortality reduction. While recognizing the dramatic progress made with supplementation coverage, the NIDs linkage should not be considered as a panacea, and new approaches should be sought.

Almost all would agree that food-based approaches (including fortification where feasible) are the logical, preferred, long term strategy. There is urgent need to expand efforts in fortification where foods reaching the target population groups are processed and where local fortification is feasible[2].

## Food-Based Strategies for Control of Iron and Vitamin A Deficiency

Recent evidence for the impact and effectiveness of food-based strategies to reduce vitamin A and iron deficiencies has been reviewed[345]. The main strategies reviewed were food-based interventions aimed at: increasing production, availability and access to vitamin A and iron-rich foods through promotion of home production; increasing intake of vitamin A and iron-rich foods through nutrition education, communication, social marketing and behaviour change programmes to improve dietary quality among vulnerable groups; and increasing bioavailability of vitamin A and iron in the diet, either through home preservation or processing techniques. Plant breeding strategies were also briefly discussed, because of their potential to increase the content of vitamin A and iron in diets. With regard to vitamin A, the literature points to the potential of home gardening, combined with promotional and education interventions. However, few of the projects that were evaluated quantified the impact of home gardening on home production, income, market sales and women's control over income. And only a few studies actually measured their impacts on vitamin A and other micronutrient status indicators.

With regard to iron, production and education interventions to increase the supply and intake of iron from plant foods have not been as popular as for vitamin A. Experience with food-based approaches to increase production and consumption of haem or nonhaem iron-rich foods is very limited. However, some lessons are clear. In addition to the well-known problem of low bioavailability with iron from plant sources, experience with animal production suggests trade-offs between increased income from selling home-produced animal products and increasing consumption of these products, to improve dietary quality. As with home gardening interventions, a strong nutrition education component is critical in animal production interventions in order to achieve improved dietary diversity.

The review[345] highlights two contrasting facts. On the one hand, it is clear that some of the technologies and strategies reviewed have the potential to address many of the concerns about both the intake and the bioavailability of vitamin A and iron among impoverished populations. On the other hand, critical information gaps still exist in relation to both the efficacy (with respect to new information on vitamin A bioavailability from plant sources) and the effectiveness of many of the strategies reviewed, even for approaches as popular as home gardening. There is potential for existing home processing technologies to address some of the concerns about the bioavailability of vitamin A and iron. Cooking, preservation techniques, home processing techniques, and food-to-food fortification (to increase promoters or to reduce inhibitors of iron) were reviewed. Many of these technologies are simple, low cost, home processing techniques and in some cases, are part of the traditional food practices of the target populations. However, there has been a limited effort to promote, to implement and to evaluate such technologies in community trials. Plant breeding strategies are at a very early stage compared to other approaches and the information is not yet available on their potential efficacy and effectiveness. Additional studies on bioavailability to humans are needed to understand the full potential of plant breeding to increase micronutrient content.

In the past 10 years, significant progress has been achieved in the design and implementation of food-based approaches, particularly with respect to the new generation of projects integrating production and nutrition education and behaviour change strategies. Yet, little has been done to evaluate their efficacy, effectiveness, feasibility, sustainability and their impact on the diets and nutritional status of populations at risk. In particular, information on the cost-effectiveness of food-based interventions is noticeably absent from the studies. Despite their complexities, it remains critical to demonstrate both the efficacy and the effectiveness of food-based strategies, in order to provide the most basic information to promote further their use in the fight against micronutrient deficiencies. Food-based approaches could be an essential part of the long term global strategy to alleviate vitamin A and iron deficiencies, but their real potential has still to be explored[345].

## Control of Iodine Deficiency Disorders

By far the main method for the control of iodine deficiency disorders (IDD) is salt iodization, although other vehicles have been used; e.g. tea in Tibet, and drinking water in Thailand.

In some countries, although the problem of iodine deficiency was known, rigorous assessments, using such indicators as goitre prevalence and urinary iodine excretion, were needed to convince policy-makers and salt producers of the need for action. The next step was to analyse these results, along with the workings of commercial salt networks and the organization of the salt industry. Using advocacy and attention to legal detail, it was also necessary to pass appropriate legislation to ensure correct levels of salt iodization, and to protect iodized salt producers by eliminating noniodized salt from the market.

It is estimated (from survey data) that 65-75% of households in Asia consume adequately iodized salt. All countries have legislation for salt iodization, and the variations come in implementation and quality control. Most constraints are known in

## BOX 5

---

### Strategy for Control of Iodine Deficiency Disorders (IDD) in Nepal

IDD strategy in Nepal comprises three pillars:

1. *The Goitre Control Project (GCP)* was established under the Salt Trading Corporation (STC) in 1973 with bilateral support of the Indian Government with the primary responsibility to coordinate and manage the salt iodization programme. Since then, the GCP/STC has been distributing iodized salt throughout the country. As of 1996, about 120,000 mt of salt has been imported from India annually, of which about 80% is iodized. Salt is distributed through 17 depots of STC and through a network of over 1,000 dealers in the country. These dealers supply salt to retailers who in turn are the primary providers of salt to the population in general. In the accessible areas of the country (60 districts), the existing marketing channels are operating satisfactorily and STC salt is readily available for purchase and consumption. In fifteen remote districts, GCP/STC has been involved directly in the distribution of iodized salt to the people by issuing sale coupons through the Chief District Office. This salt is distributed with assistance of a transport-subsidy. In addition to the transport subsidized salt, other salt is also marketed by local retailers who purchase salt from the nearest accessible areas to help to satisfy the demand in the remote areas. Information regarding the iodine content of this salt is not available.

2. *The Goitre and Cretinism Eradication Project (GCEP)*, under the Expanded Immunization Programme of the Ministry of Health was established in 1978. Forty districts located in the hill and mountain belts were targeted for iodine oil injections. Between 1983 and 1993, iodized oil injections were administrated every five years by the GCEP. In 1993, the GCEP become integrated within the Nutrition Section of the Child Health Division, Department of Health Services in the Ministry of Health, and iodine capsules administered orally were delivered through the existing network of the Primary Health Care system including mobile Village Health Workers. The number of districts targeted for supplementation has decreased significantly as infrastructure has improved and areas previously difficult to reach by road have been able to gain access to iodized salt. Iodine supplementation will remain important as a short term measure to control IDD as efforts are intensified to reach universal salt iodization, and will be phased out only once it is assured through appropriate monitoring that populations living in IDD-endemic areas have access to, and are consuming adequately iodized salt.

3. *Direct supplementation through iodized oil capsules in the most endemic and remote areas.* This intervention will be carried out only for the most difficult to reach districts on a temporary basis until iodized salt is made available. Since 1989/90, transportation facilities have improved in most districts of the country and iodized salt has also become available. The target population for iodized oil supplementation includes all children up to the age of 15 years and all women under 45 years of age. As distribution of iodized capsules is only a short term strategy, the number of districts for capsules are being decreased gradually as efforts are increased towards achieving universal salt iodization ∎

---

principle: many small producers, pricing problems, and control of imported salt.

Iodine supplementation will remain important in areas of endemic IDD as a *short term* measure as efforts are intensified to reach universal salt iodization, and should only be phased out once it is assured through appropriate monitoring that populations living in IDD-endemic areas have access to, and are consuming adequately iodized salt.

The example of IDD control strategy in Nepal (Box 5) illustrates the primacy of salt iodization as a long term strategy, with short term supplementation undertaken in parallel until the former becomes effective.

At the level of children and their families, IDD control in Asia is clearly improving lives by the thousands. The gains in salt iodization came about largely because of the work of an alliance of responsive and knowledgeable partners. WHO, in collaboration with UNICEF and the International Council for the Control of Iodine Deficiency Disorders (ICCIDD), not only helped raise awareness of the importance of IDD but also worked to ensure scientific consensus and information on standards for: levels of salt iodization, the safety of iodized salt in pregnancy, and indicators for monitoring and evaluation. UNICEF, WHO and ICCIDD also provided technical and financial support for many steps of the process.

# PRIORITIZING OPTIONS

Having discussed both the efficacy and effectiveness of different interventions, we conclude by considering processes for choosing and prioritizing actions to combat undernutrition in different situations. The choice will depend on the nature and distribution of the undernutrition problem, its causes and the type of resources which are available or mobilizable. No single intervention or mix of interventions should ever be prescribed in isolation from a participatory process of problem assessment, causal and capacity analysis and programme design.

Under the ADB-UNICEF Regional Technical Assistance (RETA) Project 5671, community-based programmes in seven Asian countries in 1998 included a wide range of activities. For children, these comprised any mix of the following: growth promotion (growth monitoring, protection and promotion of breastfeeding, and the promotion of appropriate complementary feeding practices); disease management, including feeding during and after diarrhoea and oral rehydration therapy; micronutrient supplementation, including vitamin A megadoses for children from 6 months, and possibly iron supplements where anaemia is prevalent; promotion of consumption of iodised salt; deworming; and food supplementation, where relevant, feasible and cost-effective. For women, activities within antenatal and postnatal care strategies comprised: tetanus toxoid immunization; micronutrient supplementation, including iron and folic acid tablets for pregnant women and possibly post-partum vitamin A megadoses, where VAD was known to be a problem; iodised salt consumption; food supplementation during pregnancy; malaria chemoprophylaxis in endemic areas; and reproductive health education, including the need to ensure safe birth intervals.

In any one situation of significant undernutrition, there is a series of questions to be addressed when deciding on an appropriate action or mix of actions.

These questions concern the relevance of potential interventions to the problem and to the existing context, including infrastructure for implementation and other existing resources and capacity. The most efficacious approach to combat a particular problem may not be the most appropriate. Some nutrition interventions may be essential, some merely desirable. Answers are, to a large extent, situation-specific. Participatory problem-solving approaches will reveal the main causes of undernutrition and the type and amount of resources available to combat it (Figure 5). The "Triple A" process or cycle, pioneered by UNICEF is a participatory decision-making process wherein the problem of undernutrition is *assessed* (in terms of its nature, extent, distribution etc), its causes *analyzed*, along with the available resources and capacity to combat it, followed by a decision on appropriate mix of *actions*. The process is cyclical and iterative in that once the actions have been initiated, they are subsequently monitored and evaluated (*reassessment*).

**FIGURE 5: The "Triple A" Process**

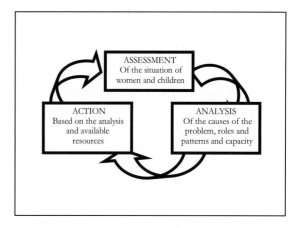

Source:  Adapted from UNICEF (1990) *Strategy for Improved Nutrition of Children and Women in Developing Countries.* New York: UNICEF.

Coverage relates to the percentage of the population at risk who are participating in the programme. Targeting concerns the degree to which this coverage is oriented towards the most needy among those who are able to respond. For example, despite evidence that undernutrition is a problem thoughout the life cycle, only 6- to 24-month old children may initially be targeted, or 6- to 36-month-olds if resources permit. These are both the most responsive and the most vulnerable age-groups. Pregnant women will also usually be included, given their relative nutrition vulnerability at this time, the known links between their nutrition status and birthweight, and the fact that they may be more accessible at this time. Adolescent girls, are often at nutrition risk, but sometimes may be targeted only later in the evolution of a programme. At a higher level, targeting may be done geographically, according to poverty criteria.

Intensity concerns how much resources are used per participant: expressed either financially, as dollar per participant per year; or with regard to population and worker ratios, e.g., number of children per community-level worker or mobilizer, number of facilitators or supervisors per mobilizer. Past experience has suggested that around US$5 to 15 per participant per year seems to be associated with effective programmes: at least those that do not include provision of additional food, which approximately doubles the cost. In many cases, well conceived programmes may be ineffective simply because their coverage is too low to have a broad impact on the problem, or because they do not reach those most in need. In other cases, the principles may be correct but the level of resources committed may be unrealistically low, so nothing much really happens. A detailed analysis of the coverage, targeting and intensity of the community-based programmes mentioned in Appendix I has been undertaken[5].

## Benefit-Cost and Cost-Effectiveness Analyses

Benefit-cost and cost-effectiveness analyses are also important, albeit not essential, for prioritizing options. Benefit-cost analysis asks whether a nutrition investment should be made in the first place or, if it exists, whether it should be expanded, contracted or terminated. A stream of benefits is calculated and discounted into a net present value. The cost stream is also calculated, discounted and summarized in a net present value. The ratio of discounted benefits to discounted costs is the benefit-cost ratio. Benefit-cost analysis is also useful for comparing interventions that have an impact on nutrition, but through very different

routes; e.g., a school-based feeding programme versus an infant growth monitoring programme. In these cases, money can often serve as a common denominator for different outcome measures; e.g., improving school attendance, increasing employment and improving child nutrition status.

Once a specific public investment in nutrition is justified, based on a sufficiently high benefit-cost ratio, cost-effectiveness analysis is used to examine project design options for delivering expected impacts at the lowest cost. A cost-effectiveness analysis can, for example, compare three different project designs and evaluate them in terms of how much they cost to increase the weight of 1,000 of the targeted preschool children by 10%.

One commonly used effectiveness measure for health interventions is the disability-adjusted life year (DALY). This combines years lost due to mortality with years lost to morbidity. Nutrition interventions (as general, preventive, public health measures) have an extensive estimated benefit in terms of reducing the burden of disease, as measured by DALYs.

### Determining Unit Costs of Interventions

The calculation of benefit-cost and cost-effectiveness measures is complex. For cost-benefit analyses, it is necessary to determine what would have happened to outcome x in the absence of the intervention. Would the private sector or an NGO have stepped in to deliver the services instead? In other words, the gross change in outcome x will not be the same as the net change. It is also necessary to decide whether to assign a higher weight to an intervention that, for a given cost, delivers a change in x to the poor as opposed to another intervention that delivers the change in x to the nonpoor. Most estimates, including those here, do not address these important considerations.

The important first step in generating benefit-cost and cost-effectiveness calculations is to obtain the unit costs of different interventions. Fortification and supplementation have low unit costs: ranging from US$0.05 per person per year for iodine fortification to US $1.70 for iron supplementation per pregnancy[492]. The unit costs of other nutrition programmes are higher. Mass-media programmes cost around US$1 per day per person, whereas community-based programmes cost about US$3-8 per day per person, depending on their intensity[492]. Feeding programmes and food subsidies undertaken since 1980s and early 1990s, (e.g., the PDS in India) have often been untargeted or poorly targeted, and have been by far the most expensive nutrition interventions. However, comparative unit cost calculations have not been undertaken for more recent, targeted, food-based programmes; e.g., Progresa in Mexico, and the Food For Education Programme in Bangladesh[9].

It is, however, misleading to rank interventions solely on the basis of cost. Perhaps the more expensive programmes are better able to reach the poor, to have a larger effect on them, and to help them reduce their future need for the intervention. To assess interventions in this light, we need to look at benefit-cost and cost-effectiveness measures.

## Cost-Effectiveness

The cost-effectiveness of various key nutrition interventions has been assessed[492]. Costs per death averted by breastfeeding promotion and IEC (PEM) are estimated as US$100-$300 in the poorest countries (Bangladesh, Cambodia, India, Viet Nam) and are also in the same range in Pakistan, which has surprisingly high levels of undernutrition given its higher per capita income. Estimated costs per death averted for vitamin A megadosing are in the same range for all countries except for Sri Lanka, which has by far the lowest infant mortality rate in this group of countries (comparing across countries, costs per death averted are inversely related to levels of mortality). The estimated costs per death averted for iron supplementation are markedly higher than for other interventions, because maternal death rates are lower than infant mortality rates. Note, however, that iron supplementation also has effects on productivity.

The results again suggest that nutrition interventions in low income Asia are a high priority in terms of high benefit-cost ratios, and low costs per death averted. If programme costs are identical across countries, then the countries where interventions are of the highest priority are those with highest current death rates and prevalences of nutrition deficiency: Bangladesh, Cambodia and Viet Nam, the poorest countries; and Pakistan, which also has surprisingly poor human resource indicators given its level of income. India is also a country of high priority, although the prevalence figures for micronutrient deficiencies appear to be underestimates. If costs of nutrition intervention are lower in countries with better primary health care systems, this would tend to improve the benefit-cost and cost-effectiveness rankings of the PRC, Sri Lanka and Viet Nam. However, good data on the variation of programme costs across countries do not exist.

Current best estimates for the cost-effectiveness of fortification programmes (Table 12) confirm previous findings[492].

Supplementation is about ten times more costly than fortification, and hence is most appropriate when the target group is less than 10% of the population; e.g., under 2-year-olds who are the target for vitamin A supplements. Supplementation is also the intervention of choice for population groups who cannot be reached by fortification.

It is important to remember that, in practice, the analysis of the cost-effectiveness of nutrition interventions is not as straightforward as is portrayed here. Context is important. The nature of the problem, the ability to target and to minimize leakage, the level of capacity to implement the intervention, and the bundling together of interventions in the field, make it very difficult to make generic statements about the cost-effectiveness of different types of intervention. All of these factors need to be taken into account more fully in the next wave of cost-effectiveness estimates.

**TABLE 12: Costs and effects of micronutrient interventions**

| Deficiency | Cost (US$)/beneficiary/year | Cost (US$)/life saved |
|---|---|---|
| Iron deficiency | | |
| Supplementation of pregnant women | 1.70 (per pregnancy) | 800 |
| Fortification | 0.09 | 2,000 |
| Iodine deficiency | | |
| Supplementation (reproductive age only) | 0.50 | 1,250 |
| Supplementation (all) | 0.50 | 4,650 |
| Fortification | 0.05 | 1,000 |
| Vitamin A deficiency | | |
| Supplementation <5 | 0.20 | 325 |
| Fortification | 0.05-0.15 | 1,000 |
| Nutrition education | 5.00 | 238 |

Source: Institute of Medicine (1998) *Prevention of Micronutrient Deficiencies.* Washington DC: National Academy Press.

## Key "Minimum Packages"

Because undernutrition is usually the result of many factors, it is not surprising that it has been attacked most effectively in situations in which several sectors and strategies have been brought to bear. Combining improved infant feeding, better household access to food, and improved and more accessible health services and sanitation, is clearly more effective in combatting undernutrition, (where food, health and care are all problems) than any of these measures taken alone. Given the well documented synergies between such actions, the combined effects are often more than additive. Actions can be initiated to impact on different levels of the problem; immediate, underlying or basic (see Figure 2).

The timing, duration, and breadth of an intervention modify its effect. Generally, the earlier and the longer an intervention, the more frequent the interpersonal contacts (i.e., more "intense"), the greater its benefits. This is true for both the initial and the later size of the effect, as well as for its duration. If timing and duration are held constant, multifocal interventions (e.g., health, nutrition, and optimal child care) will yield larger and more sustained benefits than unifocal interventions (e.g., supplementary feeding) [468]. Short term and unifocal interventions that begin during the later preschool period will do little to repair the damage from a history of undernutrition, poor health, and less than optimal caretaking. The merit of late interventions, even during the school years, is to prevent or remedy the adverse effects of concurrent health and nutrition problems that often interfere with learning and performance.

The Triple A process (Figure 5) will lead to an appropriate choice of actions in any situation, as reiterated throughout this review. It is possible, however to highlight the elements of "minimum packages" of key interventions of proven efficacy and effectiveness for different vulnerable groups in the life cycle, as follows.

For young children: promote exclusive breastfeeding for about six months; promote appropriate complementary feeding, starting at about six months, in addition to breastfeeding until 24 months; promote appropriate nutrition management during and after illness; foster psychosocial stimulation between caregivers and children; ensure adequate vitamin A intake; provide iron supplements where prevalence of deficiency is high; and promote regular use of iodized salt by all families.

For adolescent girls: improve access to family planning and to reproductive health services, aimed at delaying first pregnancy and improving knowledge and practices related to reproductive health and nutrition; provide nutrition education through schools, religious organizations, marketplaces or workplaces, and health promotion, based on research that has identified cultural and institutional constraints and detrimental attitudes and practices; prevent and treat sexually transmitted diseases, parasites, and micronutrient deficiencies; and provide supplementary food through school meals, in order to increase school attendance, and to serve as an opportunity for health and nutrition education.

For pregnant and post-partum women, provide the following through service delivery: iron and folate supplements, during pregnancy; monitoring pregnancy weight gain; antimalarials, antihelminths, and other micronutrient supplements, as appropriate, including post-partum vitamin A in VAD areas; prompt diagnosis and treatment of illness; and supplementary food, targeted to at-risk and undernourished women, using appropriate indicators for screening, and beginning as early as possible during pregnancy. The following should also be promoted: provision of counselling and education on nutrition, breastfeeding, family planning, HIV, and disease prevention education; and involvement of men and other family members in behaviour modification activities, so that they increase the demand for health services for girls and women.

Such minimum packages of interventions should be integrated into all primary health care projects, with community-based workers playing an important supportive role in catalysing improvements in home-based caring practices.

## Programme Management Principles

The main elements of successful community-based nutrition programme management practices (dealt with in greater detail in related papers[6,7]) are briefly highlighted here.

Good management is critical for sustained success in nutrition programming[455]. Progress in nutrition programming has been made where community-based programmes are linked operationally to service delivery structures, which are often village-based, primary health care outlets. Government employees at such levels may be oriented to act as *facilitators* of nutrition-relevant actions, which are coordinated and managed by community-based *mobilizers*, who are often volunteers selected by local communities. The mobilizer-facilitator nexus should be supported and managed by a series of organizational structures, from the grassroots to national level, and underpinned by broad-based social mobilization and communication strategies. Thailand has led the way in Asia with regard to such community-government partnerships.

The type and scope of relevant actions, around which community-based programmes are developed have been described above. The choice of the appropriate mix of actions and how they are to be implemented and phased over time will depend on the nature of the problems, their causes and the feasibility and cost-effectiveness of different strategies. Locally selected indicators may be used by mobilizers and facilitators, for both planning and monitoring.

At national or state levels, enabling policies and programmes are needed which explicitly consider the nature and causes of the undernutrition problem and thus the type of sectoral fine tuning that may result in improved outcomes (or at the very least will not exacerbate the problem). Policy-making should be more bottom-up than in the past, with a greater emphasis on what can be learned from community-based success and how best to enable and to accelerate it. This does not imply the exclusion of top-down, centrally derived solutions which may have a role in certain situations[7].

Contextual and programme-specific success factors have been summarized as follows[493] .

## Contextual Success Factors

- Political commitment at all levels of society was considered essential for social mobilization at the start of the programme or project and for future sustainability. The integration of nutritional goals in development programmes in general is a clear manifestation of genuine awareness and political commitment.
- A culture where people, particularly women, are involved in decision making was a prerequisite for people's participation and the creation of articulate bottom-up demands. A high level of literacy, especially among women, also associated strongly with participation and organisational capabilities.
- Community organisations e.g. womens groups, people's NGOs, credit associations, youth clubs or peasant associations, along with good infrastructure for the delivery of basic services, including committed and capable staff.
- · Charismatic community leaders, who can mobilise and motivate people to do more for themselves in a genuine self-reliant way.

- The parallel implementation of poverty-reducing programmes, particularly those integrated with nutrition-oriented programme/project.

## Programme Success Factors

- The creation of awareness of the high prevalence, serious consequences and causes of malnutrition, including the hierarchy of immediate, underlying and basic causes, and the need to address causes at all three levels.
- The initiation, promotion and support of a process whereby individuals and communities participate in assessing the nutrition problem and decide on how to use their own and additional outside resources for actions.
- Clear identification and definition of time-bound goals (targets) at all levels of the programme/ project. Young children from birth up to two to three years of age, pregnant and lactating women, and adolescent girls were normally the focus.
- The identification and support of facilitators and community mobilisers, providing a sense of joint ownership of the programme/project by the community and the Government.
- Good management of the programme/project, including effective leadership, training and supervision of facilitators and mobilizers, an appropriate balance between top-down and bottom-up actions and effective community-based monitoring.
- The involvement of local NGOs, who often provided excellent facilitators as well as culture-relevant training. They were usually accountable to the community, which facilitated sustainability.

Overall, the generic lessons to be learned from past experience with community-based nutrition programming (see bullets above) relate more to the approaches adopted than to what was actually done: more of "how" than of "what". For maximal long term sustainable impact, both process and outcome orientations need to be integrated. Ownership is fundamental to success, with respect to means and to ends. Tools such as the Triple A cycle (Figure 5) and the conceptual framework (Figure 2) are extremely useful in making the process and outcomes explicit to all stakeholders, thus improving communication and fostering ownership.

## Role of Programmes in National Nutrition Improvement

One important question concerns where, in the historical process of economic development, do nutrition programmes have their most important role? This depends to a considerable degree on the extent of administrative and physical infrastructure, its outreach, and the extent of local organizational capacity. These can then allow flows of resources to help to support nutrition activities at the local level. The following is an attempt at proposing priorities, with respect to levels to development.

For very poor regions within countries with extremely limited human, economic and organizational infrastructure, the very first priority is likely to be to establish accessible and relevant preventive and curative health care, and to ensure access to adequate food. Cost-effectiveness data suggest that many primary health interventions (e.g., immunization against diptheria, polio and tetanus (DPT), measles, TB, rotavirus and hepatitis B) should all precede programmes aimed at protein-energy undernutrition, as should other primary health care such as the treatment of measles with vitamin A, and use of antibiotics for ARI[492]. Micronutrient interventions have similar high levels of cost-effectiveness.

Once these programmes have been implemented, then it is feasible to consider extending the system and intensifying nutrition activities. This could be achieved by training existing health workers, and recruiting nutrition workers and nutrition volunteers as, for example, in Thailand[6]. The advantage is that existing health workers can provide support and supervision. This in turn requires investments in training, training materials, initial equipment (e.g., scales) as well as recurrent expenditures (micronutrient supplements, deworming tablets in endemic areas, growth charts). Although the supplies are of very modest cost per child, nonetheless these amounts become very substantial at anything approaching national scale. Countries may wish to follow the approach adopted by Thailand and the Philippines in the targeted Early Childhood Development programme (and also the PRC in the 100 counties model (see Appendix I), and begin with the highest priority areas.

Programmes also necessarily differ between urban and rural areas: in urban areas, slums are a high priority, but it may be very hard to use volunteers in such areas. By definition, high priority rural areas are most likely to be remote or difficult to access, to have dispersed populations, and to lack basic facilities, such as a local doctor, clinic, or school.

Nutrition programmes have a role whether or not the underlying trend is one of nutrition improvement. Underlying trends are too slow to combat undernutrition in Asia within an acceptable time[11]. An analogy can be drawn with public health measures, which are essential even when health conditions are tending to improve.

In upper low income countries (i.e., those with per caput GNP of about US $760-3000), programmes are more feasible, but are not so widely needed as the problem is usually less prevalent. The social and regional targeting of well organized, efficient, programmes becomes increasingly important; e.g., in the Philippines and Thailand. Nutrition programmes in this group may also have important beneficial interactions (through human capital formation) with growth. In some cases (e.g., small island developing States, such as the Republic of Fiji Islands, and Tonga) child undernutrition is not a public health problem although child obesity may be[1].

In middle income countries, such as Malaysia, nutrition programmes eventually merge with social welfare and health services. They may not be such a priority for the whole country, but need to be targeted to reduce disparity, where it exists, and to buffer any social groups that are marginalized during the growth process. As countries industrialize, food becomes more accessible and health care more extensive and better. Social welfare and services and legislation become relatively more important, and may buffer the nutrition needs of vulnerable groups during economic shocks. In such countries, where there is the economic potential to do something about undernutrition, an overriding concern is often equity, both regional and social.

The value and success of direct nutrition interventions will thus depend on factors such as their historical timing, their relevance to the extent, type and causes of undernutrition, the degree of community ownership of the programme, the infrastructure and management capacity for implementation[7] and the political will and resources to ensure sustainability.

# REFERENCES

1. Popkin, BM, Horton S, Kim S (2001) The nutrition transition and prevention of diet-related chronic diseases in Asia and the Pacific. *Food and Nutrition Bulletin.* (In press).

2. Mannar V (2001) Regional Approaches for Fortification of Staples and Complementary Foods. Paper prepared for the Asian Development Bank IFPRI Report Technical Assistance Project (RETA) 5824. Nutrition Trends, Policies and Strategies in Asia and the Pacific. Washington DC: International Food Policy Research Institute.

3. Haddad L (2001) Maximising the Nutrition Impact of Food Policy in Asia and the Pacific. Paper prepared for the Regional Technical Assistance Project RETA 5824 Nutrition Trends, Policies and Strategies in Asia and the Pacific. Manila, Philippines: Asian Development Bank.

4. Engle P (1999) The role of caring practices and resources for care in child survical, growth, and development: South and Southeast Asia. *Asian Development Review* 17 (1,2): 132-167.

5. Mason, JB, Hunt J, Parker D, Jonsson U (1999) Investing in child nutrition in Asia. *Asian Development Review* 17 (1, 2): 1-32.

6. Tontisirin K, Gillespie SR (1999) Linking community-based programs and service delivery for improving maternal and child nutrition. *Asian Development Review* 17 (1, 2): 33-65.

7. Gillespie SR (2000) *Strengthening Capacity to Improve Nutrition.* Paper prepared for the Asian Development Bank-IFPRI Regional Technical Assistance Project 5824 Nutrition Trends, Policies and Strategies in Asia and the Pacific. Washington DC: International Food Policy Research Institute.

8. UNICEF (1998) *The State of the World's Children 1998.* Oxford, UK: Oxford University Press.

9. Gillespie SR, Haddad L (2001) *Attacking the Double Burden of Malnutrition in Asia and the Pacific. Synthesis of the Regional Technical Assistance Project 5824 on Nutrition Trends, Policies and Strategies in Asia and the Pacific.* Manila: Asian Development Bank.

10. de Onis M, Blossner M., Villar J (1998) Levels and patterns of intrauterine growth retardation in developing countries. *European Journal of Clinical Nutrition* 52: S5-S15.

11. ACC/SCN (2000) *Fourth Report on the World Nutrition Situation* . Geneva: ACC/SCN in collaboration with the International Food Policy Research Institute.

12. Ramalingaswami V, Jonsson U, Rohde J (1996) The South Asian enigma. In *The Progress of Nations.* New York: UNICEF, pages 10-17.

13. ACC/SCN (2000) *Low Birthweight.* A report based on the International Low Birthweight Symposium and Workshop held June 14 – 17, 1999 in Dhaka Bangladesh. ACC/SCN Nutrition Policy Paper 18, ed. Pojda J, Kelley L. Geneva: ACC/SCN.

14. Villar J, Belizan JM (1982) The timing factor in the pathophysiology of the intrauterine growth retardation syndrome. *Obstetrical Gynecology Survey* 37: 499-506.

15. WHO (1995a) Maternal anthropometry and pregnancy outcomes: a WHO collaborative study. *Bulletin of the World Health Organization:* Supplement to Volume 73.

16. de Onis M, Habicht J-P (1996) Anthropometric reference data for international use: recommendations from a World Health Organization Expert Committee. *American Journal of Clinical Nutrition* 64: 650-658.

17. Bakketeig L (1991) Ultrasound dating of pregnancies changes dramatically the observed rates of pre-term, post-term, and small-for-gestational-term. *Iatrogenics* 1: 174-175.

18. Zhang J, Bowes WA Jr. (1995) Birth-weight-for-gestational-age patterns by race, sex, and parity in the United States population. *Obstetrical Gynecology* 86: 200-208.

19. Falkner F, Hozgreve W, Schloo RH (1994) Prenatal influences on postnatal growth: overview and pointers for needed research. *European Journal of Clinical Nutrition* 48: S15-S24.

20. Villar J, Smeriglio V, Martorell R, Brown CH, Klein RE (1984) Heterogeneous growth and mental development of intrauterine growth-

retarded infants during the first 3 years of life. *Pediatrics* 74: 783-91.

21. Kramer MS, Olivier M, McLean FH, Willis DM, Usher RH (1990) Impact of intrauterine growth retardation and body proportionality on fetal and neonatal outcome. *Pediatrics* 86: 707-713.

22. Ashworth A (1998) Effects of intrauterine growth retardation on mortality and morbidity in infants and young children. *European Journal of Clinical Nutrition* 52: S34-S42.

23. Villar J, de Onis M, Kestler E, Bolanos F, Cerezo R, Bernedes H (1990) The differential neonatal morbidity of the intrauterine growth retardation syndrome. *American Journal of Obstetrical Gynecology* 163: 151-157.

24. Caulfield LE, Haas JD, Belizan JM, Rasmussen KM, Edmonston B (1991) Differences in early postnatal morbidity risk by pattern of fetal growth in Argentina. *Paediatric Perinatal Epidemiology* 5: 263-275.

25. Cuttini M, Cortinovis I, Bossi A, de Vonderweid U (1991) Proportionality of small for gestational age babies as a predictor of neonatal mortality and morbidity. *Pediatric Perinatal Epidemiology* 5: 56-63.

26. Hoffman HJ, Bakketeig LS (1984) Heterogeneity of intrauterine growth retardation and reocurrence risks. *Seminars in Perinatology* 8: 15-24.

27. Moore SE (1998) Nutrition, immunity and the fetal and infant origins of disease hypothesis in developing countries. *Proceedings of the Nutrition Society* 57: 241-247.

28. Martorell R, Ramakrishnan U, Schroeder DG, Melgar P, Neufeld L (1998) Intrauterine growth retardation, body size, body composition and physical performance in adolescence. *European Journal of Clinical Nutrition* 52: S43-S53.

29. Albertsson-Wikland K, Karlberg J (1994) Natural growth in children born small for gestational age with and without catch-up growth. *Acta Pediatrica* 399: 64-70.

30. Harvey D, Prince J, Burton J, Parkinson C, Campbell S (1982) Abilities of children who were small-for-gestational-age babies. *Pediatrics* 69: 296-300.

31. Grantham-McGregor SM (1998) Small for gestational age, term babies, in the first six years of life. *European Journal of Clinical Nutrition* 52: S59-S64.

32. Hack M (1998) Effects of intrauterine growth retardation on mental performance and behavior, outcomes during adolescence and adulthood. *European Journal of Clinical Nutrition* 52: S65-S71.

33. Haas JD, Murdoch S, Rivera J, Martorell R (1996) Early nutrition and later physical work capacity. *Nutrition Reviews* 54: S41-8.

34. Barker DJP (1998) *Mothers, Babies and Health in Later Life*. Edinburgh: Churchill Livingstone.

35. Leon D (1998) Fetal growth and adult disease. *European Journal of Clinical Nutrition* 52: S72-S82.

36. Barker DJP (1993) Intrauterine growth retardation and adult disease. *Current Obstetrical Gynaecology* 3: 200-206.

37. Rasmussen KM (2000) The "fetal origins" hypothesis: Challenges and opportunities for maternal and child nutrition. *Annual Review of Nutrition* 2:73-95.

38. Adair LS, Kuzawa CW (2001) Early growth retardation and syndrome X: Conceptual and methodological issues surrounding the programming hypothesis. In *Nutrition and Growth*, ed. Martorell R, Haschke F. New York: Lippincott-Raven.

39. Kramer MS (1987) Determinants of low birth weight: methodological assessment and meta-analysis. *Bulletin WHO* 65: 663-737.

40. Tomkins A, Murray S, Rondo P, Filteau S (1994) Impact of maternal infection on foetal growth and nutrition. *SCN News* 11: 18-20.

41. Tomkins A, Watson F (1989) *Malnutrition and Infection*. ACC/SCN State-of-the-Art Series Nutrition Policy Discussion Paper No. 5. Geneva: ACC/SCN.

42. Kramer MS (1998) Socioeconomic determinants of intrauterine growth retardation. *European Journal of Clinical Nutrition* 52: S29-S33.

43. de Onis M, Villar J, Gülmezoglu MA (1998) Nutritional interventions to prevent intrauterine growth retardation: Evidence from randomized controlled trials. *European Journal of Clinical Nutrition* 52: S83-S93.

44. Ramakrishnan U (1999) Micronutrients and pregnancy outcome: a review of the literature. *Nutrition Research* 19: 103-159.

45. Kramer MS (1999) Balanced protein/energy supplementation in pregnancy. Oxford, UK: The Cochrane Library.

46. Girija A, Geervani P, Rao RN (1984) Influence of dietary supplementation during pregnancy on lactation performance. *Journal of Tropical Paediatrics* 30: 79-83.

47. Tontisirin K, Booranasubkajorn U, Hongsumarn A, Thewtong D (1986) Formulation and evaluation of supplementary foods for Thai pregnant women. *American Journal of Clinical Nutrition* 43: 931-939.

48. Kardjati S, Kusin JA, DeWith C (1988) Energy supplementation in the last trimester of pregnancy

in East Java. I. Effect on birthweight. *British Journal of Obstetrics and Gynaecology* 95: 783-794.

49. Rasmussen KM, Habicht J-P (1994) Summary and overview of main findings. In *Maternal and Child Nutrition in Madura, Indonesia,* ed. Kusin JA, Kardjati S. Amsterdam: Royal Tropical Institute. 21-22.

50. Ceesay SM, Prentice AM, Cole TJ, Foord F, Weaver LT, Poskitt EM, Whitehead RG (1997) Effects on birth weight and perinatal mortality of maternal dietary supplements in rural Gambia: 5-year randomised controlled trial. *British Medical Journal* 315: 786-790.

51. Prentice AM, Cole TJ, Foord FJ, Lamb WH, Whitehead RG (1987) Increased birthweight after prenatal dietary supplementation of rural African women. *American Journal of Clinical Nutrition* 46: 912-925.

52. Viegas OA, Scott PH, Cole TJ, Mansfield HN, Wharton P, Wharton BA (1982a) Dietary protein energy supplementation of pregnant Asian mothers at Sorrento, Birmingham. I: Unselective during second and third trimester. *British Medical Journal.* 285: 589-592.

53. Viegas OA, Scott PH, Cole TJ, Eaton P, Needham PG, Wharton BA (1982b). Dietary protein energy supplementation of pregnant Asian mothers at Sorrento, Birmingham. II: Selective during third trimester only. *British Medical Journal.* 285: 592-595.

54. Mardones-Santander F, Rosso P, Stekel A, Ahumada E, Llaguno S, Pizarro F, Salinas J, Vial I, Walter T (1988) Effect of a milk-based food supplement on maternal nutritional status and fetal growth in underweight Chilean women. *American Journal of Clinical Nutrition* 47: 413-419.

55. Rush D, Stein Z, Susser M (1980) A randomized controlled trial of prenatal nutritional supplementation in New York City. *Pediatrics* 65: 683-97.

56. Iyengar L (1967) Effects of dietary supplements late in pregnancy on the expectant mother and her newborn. *Indian Journal of Medical Research* 55: 85-89.

57. Anderson M (1989) The relationship between maternal nutrition and child growth in rural India. PhD dissertation. Tufts University, Boston, USA.

58. Institute of Medicine (1990) Nutrition during pregnancy. Washington DC: National Academy Press.

59. Kusin JA, Kardjati S, Renqvist UH (1994) Maternal body mass index: the functional significance during reproduction. *European Journal of Clinical Nutrition* 48 (Supplement 3): S56-S67.

60. Winkvist A, Habicht J-P, Rasmussen KM (1998) Linking maternal and infant benefits of a nutritional supplement during pregnancy and lactation. *American Journal of Clinical Nutrition* 68: 656-61.

61. Siega-Riz AM, Adair LS (1993) Biological determinants of pregnancy weight gain in a Filipino population. *American Journal of Clinical Nutrition* 57: 365-72.

62. Martínez H, Allen LH, Lung'aho M, Chávez A, Pelto GH (1994) Maternal fatness in Mexican women predicts body composition changes in pregnancy and lactation. *Advanced Experimental Medical Biology* 352: 99-107.

63. King JC, Butte NF, Bronstein MN, Kopp LE, Lindquist SA (1994) Energy metabolism during pregnancy: influence of maternal energy status. *American Journal of Clinical Nutrition* 59: 439S-445S.

64. Lawrence M, Lawrence F, Coward WA, Cole TJ, Whitehead RG (1987) Energy requirements of pregnancy in The Gambia. *The Lancet* 2: 1072-1076.

65. Williams MA, Havel PJ, Schwartz MW, Leisenring WM, King IB, Zingheim RW, Zebelman AM, Luthy DA (1999) Pre-eclampsia disrupts the normal relationship between serum leptin concentrations and adiposity in pregnant women. *Paediatrics Perinatal Epidemiology* 13: 190-204.

66. Pelto G, Dickin K, Engle P (1999) A Critical Link: Interventions for Physical Growth and Psychological Development: A Review. Geneva: Department of Child and Adolescent Health and Development, WHO.

67. Olson RK (1994) Developing indicators that predict benefit from prenatal energy supplementation. Ithaca, New York: Cornell University.

68. Susser M (1991) Maternal weight gain, infant birth weight, and diet: causal sequences. *American Journal of Clinical Nutrition* 53: 1384-1396.

69. McDonald EC, Pollitt E, Mueller WH, Hsueh AM, Sherwin R (1981) The Bacon Chow study: Nutrition supplementation and birth weight of offspring. *American Journal of Clinical Nutrition* 34: 2133-2144.

70. Li R, Haas JD, Habicht J-P (1998) Timing of the influence of maternal nutritional status during pregnancy on fetal growth. *American Journal of Human Biology* 10: 529-539.

71.  Hediger ML, Scholl TO, Belsky DH, Ances IG, Salmon RW (1989) Patterns of weight gain in adolescent pregnancy: effects on birth weight and preterm delivery. *Obstetrical Gynecology* 74: 6-12.

72.  Villar J, Rivera J (1988) Nutritional supplementation during two consecutive pregnancies and the interim lactation period: Effect on birth weight. *Pediatrics* 81: 51-57.

73.  Mahomed K (2000) Iron supplementation in pregnancy. *Cochrane Database Systematic Reviews* 2000:16.

74.  Klebanoff MA, Shiono PH, Selby JV, Trachtenberg AI, Graubard BI (1991) Anemia and spontaneous preterm birth. *American Journal of Obstetrical Gynecology* 164: 59-63.

75.  Lu ZM, Goldenberg RL, Cliver SP, Cutter G, Blankson M (1991) The relationship between maternal hematocrit and pregnancy outcome. *Obstetrical Gynecology* 77: 190-4.

76.  Scholl TO, Hediger ML, Fischer RL, Shearer JW (1992) Anemia vs iron deficiency: increased risk of preterm delivery in a prospective study. *American Journal of Clinical Nutrition* 55: 985-988.

77.  Zhou LM, Yang WW, Hua JZ, Deng CQ, Tao X, Stoltzfus RJ (1998) Relation of hemoglobin measured at different times in pregnancy to preterm birth and low birth weight in Shanghai, China. *American Journal of Epidemiology* 148: 998-1006.

78.  Menendez C, Todd J, Alonso PL, Francis N, Lulat S, Ceesay S, M'Boge B, Greenwood BM (1994) The effects of iron supplementation during pregnancy, given by traditional birth attendants, on the prevalence of anaemia and malaria. *Transactions of the Royal Society of Tropical Medicine and Hygiene* 88: 590-593.

79.  Allen LH (2000) Anemia and iron deficiency: Effects on pregnancy outcome. *American Journal of Clinical Nutrition* 71 (Supplement 5): S1280-84.

80.  Rasmussen KM (2001) Is there a causal relationship between iron deficiency or iron-deficiency anemia and weight at birth, length of gestation and perinatal mortality? *Journal of Nutrition* 131:590S-603S.

81.  Mahomed K (2000) Folic acid supplementation in pregnancy. *Cochrane Database Systematic Reviews* 2000:181.

82.  Charoenlarp P, Dhanamitta S, Kaewvichit R, Silprasert A, Suwanaradd C, Na-Nakorn S, Prawatmuang P, Vatanavicharn S, Vaniyapong T, Toe T, Valyasevi A, Baker S, Cook K, DeMaeyer EM, Garby L, Hallberg L (1988) A WHO collaborative study on iron supplementation in Burma and in Thailand. *American Journal of Clinical Nutrition* 47: 280-297.

83.  Berry RJ, Li Z, Erickson JD, Li S, Moore CA, Wang H, Mulinare J, Zhao P, Wong LY, Gindler J, Hong SX, Correa A (1999) Prevention of neural-tube defects with folic acid in China. China-U.S. Collaborative Project for Neural Tube Defect Prevention. *New England Journal of Medicine* 341: 1485-1490.

84.  Institute of Medicine (1999) Dietary reference intakes. Thiamin, riboflavin, niacin, vitamin B6, folate, vitamin B12, pantothenic acid, biotin, and choline. Washington DC: National Academy Press.

85.  Scholl TO, Hediger ML, Schall JI, Khoo CS, Fischer RL (1996) Dietary and serum folate: Their influence on the outcome of pregnancy. *American Journal of Clinical Nutrition* 63: 520-525.

86.  Kulier R, de Onis M, Gülmezoglu AM, Villar J (1998) Nutritional interventions for the prevention of maternal morbidity. *International Journal of Gynecological Obstetrics* 63: 321-246.

87.  Vollset SE, Refsum H, Irgens LM, Emblem BM, Tverdal A, Gjessing HK, Monsen ALB, Ueland PM (2000) Plasma total homocysteine, pregnancy complications, and adverse pregnancy outcomes: The Hordaland Homocystine Study. *American Journal of Clinical Nutrition* 71: 962-968.

88.  Mahomed K (2000) Zinc supplementation in pregnancy. *Cochrane Database Systematic Reviews*: 16.

89.  Garg HK, Singhal KC, Arshad Z (1993) A study of the effect of oral zinc supplementation during pregnancy on pregnancy outcome. *Indian Journal of Physiological Pharmacology* 37: 276-284.

90.  Goldenberg RL, Tamura T, Neggers Y, Copper RL, Johnston KE, DuBard MB, Hauth JC (1995) The effect of zinc supplementation on pregnancy outcome. *Journal of American Medical Association* 274: 463-468.

91.  Caulfield LE, Zavaleta N, Figueroa A, Leon Z (1999) Maternal zinc supplementation does not affect size at birth or pregnancy duration in Peru. *Journal of Nutrition* 129: 1563-1568.

92.  Osendarp SJ, van Raaij JM, Arifeen SE, Wahed M, Baqui AH, Fuchs GJ (2000) A randomized, placebo-controlled trial of the effect of zinc supplementation during pregnancy on pregnancy outcome in Bangladeshi urban poor. *American Journal of Clinical Nutrition* 71: 114-119.

93.  Christian P, West KP Jr, Khatry SK, Katz J, Shrestha SR, Pradhan EK, LeClerq SC, Pokhrel RP, (1998) Night blindness of pregnancy in rural Nepal-nutritional and health risks. *International Journal of Epidemiology* 27: 231-237.

94. West KP Jr, Katz J, Khatry SK, LeClerq SC, Pradhan EK, Shrestha SR, Connor PB, Dali SM, Christian P, Pokhrel RP, Sommer A (1999) Double blind, cluster randomised trial of low dose supplementation with vitamin A or beta carotene on mortality related to pregnancy in Nepal. The NNIPS-2 Study Group. *British Medical Journal* 318(7183): 570-575.

95. Belizán JM, Villar J, Bergel E, del Pino A, Di Fulvio S, Galliano SV, Kattan C (1997) Long-term effect of calcium supplementation during pregnancy on the blood pressure of offspring: follow up of a randomized controlled trial. *British Medical Jou*rnal 315: 281-285.

96. Purwar M, Kulkarni H, Motghare V, Dhole S (1996) Calcium supplementation and prevention of pregnancy induced hypertension. *Journal of Obstetrical Gynaecology Research* 22: 425-30.

97. Mahomed K, Gülmezoglu AM (1997) Maternal iodine supplements in areas of deficiency. *The Cochrane Library* (3):1-9.

98. Pharoah PO, Buttfield IH, Hetzel BS (1971) Neurological damage to the fetus resulting from severe iodine deficiency during pregnancy. *The Lancet* 1: 308-310.

99. Thilly CH, Delange F, Lagasse R, Bourdoux P, Ramioul L, Berquist H, Ermans AM (1978) Fetal hypothyroidism and maternal thyroid status in severe endemic goiter. *Journal of Clinical Endocrinology Metabolism* 47: 354-360.

100. Friis H, Michaelsen KF (1998) Micronutrients and HIV infection: A review. *European Journal of Clinical Nutrition* 52: 157-163.

101. Fawzi WW, Msamanga GI, Spiegelman D, Urassa EJ, McGrath N, Mwakagile D, Antelman G, Mbise R, Herrera G, Kapiga S, Willett W, Hunter DJ (1998a) Randomised trial of effects of vitamin supplements on pregnancy outcomes and T cell counts in HIV-1-infected women in Tanzania. *The Lancet* 351: 1477-1482.

102. Scholl TO, Hediger ML, Bendich A, Schall JI, Smith WK, Krueger PM (1997) Use of multivitamin/mineral prenatal supplements: Influence on the outcome of pregnancy. *American Journal of Epidemiology* 146: 134-141.

103. Gopalan C (2000) Multiple micronutrient supplementation in pregnancy. Nutrition Foundation of India. (www.nutritionfoundationin.org).

104. Allen LH (1994) Maternal micronutrient malnutrition: Effects on breast milk and infant nutrition, and priorities for intervention. *ACC/ SCN Second Report on the World Nutrition Situation* 1: 21-24.

105. Gülmezoglu M, de Onis M, Villar J (1997) Effectiveness of interventions to prevent or treat impaired fetal growth. *Obstetrical Gynecological Survey* 52: 139-49.

106. Garner, P, Gülmezoglu AM (2000) *Prevention Versus Treatment for Malaria in Pregnant Women.* Cochrane Review. Oxford, UK: The Cochrane Library. Update Software.

107. Launer LJ, Villar J, Kestler E, de Onis M (1990) The effect of maternal work on fetal growth and duration of pregnancy: a prospective study. *British Journal of Obstetrical Gynaecology* 97: 62-70.

108. Naeye RL, Peters EC (1982) Working during pregnancy: Effects on the fetus. *Pediatrics 69*: 724-7.

109. Henriksen TB, Hedegaard M, Secher NJ (1995) Standing and walking at work and birthweight. *Acta Obstetrical Gynecology Scan*dinavia 74: 509-516.

110. Dewey KG, McCrory MA (1994) Effects of dieting and physical activity on pregnancy and lactation. *American Journal of Clinical Nutrition* 59: 446S-452S.

111. Brasel J (1982) Changes in body composition during adolescence. In *Adolescent Nutrition*, ed. Winick M. New York: John Wiley and Sons.

112. Garn SM, Wagner B (1969) The adolescent growth of the skeletal mass and its implications for mineral requirements. In *Adolescent Nutrition and Growth*, ed. Heald FP. New York: Meredith. 139 – 161.

113. Roche AF, Davila GH (1972) Late adolescent growth in stature. *Pediatrics* 50: 874-880.

114. Moerman ML (1982) Growth of the birth canal in adolescent girls. *American Journal of Obstetrical Gynecology* 143: 528-532.

115. Harrison DA, Fleming AF,Briggs ND, Rossiter CE (1985) Growth during pregnancy in pregnant Nigerian primagravidae. *British Journal of Obstetrical Gynecology* 5: 32-39.

116. FNB/NAS/NRC (1989) *Osteoporosis.* Chapter 23. In Diet and Health: Implications for Reducing Chronic Disease Risk. Food and Nutrition Board/ National Academy of Sciences/National Research Council (FNB/NAS/NRC). Washington DC: National Academy Press. 615 – 626.

117. Kanade AN (1994) Studies in inter and intra individual variations in growth and dietary intake of adolescents. PhD thesis, Agharkar Research Institute, Pune, India.

118. Kulin HE, Bwibo N, Mutie D, Santner S (1982) The effect of chronic childhood malnutrition on pubertal growth and development. *American Journal of Clinical Nutrition* 36: 527-536.

119. Eveleth PB, Tanner JM (1990) *Worldwide Variation in Human Growth*. Cambridge: Cambridge University Press.

120. Brabin L, Brabin BJ (1992) The cost of successful adolescent growth and development in girls in relation to iron and vitamin A status. *American Journal of Clinical Nutrition*, 55: 955-958.

121. Gopalan C (1987) Motherhood in early adolescence. In *Combating Undernutrition. Nutrition Foundation India Special Publication Series No. 3*. New Delhi, India: Nutrition Foundation of India.

122. Kushwaha KP, Rai AK, Rath AK, Singh YD, Sirohi R (1993) Pregnancies in adolescents: Fetal, neonatal and maternal outcome. *Indian Pediatrics* 30: 501-5.

123. ICMR (1990) A national collaborative study of identification of high risk families, mothers and outcome of their offspring with particular reference to the problem of maternal nutrition, low birth weight, perinatal and infant morbidity and mortality in rural and urban slum communities. New Delhi, India: Indian Council of Medical Research.

124. Senderowitz J (1995) *Adolescent Health: Reassessing the Passage to Adulthood*. World Bank Discussion Paper No. 272. Washington DC: The World Bank.

125. Westoff C, Ochoa L (1991) As reported in Tinker, A., P. Daly, C. Green, H. Saxenian, R. Lakshminarayanan, and K. Gill, 1994. *Women's Health and Nutrition: Making a Difference*. World Bank Discussion Paper No. 256. Washington DC.: The World Bank.

126. Frisancho AR, Matos J, Leonard WR and Yaroch LA (1985) Developmental and nutritional determinants of pregnancy outcome among teenagers, *American Journal of Physical Anthropology* 66: 247-261.

127. WHO (1995b) Physical status: The use and Interpretation of Anthropometry: Report of a WHO Expert Committee. WHO Technical Report Series No. 854. Geneva: WHO.

128. Scholl TO, Hediger ML, Ances IG, Belsky DH, Salmon RW (1990) Weight gain during pregnancy in adolescence: predictive ability of early weight gain. *Obstetrical Gynecology* 75: 948-953.

129. Olson CM (1987a) Pregnancy in adolescents: A cause for nutritional concern? *Professional Perspectives* 1: 1-5.

130. Zeitlin, M. F., J. D. Wray, J. B. Stanbury, N. P. Schlossman, Meurer JJ (1982) *Nutrition and Population Growth: The Delicate Balance*. Cambridge UK: Oelgeschlager, Gunn and Hain.

131. Vir, S (1990) Adolescent growth in girls - the Indian perspective. *Indian Paediatrics* 27: 1249-1255.

132. UN (1989) *Adolescent Reproductive Behaviour*, Vol. II: *Evidence from developing countries*. New York: United Nations ST/ESA/SER.A/109/Add.1..

133. WHO (1989) WHO/UNFPA/UNICEF Statement. The reproductive health of adolescents. Geneva: WHO.

134. Leslie J (1995) Improving the nutrition of women in the Third World. 117-138. In *Child Growth and Nutrition in Developing Countries: Priorities for Action*, ed. Pinstrup-Andersen P. Ithaca, New York: Cornell University Press. 117 – 138.

135. Geervani P, Jayashree G (1988) A study of nutritional status of adolescent and adult pregnant and lactating women and growth of their infants. *Journal of Tropical Paediatrics* 34: 234-237.

136. Bailey W (1981) Malnutrition among babies born to adolescent mothers. *West Indian Medical Journal* 30: 72-76.

137. Chan GM, McMurry M, Westover K, Engelbert-Fenton K, Thomas MR (1987) Effects of increased dietary calcium intake upon the calcium and bone mineral status of lactating adolescent and adult women. *American Journal of Clinical Nutrition* 46: 319-323.

138. Olson CM (1987b) Breastfeeding by adolescent mothers: Potential benefits and concerns. *Professional Perspectives* 2: 1-4.

139. Kurz KM, Johnson-Welch C (1994) The nutrition and lives of adolescents in developing countries: Findings from the nutrition of adolescent girls research program. Washington DC: International Center for Research on Women.

140. DeMaeyer E, Adiels-Tegman M (1985) The prevalence of anaemia in the world. *World Health Statistics Quarterly* 38: 302-316.

141. Rani S, Sehgal S (1995) Nutritional intake of rural and urban adolescent girls of Haryana (India). *Ecology of Food and Nutrition* 34: 211-216.

142. Ravindran S (1986) Health implications of sex discrimination among childhood: A review paper and annotated bibliography. Geneva: WHO.

143. Satyanarayana K, Nadamuni Naidu A, Swaminathan MC, Narasinga Rao BS (1981) Effect of nutritional deprivation in early childhood on later growth. A community study without intervention. *American Journal of Clinical Nutrition* 34: 1636-1637.

144. Martorell R, Rivera J, Kaplowitz H (1990) Consequences of stunting in early childhood for adult body size in rural Guatemala. *Annales Nestle* 48: 85-92.

145. Martorell R, Kettel Khan L, Schroeder DG (1994) Reversibility of stunting: Epidemiological findings in children from developing countries. *European Journal of Clinical Nutrition* 48 (Supplement 1): S45-S57.

146. Proos LA, Hofvander Y, Wennqvist K, Tuvemo T (1992) A longitudinal study on the anthropometric and clinical development of Indian children adopted in Sweden. *Uppsala Journal of Medical Science* 97: 93 - 106.

147 Gopalan C (1994) Low birth weights — significance and implications. In *Nutrition in Children: Developing Country Concerns*, ed. Sachdev HPS, Choudury P. New Delhi, India: Cambridge Press. 1-33.

148. ACC/SCN (1992) *Second Report on the World Nutrition Situation: Volume I: Global and Regional Results*. Geneva: ACC/SCN.

149. NNMB (1980) National Nutrition Monitoring Bureau Report for 1974-79. Hyderabad, India: National Institute of Nutrition.

150. Bouis HE, Palabrica-Costello M, Solon O, Limbo AB (1994) Understanding the gender-differentiated constraints to Philippine farm household investments in adolescents: Implications for their nutritional status. Washington DC: Nutrition of Adolescent Girls Research Program, No. 7, International Center for Research on Women.

151. Chavez A, Martinez C, Soberanes B, Dominguez L, Avila A (1994) Early nutrition and physical and mental development in Mexican rural adolescent females. Washington DC: Nutrition of Adolescent Girls Research Program, No. 4. International Center for Research on Women.

152. Mendez MA, Adair LS (1999) Severity and timing of stunting in the first two years of life affect performance on cognitive tests in late childhood. *Journal of Nutrition* 129 (8):1555-1562.

153. Lumey LH (1985) Famine and birth weight in the second generation: Maternal transmission of environmental experience. *Human Biology* 12 (Supplement 1): 42.

154. Lumey LH (1988) Obstetric performance of women after in utero exposure to the dutch famine (1944-45). PhD Thesis, Columbia University.

155. Ramachandran P (1989) Nutrition in pregnancy. In *Women and Nutrition in India*, ed. Gopalan C, Suminder Kaur. Special Publication Series No. 5. New Delhi, India: Nutrition Foundation of India.

156. Martorell R, Habicht J-P, Rivera JA (1995) History and design of the INCAP longitudinal study (1969-77) and its follow-up (1988-89). *Journal of Nutrition* 125: 1027S-1041S.

157. Lind T (1984) Could more calories per day keep low birth weight at bay? *The Lancet* 1: 501-502.

158. Torun B, Viteri FE, Ramirez-Zea M, Rodriguez MM, Guptill K (1995) Response of endogenous growth factors to exercise and food supplementation in stunted pubertal girls in Guatemala. Nutrition of Adolescent Girls Research Program, No. 2. Washington DC: International Center for Research on Women.

159. Golden MHN (1994) Is complete catch-up possible for stunted malnourished children? *European Journal of Clinical Nutrition* 48 (Supplement): S58-S71.

160. Kurz KM, Dusch E (2000) Exploring reductions in low birth weight through interventions during adolescence. Background paper for the UNICEF/World Bank/USDA Meeting on low birth weight, 30-31 March 2000. New York: UNICEF.

161. Viteri FE (1994) The consequences of iron deficiency and anaemia in pregnancy on maternal health, the foetus and the infant. SCN News 11: 14-17.

162. Viteri FE, Ali F, Tujagne J (1999) Long term weekly iron supplementation improves and sustains nonpregnant women's iron status as well or better than currently recommended short-term daily supplementation. *Journal of Nutrition.* 129: 2013-2020.

163. Lynch SR (2000) The potential impact of iron supplementation during adolescence on iron status in pregnancy. *Journal of Nutrition* (Supplement) 130: S448-S451.

164. UN (1989) Convention on the Rights of the Child. Adopted by the General Assembly of the United Nations on 20 November 1989. New York: UN.

165. Mensch BS, Bruce J, Greene ME (1998) *The Uncharted Passage: Girls' Adolescence in the Developing World*. New York: Population Council.

166. Scholl TO, Hediger ML, Belsky DH (1994) Prenatal care and maternal health during adolescent pregnancy: a review and meta-analysis. *Journal of Adolescent Health* 15 (6): 444-456.

167. NCHS (2000) http://www.cdc.gov/growthcharts

168. Dewey KG (2001). Approaches for improving complementary feeding of infants and young children. Background paper for the WHO/

UNICEF Technical Consultation on Infant and Young Child Feeding. Geneva: WHO. (In press).

169. Garza C, de Onis M (1999) A new international growth reference for young children. *American Journal of Clinical Nutrition* 70: 169S-1672S.

170. Frongillo EA Jr, de Onis M, Hanson KM (1997) Socioeconomic and demographic factors are associated with worldwide patterns of stunting and wasting of children. *Journal of Nutrition* 127: 2302-2309.

171. Pelletier DL, Frongillo EA Jr, Schroeder DG, Habicht J-P (1994) A methodology for estimating the contribution of malnutrition to child mortality in developing countries. *Journal of Nutrition* 124: 2106S-2122S.

172. World Bank (1993) *World Development Report*. Washington DC.: The World Bank.

173. Murray CJL, Lopez AD (1996) *The Global Burden of Disease*. Cambridge MA: Harvard University Press. 312.

174. WorldWatch. 2000. *Underfed and Overfed: The Global Epidemic of Malnutrition*. Gardner G, Halweil B. Paper Number 150. Washington DC: The WorldWatch Institute.

175. Haas JD, Martinez EJ, Murdoch S, Conlisk E, Rivera JA, Martorell R (1995) Nutritional supplementation during the preschool years and physical work capacity in adolescent and young adult Guatemalans. *Journal of Nutrition* (Supplement) 125: S1078-S1089.

176. Rivera JA, Martorell R, Ruel MT, Habicht J-P, Haas JD (1995) Nutritional supplementation during the preschool years influences body size and composition of Guatemalan adolescents. *Journal of Nutrition* 125: 1068S-1077S.

177. Aylward GP, Pfeiffer SI, Wright A, Verhulst SJ (1989) Outcome studies of low birth weight infants published in the last decade: A meta-analysis. *Journal of Pediatrics* 115: 515-520.

178. Martorell R (1996) Undernutrition during pregnancy and early childhood and its consequences for cognitive and behavioral development. Paper prepared for the World Bank Conference, Early Childhood Development: Investing in the Future, Atlanta, Georgia, 8-9 April, 1996. Washington DC: The World Bank.

179. Pollitt E (1984) Methods for the behavioral aseessment of the consequences of malnutrition. In *Methods for the Evaluation of the Impact of Food and Nutrition Programmes*. ed. Sahn DE, Lockwood R, Scrimshaw NS. Tokyo, Japan: United Nations University.

180. Pollitt E, Gorman KS, Engle PL, Martorell R, Rivera J (1993) Early supplementary feeding and cognition: Effects over two decades. *Monographs of the Society for Research in Child Development* 58: 1-99.

181. Grantham-McGregor SM, Powell CA, Walker SP, Himes JH (1991) Nutritional supplementation, psychosocial stimulation and mental development of stunted children: the Jamaican study. *The Lancet* 388: 1-5.

182. Brown JL and Pollitt E (1996) Malnutrition, poverty and intellectual development. *Scientific American* 274: 38-43.

183. Gorman KS, Pollitt E (1996) Does schooling buffer the effects of early risk? *Child Development* 67: 314-326.

184. Engle P, Bentley M, Pelto G (2000) The role of care in nutrition programmes. *Proceedings of the Nutrition Society* 59: 25-35.

185. Engle P, Lhotska L, Armstrong H (1997) The care initiative: Assessment, analysis and action to improve care for nutrition. New York: UNICEF.

186. UNICEF (2001) *The State of the World's Children*. New York: UNICEF.

187. Ruel MT, Levin C, Armar-Klemesu M, Maxwell D, Morris SS (1999) Good care practices can mitigate the negative effects of poverty and low maternal schooling on children's nutritional status: Evidence from Accra. Food Consumption and Nutrition Division Discussion Paper 62. Washington DC: International Food Policy Research Institute.

188. Brown KH, Black RE, Lopez de Romaña G, Creed de Kanashiro H (1989) Infant-feeding practices and their relationship with diarrheal and other diseases in Huascar (Lima), Peru. *Pediatrics* 83: 31-40

189. Popkin BM, Adair L, Akin JS, Black R, Briscoe J, Flieger W (1990) Breast-feeding and diarrheal morbidity. *Pediatrics* 86: 874-882.

190. Brown KH, Stallings RY, de Kanashiro HC, Lopez de Romaña G, Black RE (1990) Effects of common illnesses on infants' energy intakes from breast milk and other foods during longitudinal community-based studies in Huascar (Lima), Peru. *American Journal of Clinical Nutrition* 52: 1005-1013.

191. Brown KH, Dewey KG, Allen LH (1998) Complementary feeding of young children in developing countries: A review of current scientific knowledge. Geneva: WHO.

192. Armstrong H (1995) Breastfeeding as the foundation of care. *Food and Nutrition Bulletin* 16: 299-312.

193. de Andraca I, Peirano P, Uauay R (1998) Nutrition and care in the preterm and neonatal periods and later development: human milk is

best for optimal mental development. Nutrition, health, and child development: research advances and policy recommendations. Washington DC: Pan American Health Organization.

194. WHO (2001) *The Optimal Duration of Exclusive Breastfeeding: Results of a WHO Systematic Review.* Note for the Press No. 7, 2 April 2001, www.who.int/inf-pr-2001/en/note2001-07.html

195. Dewey KG, Cohen RJ, Brown KH, Rivera LL (1999) Age of introduction of complementary foods and growth of term, low-birth-weight, breast-fed infants: A randomized intervention study in Honduras. *American Journal of Clinical Nutrition* 69: 679-686.

196. WHO (2000) *Malnutrition, the Global Picture.* Geneva: WHO.

197 Fomon SJ, Filer LJ Jr, Thomas LN, Anderson TA, Nelson SE (1975) Influence of formula concentration on caloric intake and growth of normal infants. *Acta Paediatrica Scandinavica* 64: 172-181.

198. Fomon SJ, Filer LJ, Ziegler EE, Bergmann KE, Bergmann RL (1977) Skim milk in infant feeding. *Acta Paediatrica Scandinavica* 66: 17-30.

199. Lampl M, Johnston FE, Malcolm LA (1978) The effects of protein supplementation on the growth and skeletal maturation of New Guinean school children. *Annals of Human Biology* 5: 219-227.

200. Malcolm LA (1970) Growth retardation in a New Guinea boarding school and its response to supplementary feeding. *British Journal of Nutrition* 24: 297-305.

201. Gopalan C, Swaminathan MC, Kumari VKK, Rao DH, Vijayaroghavan K (1973) Effect of calorie supplementation on growth of undernourished children. *American Journal of Clinical Nutrition* 26: 563-566.

202. Beaton GH, Calloway D, Murphy SP (1992) Estimated protein intakes of toddlers: predicted prevalence of inadequate intakes in village populations in Egypt, Kenya, and Mexico. *American Journal of Clinical Nutrition* 55: 902-911.

203. Marquis GS, Habicht J-P, Lanata CF, Black RE, Rasmussen KM (1997) Breast milk or animal-product foods improve linear growth of Peruvian toddlers consuming marginal diets. *American Journal of Clinical Nutrition* 66: 1102-1109.

204. Martorell R, Klein RE (1980) Food supplement and growth rates in preschool children. *Nutrition Reports International* 21: 447-454.

205. Martorell R, Habicht J-P (1996) Growth in early

childhood in developing countries. In *Human Growth. A Comprehensive Treatise*, Vol. 3, ed. Falkner F, Tanner JM. New York: Plenum Press. 241 – 262.

206. Mitzner K, Scrimshaw N, Morgan R (1984) Improving the nutritional status of children during the weaning period. A manual for policymakers, program planners and field workers. Cambridge MA: International Food and Nutrition Program, MIT.

207. Huffman SL, Oniong'o R, Quinn V (2000) Improving young child feeding with processed complementary cereals and behaviour change in urban Kenya. *Food and Nutrition Bulletin.* (In press).

208. Brown KH, Lutter CK (2001) The potential for processed complementary foods in Latin America to improve early childhood nutrition. *Food and Nutrition Bulletin.* (In press).

209. Lutter CK (2000) Processed complementary foods: Summary of nutritional characteristics, methods of production and distribution, and costs. *Food and Nutrition Bulletin* 21: 95 – 100.

210. Clark D, Shrimpton R (2000) Complementary feeding, the code and codex. *Food and Nutrition Bulletin* 21: 25-29.

211. Allen LH, Ahluwalia N (1997) *Improving Iron Status through Diet. The Application of Knowledge Concerning Dietary Iron Bioavailability in Human Populations.* Arlington VA: Management of Social Transformation Programme.

212. Gillespie SR (1998) *Major Issues in the Control of Iron Deficiency.* Ottawa: The Micronutrient Initiative/UNICEF.

213. Allen LH, Backstrand JR, Stanek EJ, Pelto GH, Chavez A, Molina E (1992) The interactive effects of dietary quality on the growth and attained size of young Mexican children. *American Journal of Clinical Nutrition* 56: 353-364.

214. Allen LH (1993) The Nutrition CRSP: What is marginal malnutrition, and does it affect human function? *Nutrition Reviews* 51: 255-67.

215. Dagnelie PC, van Dusseldorp M, van Staveren WA, Hautvast JG (1994) Effects of macrobiotic diets on linear growth in infants and children until 10 years of age. *European Journal of Clinical Nutrition* 48 (Supplement 1): S103-111.

216. Dagnelie PC, van Staveren WA (1994) Macrobiotic nutrition and child health: Results of a population-based, mixed-longitudinal cohort study in The Netherlands. *American Journal of Clinical Nutrition* 59: 1187S-1196S.

217. Dagnelie PC, van Staveren WA, Vergote FJ, Hautvast JG (1989) Nutritional status of infants aged 4 to 18 months on macrobiotic diets and

matched omnivorous control infants: A population-based mixed-longitudinal study. II. Growth and psychomotor development. *European Journal of Clinical Nutrition* 43: 325-338.

218. Louwman MWJ, van Dusseldorp M, van de Vijver FJR, Thomas CM, Schneede J, Ueland PM, Refsum H, van Staveren WA (2000) Signs of impaired cognitive function in adolescents with marginal cobalamin status. *American Journal of Clinical Nutrition* 72: 762-769.

219. Haskell MJ, Brown KH (1997) The nutritional value of animal products and their role in the growth and development of young children in developing countries. Unpublished review, University of California Davis.

220. Lartey A, Manu A, Brown KH, Peerson JM, Dewey KG (1999) A randomized, community-based trial of the effects of improved, centrally processed complementary foods on growth and micronutrient status of Ghanaian infants from 6 to 12 mo of age. *American Journal of Clinical Nutrition* 70: 391-404.

221. Dewey KG, Romero-Abal ME, Quan de Serrano J, Bulux J, Peerson JM, Engle P, Domeloff M, Solomons NW (1997). Effects of discontinuing coffee intake on iron status of iron-deficient Guatemalan toddlers: A randomized intervention study. *American Journal of Clinical Nutrition* 66: 168-176.

222. Allen LH (1998) Iron-ascorbic acid and iron-calcium interactions and their relevance in complementary feeding. In *Micronutrient Interactions. Impact on Child Health and Nutrition*, International Life Sciences Institute, Washington DC. 11 – 20.

223. Stekel A, Olivares M, Pizarro F, Chadud P, Lopez I, Amar M (1986) Absorption of fortification iron from milk formulas in infants. *American Journal of Clinical Nutrition* 43: 917-922.

224. Shankar AV, West KP Jr, Gittelsohn J, Katz J, Pradhan R (1996) Chronic low intakes of vitamin A-rich foods in households with xerophthalmic children: A case-control study in Nepal. *American Journal of Clinical Nutrition* 64: 242-248.

225. Rahman MM, Mahalanabis D, Islam MA, Biswas E (1992) Can infants and young children eat enough green leafy vegetables from a single traditional meal to meet their daily vitamin A requirements? *European Journal of Clinical Nutrition* 46: 68-72.

226. de Pee S, West CE, Muhilal, Karyadi D, Hautvast JG (1995) Lack of improvement in vitamin A status with increased consumption of dark-green leafy vegetables. *The Lancet* 346: 75-81.

227. Gibson RS (1994) Zinc nutrition in developing countries. *Nutrition Research Reviews* 7: 151-173.

228. Michaelsen KF, Weaver L, Branca F, Robertson A (1999) Guidelines on complementary feeding and control of iron deficiency for 0-3 year olds in the WHO European region. Geneva: WHO.

229. Becroft T, Bailey KV (1965) Supplementary feeding trial in New Guinea highland infants. *Journal of Tropical Pediatrics and African Child Health* 11:28-34.

230. Vaughan JP, Zumrawi F, Waterlow JC, Kirkwood BR (1981) An evaluation of dried skimmed milk on children's growth in Khartoum province, Sudan. *Nutrition Research* 1:243-252.

231. Gershoff SN, McGandy RB, Nondasuta A, Tantiwongse P (1988) Nutrition studies in Thailand: effects of calories, nutrient supplements, and health interventions on growth of preschool Thai village children. *American Journal of Clinical Nutrition* 48: 1214-1218.

232. Lutter CK, Mora JO, Habicht J-P, Rasmussen KM, Robson DS, Herrera MG (1990) Age-specific responsiveness of weight and length to nutritional supplementation. *American Journal of Clinical Nutrition* 51: 359-364.

233. Schroeder DG, Martorell R, Rivera JA, Ruel MT, Habicht J-P (1995) Age differences in the impact of nutritional supplementation on growth. *Journal of Nutrition* 125: 1051S-1059S.

234. Hussaini MA, Karyadi L, Husain Sandjaja YK, Karyadi D, Pollitt E (1991) Developmental effects of short-term supplementary feeding in nutritionally-at-risk Indonesian infants. *American Journal of Clinical Nutrition* 54: 799-804.

235. Walker SP, Powell CA, Grantham-McGregor SM, Himes JH, Chang SM (1991) Nutritional supplementation, psychosocial stimulation, and growth of stunted children: The Jamaican study. *American Journal of Clinical Nutrition* 54: 642-648.

236. Liu DS, Bates CJ, Yin TA, Wang XB, Lu CQ (1993) Nutritional efficacy of a fortified weaning rusk in a rural area near Beijing. *American Journal of Clinical Nutrition* 57: 506-511.

237. Simondon KB, Gartner A, Berger J, Cornu A, Massamba JP, San Miguel JL, Coudy L, Misotte I, Simondon F, Traissac P, Delpeuch F, Maire B (1996) Effect of early, short-term supplementation on weight and linear growth of 4-7-mo-old infants in developing countries: A four-country randomized trial. *American Journal of Clinical Nutrition* 64: 537-545.

238. Engelmann MDM, Sandstrom B, Michaelsen KF (1998) Meat intake and iron status in late

infancy: An intervention study. *European Journal of Clinical Nutrition* 67: 26-33.

239.   Cohen RJ, Brown KH, Canahuati J, Rivera LL, Dewey KG (1994) Effects of age of introduction of complementary foods on infant breast milk intake, total energy intake, and growth: a randomised intervention study in Honduras. *The Lancet* 344: 288-293.

240.   Kusin JA, Kardjati S, Houtkooper JM, Renqvist UH (1992) Energy supplementation during pregnancy and postnatal growth. *The Lancet* 340: 623-626.

241.   Mora J, de Paredes B, Wagner M, de Navarro L, Suescun J, Christiansen N, Herrera MG (1979) Nutritional supplementation and the outcome of pregnancy. I. Birth weight. *American Journal of Clinical Nutrition* 32: 455-462.

242.   Domeloff M, Cohen RJ, Dewey KG, Hernell O, Landa Rivera L, Lonnerdal B (2000) Hematologic responses to iron supplementation in Swedish and Honduran children. *Federation of American Societies for Experimental Biology Journal* 14: (Abstract) A561.

243.   Allen LH (1994) Nutritional influences on linear growth: a general review. *European Journal of Clinical Nutrition* 48 (Supplement 1): S75-89.

244.   Dewey KG, Domeloff M, Cohen RJ, Rivera LL, Hernell O, Lonnerdal BL (2000) Effects of iron supplementation on growth and morbidity of breastfed infants: A randomized trial in Sweden and Honduras. *Federation of American Societies for Experimental Biology Journal* 14: (Abstract) A509.

245.   Walravens PA, Krebs NF, Hambidge KM (1983) Linear growth of low income preschool children receiving a zinc supplement. *American Journal of Clinical Nutrition* 38: 195-201.

246.   Dirren H, Barclay D, Ramos JG, (1994) Zinc supplementation and child growth in Ecuador. *Advances in Experimental Medicine and Biology* 352: 215-222.

247.   Rivera JA, Ruel MT, Santizo CM, Lonnerdal B, Brown KH (1998) Zinc supplementation improves the growth of stunted rural Guatemalan infants. *Journal of Nutrition* 128: 556-562.

248.   Rosado JL, Lopez P, Munoz E, Martinez H, Allen LH (1997) Zinc supplementation reduces morbidity, but neither zinc nor iron supplementation affected growth or body composition of stunted Mexican preschoolers. *American Journal of Clinical Nutrition* 65: 13-19.

249.   Brown KH, Peerson JM, Allen LH (1997) Effect of zinc supplementation on children's growth: A meta-analysis of intervention trials. *Bibliotheca Nutritio et Dietetica* 54: 76-83.

250.   Black RE (1998) Therapeutic and preventive effects of zinc on serious childhood infectious diseases in developing countries. *American Journal of Clinical Nutrition* 68: 476S-479S.

251.   Sazawal S, Black RE, Bhan MK, Jalla S, Bhandari N, Sinha A, Majumdar S (1996) Zinc supplementation reduces the incidence of persistent diarrhea and dysentery among low socioeconomic children in India. *Journal of Nutrition* 126: 443-450.

252.   Sazawal S, Black RE, Jalla S, Mazumdar S, Sinha A, Bhan MK (1998) Zinc supplementation reduces the incidence of acute lower respiratory infections in infants and preschool children: A double-blind, controlled trial. *Pediatrics* 102: 1-5.

253.   Bloem MW, Hye A, Wijnroks M, Ralte A, West KP Jr, Sommer A (1995) The role of universal distribution of vitamin A capsules in combatting vitamin A deficiency in Bangladesh. *American Journal of Epidemiology* 142: 843-55.

254.   Beaton GH, Martorell R, Aronson KJ (1993). *Effectiveness of vitamin A supplementation in the control of young childhood morbidity and mortality in developing coun*tries. State-of-the-Art Series Nutrition Policy Discussion Paper No. 13. Geneva: ACC/SCN.

255.   WHO/CHD (1998) Immunization-linked vitamin A supplementation study group. Randomised trial to assess benefits and safety of vitamin A supplementation linked to immunization in early infancy. *The Lancet* 352: 1257-1263.

256.   Allen LH, Haskell M (2001) Vitamin A requirements of infants under six months. *Food and Nutrition Bulletin* (In press).

257.   Tarwotjo I, Katz J, West WP Jr, Tielsch JM, Sommer A (1992) Xerophthalmia and growth in preschool Indonesian children. *American Journal of Clinical Nutrition* 55: 1142-1146.

258.   Muhilal, Permeisih D, Idjradinata YR, Muherdiyantiningsih, Karyadi D (1988) Vitamin A-fortified monosodium glutamate and health growth, and survival of children: a controlled field trial. *American Journal of Clinical Nutrition* 48: 1271-1276.

259.   West KP, Djunaedi E, Pandji A, Kusdiono, Tarwotjo I, Sommer A (1988) Vitamin A supplementation and growth: A randomized community trial. *American Journal of Clinical Nutrition* 48: 1257-1264.

260.   Rahmathullah L, Underwood BA, Thulasiraj RD, Milton RC (1991). Diarrhea, respiratory infections, and growth are not affected by a weekly low-dose vitamin A supplement: A masked, controlled field trial in children in

southern India. *American Journal of Clinical Nutrition* 54: 568-577.

261. Lie C, Ying C, Wang EL, Brun T, Geissler C (1993) Impact of large-dose vitamin A supplementation on childhood diarrhoea, respiratory disease and growth. *European Journal of Clinical Nutrition* 47: 88-96.

262. Ramakrishnan U, Latham MC, Abel R (1994) Vitamin A supplementation does not improve growth of preschool children: A randomized double-blind field trial in South India. *Journal of Nutrition* 125: 202-211.

263. Hadi H, Stoltzfus RJ, Dibley MJ, Moulton LH, West KPJ, Kjolhede CL (2000) Vitamin A supplementation selectively improves the linear growth of Indonesian preschool children: Results from a randomized controlled trial. *American Journal of Clinical Nutrition* 71: 507-513.

264. Prentice A, Bates CJ (1994) Adequacy of dietary mineral supply for human bone growth and mineralisation. *European Journal of Clinical Nutrition* 48: S161-S177.

265. Akroyd WR, Krishnan BG (1939). Effect of calcium lactate on children in a nursery school. *The Lancet* ii: 153-155.

266. Dibba B, Prentice A, Ceesay M, Stirling DM, Cole TJ, Poskitt EM (2000) Effect of calcium supplementation on bone mineral accretion in Gambian children accustomed to a low-calcium diet. *American Journal of Clinical Nutrition* 71:544-549.

267. Neumann CG, Harrison GG (1994) Onset and evolution of stunting in infants and children. Examples from the Human Nutrition Collaborative Research Support Program. Kenya and Egypt studies. *European Journal of Clinical Nutrition* 48: S90-S102.

268. Thilly CH (1983) Prevention of myxedematous cretinism with iodized oil during pregnancy. Current problems in thyroid research. *Excerpta Medica* 386-389.

269. Ramirez I, Fierro-Benitez R, Estrella E, Gomez A, Jaramillo C, Hermida C, Moncayo F (1969) Iodized oil in the prevention of endemic goiter and associated defects in the Andean region of Ecuador. *In Endemic Goiter*, ed. Stanbury JB, Kroc RL. New York: Plenum.

270. Bautista A, Barker PA, Dunn JT, Sanchez M, Kaiser DL (1982). The effects of oral iodized oil on intelligence, thyroid status, and somatic growth in school-age children from an area of endemic goiter. *American Journal of Clinical Nutrition* 35: 127-34.

271. Murphy SP, Beaton GH, Calloway DH (1992) Estimated mineral intakes of toddlers: predicted prevalence of inadequacy in village populations in Egypt, Kenya, and Mexico. *American Journal of Clinical Nutrition* 56: 565-572.

272. Calloway DH, Murphy SP, Beaton GH, Lein D (1993) Estimated vitamin intakes of toddlers: Predicted prevalence of inadequacy in village populations in Egypt, Kenya, and Mexico. *American Journal of Clinical Nutrition* 58: 376-384.

273. Thu BD, Schultink W, Dillon D, Gross R, Leswara ND, Khoi HH (1999) Effect of daily and weekly micronutrient supplementation on micronutrient deficiencies and growth in young Vietnamese children. *American Journal of Clinical Nutrition* 69: 80-86.

274. Rivera JA, Gonzales-Cossio T, Flores M (2001). Multiple micronutrient supplementation improves the growth of Mexican infants. *American Journal of Clinical Nutrition*. (In press).

275. Penny ME, Brown KH, Lanata CL, Peerson JM, Marin RM, Duran A, Lonnerdal B, Black RE (1997) Community-based trial of the effect of zinc supplements with and without other micronutrients on the duration of persistent diarrhea, and the prevention of subsequent morbidity. *Federation of American Societies for Experimental Biology Journal* 11: A655.

276. Brown KH, Santizo MC, Begin F, Torun B (2000) Effect of supplementation with multiple micronutrients and/or bovine serum concentrate on the growth of low-income, peri-urban Guatemalan infants and young children. *Federation of American Societies for Experimental Biology Journal* 14: A534.

277. Briend A, Lacsala R, Prudhon C, Mounier B, Grellety Y, Golden MH (1999) Ready-to-use therapeutic food for treatment of marasmus. *The Lancet* 353: 1767-1768 (Letter).

278. Branca F, Lopriore C, Briesid A, Golden MH (1999) Multi-micronutrient fortified food reverses growth failure and anaemia in 2 – 5 year-old stunted refugee children. *Scandinavian Journal of Nutrition* 43 (25): 51S.

279. Stoltzfus RJ, Dreyfuss ML (1998) *Guidelines for the Use of Iron Supplements to Prevent and Treat Iron Deficiency Anemia*. Geneva: International Nutritional Anemia Consultative Group/ UNICEF/WHO.

280. Grajeda R, Perez-Escamilla R, Dewey KG (1997) Delayed clamping of the umbilical cord improves hematologic status of Guatemalan infants at 2 mo of age. *American Journal of Clinical Nutrition* 65: 425-431.

281. Gillespie SR, Johnston I (1998) *Expert Consultation on Anemia Determinants and Interventions*. Ottawa: The Micronutient Initiative.

282. Ross JS, Thomas EL (1996) Iron deficiency anemia and maternal mortality. Washington DC: Academy of Educational Development.

283. Brabin BJ, Hakimi M, Pelletier D (2001) An analysis of anemia and pregnancy-related maternal mortality. *Journal of Nutrition* 131: S604-S615.

284. de Benaze C, Galan P, Wainer R, Hercberg S (1989) Prévention de l'anémie ferriprivée au cours de la grossesse par une supplémentation martiale précoce: Un essaie contrôle. *Revue Epidémiologique de la Santé Publique* 27: 109-119.

285. Hemminki E, Rimpelä U (1991) A randomized comparison of routine versus selective iron supplementation during pregnancy. *American Journal of Clinical Nutrition* 10: 3-10.

286. Draper A (1997) *Child Development and Iron Deficiency: the Oxford Brief.* Washington DC: USAID, Opportunities for Micronutrient Interventions, and Partnership for Child Development.

287. Grantham-McGregor SM, Ani C (2001) A review of studies on the effect of iron deficiency on cognitive development in children. *Journal of Nutrition* 131 (2S-2): 649S – 666S; Discussion 666S – 668S.

288. Clark M, Royal J, Seeler R (1988) Interaction of iron deficiency and lead and the hematologic findings in children with severe lead poisoning. *Pediatrics* 81: 247-254.

289. Basta SS, Soekirman MS, Karyadi D, Scrimshaw NS (1979) Iron deficiency anemia and the productivity of adult males in Indonesia. *American Journal of Clinical Nutrition* 32: 916-925.

290. Scholz BD, Gross R, Schultink W, Sastroamidjojo S (1997) Anaemia is associated with reduced productivity of women workers even in less-physically-strenuous tasks. *British Journal of Nutrition* 77: 47-57.

291. Zhu YI, Haas JD (1997) Iron depletion without anemia and physical performance in young women. *American Journal of Clinical Nutrition* 66: 334-341.

292. SEAMEO-TROPMED, H. K. International (1999) Integrated iron supplementation for women: A new approach for iron deficiency control. Jakarta, Indonesia: SEAMEO-TROPMED, H. K. International.

293. UNICEF/UNU/WHO/MI (1999) *Preventing Iron Deficiency in Women and Children. Technical Consensus on Key Issues.* Boston MA and Ottawa, Canada: International Nutrition Foundation and The Micronutrient Initiative.

294. Mahomed K (1998) Routine iron supplementation during pregnancy. Oxford UK: Cochrane review. Update Software.

295. Sloan NL, Jordan EA, Winikoff B (1995) *Does Iron Supplementation Make a Difference?* Arlington VA: MotherCare Project, John Snow Inc.

296. Beaton GH, McCabe GP (1999) Efficacy of intermittent iron supplementation in the control of iron deficiency anemia in developing countries: an analysis of experience. Ottawa: Micronutrient Initiative.

297. Ekstrom EC, Kavishe FP, Habicht J-P, Frongillo EA, Rasmussen K, Hemed L (1996) Adherence to iron supplementation during pregnancy in Tanzania: Determinants and haematological consequences. *American Journal of Clinical Nutrition.* 64: 368-374.

298. Ekstrom EC (2001) Supplementation for nutritional anemias. In *Nutritional Anemias*, ed. Ramakrishnan U. Boca Raton Florida: CRC Press. 129 – 151.

299. Agarwal KN, Agarwal DK, Mishra KP (1991) Impact of anaemia prophylaxis in pregnancy on maternal hemoglobin, serum ferritin, and birth weight. *Indian Journal of Medical Research* 94: 277-280.

300. Colomer J, Colomer C, Gutierrez D, Jubert A, Nolasco A, Donat J, Fernandez-Delgado R, Donat F, Alvarez-Dardet C (1990) Anaemia during pregnancy as a risk factor for infant iron deficiency: Report from the Valencia Infant Anaemia Cohort (VIAC) study. *Pediatric Perinatal Epidemiology* 4: 196-204.

301. Puolakka, J, Jänne O, Pakarinen A, Järvinen PA, Vihko R (1980) Serum ferritin as a measure of iron stores during and after normal pregnancy with and without iron supplements. *Acta Obstetrica Gynecology Scandinavica* 95: 43-51.

302. Preziosi P, Prual A, Galan P, Daouda H, Boureima H, Hercberg S (1997) Effect of iron supplementation on the iron status of pregnant women: consequences for newborns. *American Journal of Clinical Nutrition* 66: 1178-1182.

303. Suharno D, West CE, Muhilal, Karyadi D, Hautvast JG (1993) Supplementation with vitamin A and iron for nutritional anaemia in pregnant women in West Java, Indonesia. *The Lancet* 342 (8883): 1325-1358.

304. Stoltzfus RJ, Albonico M, Chwaya HM, Tielsch JM, Schulze KJ, Savioli L (1998) Effects of the Zanzibar school-based deworming program on iron status of children. *American Journal of Clinical Nutrition* 68 (1): 179-186.

305. Idjradinata P, Pollitt E (1993) Reversal of developmental delays in iron-deficient anaemic infants treated with iron. *The Lancet* 341(8836): 1-4.

306. Palupi L, Schultink W, Achadi E, Gross R (1997) Effective community intervention to improve hemoglobin status in preschoolers receiving once-weekly iron supplementation. *American Journal of Clinical Nutrition* 65: 1057-1061.

307. Allen LH, Rosado JL, Casterline JE, Lopez P, Munoz E, Garcia OP, Martinez H (2000) Lack of hemoglobin response to iron supplementation in anemic Mexican preschoolers with multiple micronutrient deficiencies. *American Journal of Clinical Nutrition* 71: 1485-1494.

308. Reid E, Lopez P, Galavez IA, Isoard F, Rosado JL, Allen LH (2001) Hematological and biochemical responses of rural Mexican preschoolers to iron alone or iron plus micronutrients. *Federation of American Societies for Experimental Biology Journal* 15 (Abstract): A371.

309. Lozoff B, Jimenez E, Wolf AW (1991) Long-term developmental outcome of infants with iron deficiency. *New England of Journal of Medicine* 325: 687-694.

310. Lozoff B, Wolf AW, Jimenez E (1996) Iron-deficiency anemia and infant development: effects of extended oral iron therapy. *Journal of Pediatrics* 129: 382-389.

311. Moffatt ME, Longstaffe S, Besant J, Dureski C (1994) Prevention of iron deficiency and psychomotor decline in high-risk infants through use of iron-fortified infant formula: A randomized clinical trial. *Journal of Pediatrics* 125: 527-34

312. Nestel P, Alnwick D (1997) Iron/multi-micronutrient supplements for young children: summary and conclusions of a consultation held at UNICEF Copenhagen, 1996. Washington DC: OMNI/USAID.

313. Ballin A, Berar M, Rubinstein U, Kleter Y, Hershkovitz A, Meytes D (1992). Iron state in female adolescents. *American Journal of Diseases in Childhood* 146: 803-805.

314. Bruner AB, Joffe A, Duggan AK, Casella JF, Brandt J (1996) Randomised study of cognitive effects of iron supplementation in non-anaemic iron-deficient adolescent girls. *The Lancet* 348: 992-996.

315. Seshadri S, Gopaldas T (1989) Impact of iron supplementation on cognitive functions in preschool and school-aged children: the Indian experience. *American Journal of Clinical Nutrition* 50: 675-684.

316. Latham MN, Stephenson LS, Kinoti SN, Zaman MS, Kurtz KM (1990) Improvements in growth following iron supplementation in young Kenyan school children. *Nutrition* 6: 159-165.

317. Hodges RE, Sauberlich HE, Canham JE, Wallace DL, Rucker RB, Mejia LA, Mohanram M (1978) Hematopoietic studies in vitamin A deficiency. *American Journal of Clinical Nutrition* 31: 876-885.

318. Sommer A, West KP (1996) *Vitamin A Deficiency: Health, Survival and Vision*. New York: Oxford University Press.

319. Campbell TC, Brun T, Chen JS, Feng ZL, Parpia B (1990) Questioning riboflavin recommendations on the basis of a survey in China. *American Journal of Clinical Nutrition* 51: 436-445.

320. Boisvert WA, Castañeda C, Mendoza I, Langeloh G, Solomons NW, Gershoff SN, Russell RM (1993) Prevalence of riboflavin deficiency among Guatemalan elderly people and its relationship to milk intake. *American Journal of Clinical Nutrition* 58: 85-90

321. Allen LH, Ruel MT. Supplementation of anemic lactating Guatemalan women with riboflavin improves erythrocyte riboflavin concentrations and ferritin response to iron treatment. *Journal of Nutrition.*(In press.)

322. Bates CJ, Prentice AM, Paul AA, Sutcliffe BA, Watkinson M, Whitehead RG (1981) Riboflavin status in Gambian pregnant and lactating women and its implications for Recommended Dietary Allowances. *American Journal of Clinical Nutrition* 34: 928-935.

323. Powers HJ, Weaver LT, Austin S, Beresford JK (1993) A proposed intestinal mechanism for the effect of riboflavin deficiency on iron loss in the rat. *British Journal of Nutrition* 69: 553-561.

324. Powers HJ, Bates CJ, Prentice AM, Lamb WH, Jepson M, Bowman H (1983) The relative effectiveness of iron and iron with riboflavin in correcting a microcytic anaemia in men and children in rural Gambia. *Human Nutrition: Clinical Nutrition* 37: 413-425.

325. Powers HJ, Bates CJ (1984) Effects of pregnancy and riboflavin deficiency on some aspects of iron metabolism in rats. *International Journal of Vitamin Nutrition Research* 54: 179-183.

326. Buzina R, Jusic M, Milanovic N, Sapunar J, Brubacher G (1979) The effects of riboflavin administration on iron metabolism parameters in a school-going population. *International Journal of Vitamin Nutrition Research* 49: 136-143.

327. Areekul S (1982) Folic acid deficiency in Thailand. *Journal of Medical Association of Thailand* 65: 1-5.

328. Franzetti S, Mejia LA, Viteri FE, Alvarez E (1984) Body iron reserves of rural and urban uatemalan women of reproductive age. *Archives of Latin Nutrition*: 69-74.

329. Black AK, Allen LH, Pelto GH, de Mata MP, Chávez A (1994) Iron, vitamin B-12 and folate status in Mexico: Associated factors in men and women and during pregnancy and lactation. *Journal of Nutrition* 124: 1179-88.

330. Jackson RT, Latham MC (1982) Anemia of pregnancy in Liberia, West Africa: A therapeutic trial. *American Journal of Clinical Nutrition* 35: 710-714.

331. Basu RN, Sood SK, Ramachandran K, Mathur M, Ramalingaswami V (1973) Etiopathogenesis of nutritional anemia in pregnancy: a therapeutic approach. *American Journal of Clinical Nutrition* 26: 591-594.

332. Iyengar L, Arte S (1970) Prophylaxis of anemia in pregnancy. *American Journal of Clinical Nutrition* 23: 725-730.

333. Batu AT, Toe T, Pe H, Nyunt KK (1976) A prophylactic trial of iron and folic acid supplements in pregnant Burmese women. *Israel Journal of Medical Sciences* 12: 1410-1417.

334. Sirisupandit S, Pottrakul P, Areekul S, Neungton S, Mokkavs J, Kiriwat O, Kanonkpongsukdi S (1983) A prophylactic supplementation of iron and folate in pregnancy. *Southeast Asian Journal of Tropical Medical Public Health* 14: 317-323.

335. Stevens D, Burman D, Strelling MK, Morris A (1979) Folic acid supplementation in low birth weight infants. *Pediatrics* 64: 333-335.

336. Allen LH, Rosado JL, Casterline JE, Martinez H, Lopez P, Muñoz E, Black AK (1995) Vitamin B-12 deficiency and malabsorption are highly prevalent in rural Mexican communities. *American Journal of Clinical Nutrition* 62(5):1013-9.

337. Casterline JE, Allen LH, Ruel MT (1997) Vitamin B-12 deficiency is very prevalent in lactating Guatemalan women and their infants at three months postpartum. *Journal of Nutrition* 127: 1966-1972.

338. Lindenbaum J, Rosenbergh IH, Wilson PWF (1994) Prevalence of cobalamin deficiency in the Framingham elderly population. *American Journal of Clinical Nutrition* 60: 2 – 11.

339. King JE, Mazariegos M, Valdez C, Castañeda C, Solomons NW (1997) Nutritional status indicators and their interactions in rural Guatemalan elderly: a study in San Pedro Ayampuc. *American Journal of Clinical Nutrition* 66: 795-802.

340. Hallberg L, Brune M, Rossander L (1986) Effect of ascorbic acid on iron absorption from different types of meals. Studies with ascorbic-acid-rich foods and synthetic ascorbic acid given in different amounts with different meals. *Human Nutrition: Applied Nutrition* 40: 97-113.

341. Garcia OP, Allen LH, Diaz M, Rosado JL (1999) Community trial of the efficacy of a local food source of ascorbic acid for improving iron status of iron deficient Mexican women. *Federation of American Society for Experimental Biology Journal* 13 (Abstract): A207.

342. Seshadri S, Shah A, Bhade S (1985) Haematologic response of anaemic preschool children to ascorbic acid supplementation. *Human Nutrition: Applied Nutrition* 39A: 151-154.

343. Walter T, Dallman PR, Pizarro F, Velozo L, Pena G, Bartholmey SJ, Hertrampf E, Olivares M, Leteelier A, Arredondo M (1993) Effectiveness of iron-fortified infant cereal in prevention of iron deficiency anemia. *Pediatrics* 91: 976-982.

344. Hallberg L, Björn-Rasmussen E, Garby L, Pleehachinda R, Suwanik R (1978) Iron absorption from South-East Asian diets and the effect of iron fortification. *American Journal of Clinical Nutrition* 31: 1403-8.

345. Ruel MT, Levin CE, (2000) Assessing the potential for food-based strategies to reduce vitamin A and iron deficiencies: a review of recent evidence. Food Consumption and Nutrition Division Discussion Paper No. 92. Washington DC: International Food Policy Research Institute.

346. English R, Badcock J, Tu Giay, Tu Ngu, Waters AM, Bennett SA (1997) Effect of nutrition improvement projecton morbidity from infectious diseases in preschool children in Viet Nam: comparison with control commune. *British Medical Journal* 315: 1122-1125.

347. Carrasso Sanez NC, deUbillas RM, Guillen IS, Ferreira SM (1998) Increasing women's involvement in community decision-making, a means to improve iron status. Washington DC: OMNI Research Project Series no. 1, International Center for Research on Women.

348. International Food Policy Research Institute, Bangladesh Institute of Development Studies, Institute of Nutrition and Food Science, Data Analysis and Technical Assistance and Research Department of Human Nutrition, Royal Veterinary and Agricultural University (1998) Commercial vegetable and polyculture fish production in Bangladesh: The impacts on income, household resource allocation, and

nutrition. Report, Volume 1. Washington DC: International Food Policy Research Institute.

349. Smitasiri S, Dhanamitta S (1999) *Sustaining Behavior Change to Enhance Micronutrient Status: Community- and Women-based Interventions in Thailand*. OMNI Research Report Series No. 2, Washington DC: International Center for Research on Women.

350. Mendoza C, Viteri FE, Lonnerdal B, Young KA, Raboy V, Brown KH (1998) Effect of genetically-modified, low-phytic acid maize on absorption of iron from tortillas. *American Journal of Clinical Nutrition* 68:1123-1127.

351. Goto, F, Yoshihar I, Shigemoto N, Toki S, Takaiwa F (1999) Iron fortification of rice seed by the soybean ferritin gene. *Nature Biotechnology* 17: 282 – 286.

352. Gura J (1999) New genes boost rice nutrients. *Science* 285: 994-995.

353. Bovell-Benjamin AC, Viteri FE, Allen LH (2000) Iron absorption from ferrous bisglycinate and ferric trisglycinate in whole maize is regulated by iron status. *American Journal of Clinical Nutrition* 71: 1563-1569.

354. Layrisse M, Garcia-Casal MN, Solano L, Barón MA, Arguello F, Llovera D, Ramírez J, Leets I, Tropper E (2000) Iron bioavailability in humans from breakfasts enriched with iron bis-glycine chelate, phytates and polyphenols. *Journal of Nutrition* 130: 2195-2199.

355. Bovell-Benjamin AC, Allen LH, Frankel EN, Guinard JX (1999). Sensory quality and lipid oxidation of maize porridge as affected by iron amino acid chelates and EDTA. *Journal of Food Sciences* 64:371-376 and Bovell-Benjamin, AC, Allen LH, Guinard JX (1999) Toddler's acceptance of whole-maize meal porridge fortified with ferrous bisglycinate. *Food Quality and Preference* 10: 123-128.

356. Sattarzadeh M, Zlotkin SH (1999) Iron is well absorbed by healthy adults after ingestion of double-fortified (iron and dextran-coated iodine) table salt and urinary iodine excretion is unaffected. *Journal of Nutrition* 129: 117-121.

357. Nair KM, Brahmam GM, Ranganathan S, Vijayaraghavan K, Suvakumar B, Krishnaswamy K (1998) Impact evaluation of iron and iodine fortified salt. *Indian Journal of Medical Research* 108: 203-211.

358. Layrisse M, Chaves JF, Mendez-Castellano H, Bosch V, Tropper E, Bastardo B, Gonzalez E (1996) Early response to the effect of iron fortification in a Venezuelan population. *American Journal of Clinical Nutrition* 64: 903-907.

359. Walter T, Olivares M, Pizarro G, Hertrampf E (2001) Fortification. In *Nutritional Anemias*, ed. Ramakrishnan U. Boca Raton, Louisiana: CRC Press. 153 – 183.

360. Viteri FE, Alvarez E, Batres R, Torún B, Pineda O, Mejía LA, Sylvi J (1995) Fortification of sugar with iron sodium ethylenediaminotetraacetate (FeNaEDTA) improves iron status in semirural Guatemalan populations. *American Journal of Clinical Nutrition* 61: 1153-1163.

361. Garby L, Areekul S (1974) Iron supplementation in Thai fish-sauce. *Annals of Tropical Medical Parasitology* 68: 467-476.

362. Ballot DE, MacPhail AP, Bothwell TH, Gillooly M, Mayet FG (1989) Fortification of curry powder with NaFe(111)EDTA in an iron-deficient population: Report of a controlled iron-fortification trial. *American Journal of Clinical Nutrition* 49: 162-169.

363. Hurrell RF, Furniss DE, Burri J, Whittaker P, Lynch SR, Cook JD (1989) Iron fortification of infant cereals: a proposal for the use of ferrous fumarate or ferrous succinate. *American Journal of Clinical Nutrition* 49: 1274-82.

364. Rush D, Leighton J, Sloan NL, Alvir JM, Garbowski GC (1988) The National WIC Evaluation: Evaluation of the Special Supplemental Food Program for Women, Infants, and Children. II. Review of past studies of WIC. *American Journal of Clinical Nutrition* 48: 394-411.

365. British Nutrition Foundation (1995) Iron: Nutritional and physiological significance: Report of the British Nutrition Foundation Task Force. London: Chapman and Hall.

366. WHO (1998) *Global Database on Anaemia and Iron Deficiency*. Geneva: WHO.

367. Yip R, Parvanta Y, McDonnell S, Trowbridge F (1996) CDC recommendations for the prevention and management of iron deficiency and iron overload. Atlanta GA: Centers for Disease Control and Promotion.

368. Hallberg L, Bjorn-Rasmussen E, Junger I (1989) Prevalence of hereditary hemochromatosis in two Swedish urban areas. *Journal of International Medical Research* 25:249-255.

369. Oppenheimer SJ (2001) Iron, and its relation to immunity and infectious disease. Journal of Nutrition 131: 616S-635S.

370. WHO/UNICEF/ICCIDD (1993) *Global Prevalence of Iodine Deficiency Disorders*. Geneva: WHO.

371. Maberly GF, Eastman CJ, Waite KV, Corcoran J, Rashford V (1983) The role of cassava. Current problems. In *Thyroid Research*, ed. Ui N, Torizuka K, Nagataki S, Miyai K. Amsterdam: Excerpta Medica.

372. Hofbauer LC, Spitzweg C, Magerstädt RA, Heufelder AE (1997) Selenium-induced thyroid dysfunction. *Postgraduate Medical Journal* 73 (856): 103-104.

373. Köhrle J (1999) The trace element selenium and the thyroid gland. *Biochimie* 81: 527-533.

374. Brätter P, Negretti de Brätter VE (1996) Influence of high dietary selenium intake on the thyroid hormone level in human serum. *Journal of Trace Elements in Medical Biology* 10: 163-166.

375. Zimmermann M, Adou P, Torresani T, Zeder C, Hurrell R (2000) Persistence of goiter despite oral iodine supplementation in goitrous children with iron deficiency anemia in Côte d'Ivoire. *American Journal of Clinical Nutrition* 71: 88-93.

376 Tiwari BD, Godbole MM, Chattopadhyay N, Mandal A, Mithal A (1996) Learning disabilities and poor motivation to achieve due to prolonged iodine deficiency. *American Journal of Clinical Nutrition* 63: 782-786.

377. Huda SN, Gratham-McGregor SM, Rahman KM, Tomkins A (1999) Biochemical hypothyroidism secondary to iodine deficiency is associated with poor school achievement and cognition in Bangladeshi children. *Journal of Nutrition* 129: 980-987.

378. Stanbury JB (1994) *The Damaged Brain of Iodine Deficiency*. New York: Cognizant Communications.

379. Bleichrodt N, Born PM (1994) A meta-analysis of research on iodine and its relationship to cognitive development. In *The Damaged Brain of Iodine Deficiency: Neuromotor, Cognitive, Behavioural and Educative Aspects*, ed. Stanbury JB. Port Washington, NY: Cognizant Communication Corp.

380. Pharoah POD, Ellis SM, Ekins RP, Williams ES (1976) Maternal thyroid function, iodine deficiency and fetal development. *Clinical Endocrinology* 5: 159-166.

381. Suwanik R, Pleehachinda R, Pattanachak C (1989) Simple technology provides effective IDD control at the village level in Thailand. *IDD Newsletter* 5: 1-6.

382. Cao XY, Jiang XM, Dou ZH, Rakeman MA, Zhang ML, O'Donnell K, Ma T, Amette K, DeLong N, DeLong GR (1994a) Timing of vulnerability of the brain to iodine deficiency in endemic cretinism. *New England Journal of Medicine* 331: 1739-1744.

383. Jooste PL, Weight MJ, Kriek JA (1997) Iodine deficiency and endemic goitre in the Langkloof area of South Africa. *South Africa Medical Journal* 87: 1374-1379.

384. Li J, Wang X (1987) Jixian: a success story in IDD control. *IDD Newsletter* 3: 4-5.

385. Zhao J, Xu F, Zhang Q, Shang L, Xu A, Gao Y, Chen Z, Sullivan K, Maberly GF (1999) Randomized clinical trial comparing different iodine interventions in school children. *Public Health Nutrition* 2: 173-178.

386. van Stuijvenberg ME, Kvalsvig JD, Faber M, Kruger M, Kenoyer DG, Benadé AJ (1999) Effect of iron-, iodine-, and beta-carotene-fortified biscuits on the micronutrient status of primary school children: a randomized controlled trial. *American Journal of Clinical Nutrition* 69: 497-503.

387. Pharoah PO, Connolly KF (1987) A controlled trial of iodinated oil for the prevention of endemic cretinism: a long-term follow-up. *International Journal of Epidemiology* 16: 68-73.

388. Thilly CH (1981) Endemic goiter and cretinism; etiologic role of the consumption of cassava, and eradication strategy. *Bulletin of the Members of the Royal Academy of Belgium* 136: 389-412.

389. Pretell EA, Torres T, Zenteno V, Cornejo M (1972) Prophylaxis of endemic goiter with iodized oil in rural Peru. *Advanced Experimental Medical Biology* 30:246-265.

390. Ma T, Yu ZH, Lu TZ, Wang SY, Dong CF, Hu XY, Zhu HC, Liu RN, Yuan CY, Wang GQ, Cai HZ, Wang Q (1982) High-iodide endemic goiter. *Chinese Medical Journal* (Engl.) 95: 692-696.

391. Dulberg EM, Widjaja K, Djokomoeljanto R, Hetzel BS, Belmont I (1983) Evaluation of the iodization program in Central Java with reference to the prevention of endemic cretinism and motor coordination defects. In *Current Problems in Thyroid Research*, ed. Ui N, Torizuka K, Nagataki S, Miyai K. Amsterdam: Excerpta Medica. 19-20.

392. Glinoer D (1997) Maternal and fetal impact of chronic iodine deficiency. *Clinical Obstetrical Gynecology* 40: 102-116.

393. Cao XY, Jiang XM, Kareem A, Dou ZH, Rakeman MA, Zhang ML, Ma T, O'Donnell K, DeLong N, DeLong GR (1994b) Iodination of irrigation water as a method of supplying iodine to severely iodine-deficient population in Xinjiang, China. *The Lancet* 344: 107-110.

394. Connolly KJ, Pharoah PO, Hetzel BS (1979) Fetal iodine deficiency and motor performance during childhood. *The Lancet* 2 (8153): 1149-1151.

395. Cobra C, Muhilal K, Rusmil D, Rustama, Djatnika, Suward S, Permaesih D, Muherdiyantiningsih, Marturi S, Semba RD (1997) Infant survival is improved by oral iodine supplementation. *Journal of Nutrition* 127: 574-578.

396. Delange F (1999) Neonatal thyroid screening as a monitoring tool for the control of iodine deficiency. *Acta Paediatrica*, Supplement 88 (432): 21-24.

397. Dodge PR, Palkes H, Fierro-Benitez R, Ramirez I (1969) Effect on intelligence of iodine in oil administered to young Andean children - a preliminary report. In Endemic Goiter, ed. Stanbury JB. Washington DC: Pan American Health Organization. 378 – 380.

398. Shrestha, R. M. and C. E. West. (1994) *Role of Iodine in Mental and Psychomotor Development: an Overview*. Wageningen, Netherlands: Grafisch Service Centrum.

399. Delange F, de Benoist B, Alnwick D (1999) Risks of iodine-induced hyperthyroidism after correction of iodine deficiency by iodized salt. *Thyroid* 9: 545-556.

400. Stanbury JB, Ermans AE, Bourdoux P, Todd C, Oken E, Tonglet R, Vidor Braverman LE, and Medeiros-Neto G (1999) Iodine-induced hyperthyroidism: Occurrence and epidemiology. *Thyroid* 8:83-100.

401. ACC/SCN (1997) *Third Report on the World Nutrition Situation*. Geneva: ACC/SCN.

402. MI/UNICEF/Tulane University (1998) *Progress in Controlling Vitamin A Deficiency*. Ottawa: The Micronutrient Initiative, UNICEF.

403. Beaton GH (1999) Comparative evaluation of WHO/UNICEF and UNICEF/MI/Tulane estimations of the magnitude of the problem of vitamin A deficiency. Toronto, Canada: WHO/GHB Consulting.

404. Sommer A (1982) *Field Guide to the Detection and Control of Xerophthalmia*. Geneva: WHO.

405. Tarwotjo I, Sommer A, Soegiharto T, Susanto D, Muhilal (1982) Dietary practices and xerophthalmia among Indonesian children. *American Journal of Clinical Nutrition* 35: 574-581.

406. Jalal F, Nesheim MC, Agus Z, Sanjur D, Habicht J-P (1997) Serum retinol levels in children are affected by food sources of beta-carotene, fat intake, and anti-heminthic drug treatment. Ithaca, New York: Division of Nutritional Sciences, Cornell University.

407. Tanumihardjo SA, Permaesih D, Muherdiyantiningsih, Rustan E, Rusmil K, Fatah AC, Wilbur S, Muhilal, Karyadi D, Olson JA (1996) Vitamin A status of Indonesian children infected with Ascaris lumbricoides after dosing with vitamin A supplements and albendazole. *Journal of Nutrition* 126: 451-457.

408. Gebre-Medhin M, Vahlquist A (1984) Vitamin A nutrition in the human foetus. A comparison of Sweden and Ethiopia. *Acta Paediatrica Scandinavica* 73: 333-340.

409. Sommer A, Rahmathullah L, Underwood B, Milton R, Reddy V, West K, Daulaire N, Stutkel T, Herrera G, Stansfield S, Ross D, Kirkwood BR, Arthur P, Morris S, Kjolhede C, Dibley M, Barreto M, Bhan MK, Gove S, the Vitamin A and Pneumonia Working Group (1995) Potential interventions for the prevention of childhood pneumonia in developing countries: a meta-analysis of data from field trials to assess the impact of vitamin A supplementation on pneumonia morbidity and mortality. *Bulletin of the World Health Organization* 73: 609 – 619.

410. Katz J, Khatry SK, West KP, Humphrey JH, Leclerq SC, Kimbrough E, Pohkrel PR, Sommer A (1995) Night blindness is prevalent during pregnancy and lactation in rural Nepal. *Journal of Nutrition* 125: 2122-2127.

411. Jayasekera JP, Atukorala TM, Seneviratne HR (1991) Vitamin A status of pregnant women in five districts of Sri Lanka. *Asia-Oceania Journal of Obstetrics and Gynaecology* 17: 217-224.

412. Bloem MW, Hye A, Wijnroks M, Ralte A, West KP Jnr, Sommer A (1995) The role of universal distribution of vitamin A capsules in combatting Vitamin A deficiency in Bangladesh. *American Journal of Epidemiology* 142: 843 – 855.

413. Sachdev HPS (1999) Effect of supplementation with vitamin A or B-carotene on mortality related to pregnancy. No magic pills exist for reducing mortality related to pregnancy. *British Medical Journal* 319:1202.

414. Humphrey JH, Agoestina T, Wu L, Usman A, Nurachim M, Subardja D, Hidayat S, Tielsch J, West KP Jr, Sommer A (1996) Impact of neonatal vitamin A supplementation on infant morbidity and mortality. *Journal of Pediatrics* 128: 489-496.

415. Daulaire NM, Starbuck ES, Houston RM, Church MS, Stukel TA, Pandey MR (1992) Childhood mortality after a high dose of vitamin A in a high risk population. *British Medical Journal* 304(6821): 207-210.

416. West KP Jr, Katz J, Shrestha SR, LeClerq SC, Khatry SK, Pradhan EK, Adhikari R, Wu LS, Pokhrel RP, Sommer A (1995) Mortality of infants < 6 mo of age supplemented with vitamin A: a randomized, double-masked trial in Nepal. *American Journal of Clinical Nutrition* 62: 143-148.

417. McNally L, Tomkins A (2000) A review of the evidence on the benefits and safety of adding vitamin A to the treatment of six common health problems in children. Prepared for the WHO

consultation on vitamin A for children under 6 months, Geneva, March 2000. London: Centre for International Child Health, Institute of Child Health.

418. Hussey GD, Klein M (1990) A randomized, controlled trial of vitamin A in children with severe measles. *New England Journal of Medicine* 323: 160-164.

419. Barclay AJ, Foster A, Sommer A (1987) Vitamin A supplements and mortality related to measles: a randomised clinical trial. *British Medical Journal* 294(6567): 294-296.

420. Hussey GD, Klein M (1993) Routine high-dose vitamin A therapy for children hospitalized with measles. *Journal of Tropical Pediatrics* 39: 342-345.

421. Rosales FJ, Kjolhede C, Goodman S (1996) Efficacy of a single oral dose of 200,000 IU of oil-soluble vitamin A in measles-associated morbidity. *American Journal of Epidemiology* 143: 413-422.

422. Henning B, Stewart K, Zaman K, Alam AN, Brown KH, Black RE (1992) Lack of therapeutic efficacy of vitamin A for non-cholera, watery diarrhoea in Bangladeshi children. *European Journal of Clinical Nutrition* 46: 437-443.

423. Faruque AS, Mahalanabis D, Haque SS, Fuchs GJ, Habte D (1999) Double-blind, randomized, controlled trial of zinc or vitamin A supplementation in young children with acute diarrhoea. *Acta Paediatrica* 88: 154-160.

424. Dewan, V, Patwari AK, Jain M, Dewan N (1995) A randomized controlled trial of vitamin A supplementation in acute diarrhea. *Indian Pediatrics* 32: 21-25.

425. Hossain S, Biswas R, Kabir I, Sarker S, Dibley M, Fuchs G, Mahalanabis D (1998) Single dose vitamin A treatment in acute shigellosis in Bangladesh children: randomised double blind controlled trial. *British Medical Journal* 316 (7129): 422-426.

426. Donnen P, Dramaix M, Brasseur D, Bitwe R, Vertongen F, Hennart P (1998) Randomized placebo-controlled clinical trial of the effect of a single high dose or daily low doses of vitamin A on the morbidity of hospitalized, malnourished children. *American Journal Clinical Nutrition* 68: 1254-1260.

427. Nacul LC, Kirkwood BR, Arthur P, Morris SS, Magalhães M, Fink MC (1997) Randomised, double blind, placebo controlled clinical trial of efficacy of vitamin A treatment in non-measles childhood pneumonia. *British Medical Journal* 315(7107): 505-510.

428. Kjolhede CL, Chew FJ, Gadomski AM, Marroquin DP (1995) Clinical trial of vitamin A as adjuvant treatment for lower respiratory tract infections. *Journal of Pediatrics* 126: 807-812.

429. Fawzi WW, Mbise RL, Fataki MR, Herrera MG, Kawau F, Hertzmark E, Spiegelman D, Ndossi G (1998b) Vitamin A supplementation and severity of pneumonia in children admitted to the hospital in Dar es Salaam, Tanzania. *American Journal Clinical Nutrition* 68: 187-192.

430. Si NV, Grytter C, Vy NN, Hue NB, Pedersen FK (1997) High dose vitamin A supplementation in the course of pneumonia in Vietnamese children. *Acta Paediatrica* 86: 1052-1055.

431. Coutsoudis A (2000) The relationship between vitamin A deficiency and HIV infection: review of scientific studies. Report prepared for the WHO Consultation on Vitamin A in the First Six Months of Life. Geneva: WHO.

432. Stallings RY, Stoltzfus RJ, Schulze K, Miotti P (1997) Negative association of an acute phase protein with maternal serum retinol in HIV infection. Abstracts of the 18th International Vitamin A Consultative Group Meeting, Cairo, Egypt. Washington DC: International Life Sciences Institute.

433. Coutsoudis A, Pillay K, Spooner E, Kuhn L Coovadia HM (1999) Randomized trial testing the effect of vitamin A supplementation on pregnancy outcomes and early mother-to-child HIV-1 transmission in Durban, South Africa. South African Vitamin A Study Group. *AIDS* 13: 1517-1524.

434. Semba RD (1997) Overview of the potential role of vitamin A in mother-to-child-transmission of HIV-1. *Acta Paediatrica* (Supplement) 421: 107-112.

435. Coutsoudis A, Bobat RA, Coovadia HM, Kuhn L, Tsai WY, Stein ZA (1995) The effects of vitamin A supplementation on the morbidity of children born to HIV-infected women. *American Journal of Public Health* 85: 1076-1081.

436. Rollins NC, Filteau SM, Elson EI, Tomkins AM (2000) Vitamin A supplementation of South African children with severe diarrhea: optimum timing for improving biochemical and clinical recovery and subsequent vitamin A status. *Pediatric Infectious Disease Journal* 19:284-289.

437. Soleri D, Cleveland DA, Wood A (1991) Vitamin A Nutrition and Gardens Bibliography, Vitamin A Field Support Project (VITAL) Report No. IN-I Washington DC: International Life Sciences Institute.

438. Gillespie SR, Mason JB (1994) *Controlling Vitamin A Deficiency*. ACC/SCN State-of-the-Art Series Nutrition Policy Discussion Paper No 14. Geneva: ACC/SCN.

439. Castenmiller JJ; West CE (1998) Bioavailability and bioconversion of carotenoids. *Annual Review of Nutrition*, 18:19-38.

440. Pollard, R. 1989. The West Sumatra vitamin A social marketing project. Jakarta, Indonesia: Department of Health and Helen Keller International.

441. de Pee, S., M. W. Bloem, Satoto, R. Yip, A. Sukaton, R. Tjiong, R. Shrimpton, Muhilal, B. Kodyat (1998) Impact of social marketing campaign promoting dark green leafy vegetables and eggs in Central Java, Indonesia. *International Journal of Vitamin and Nutrition Research* 68: 389-398.

442. Marsh R (1998) Building on traditional gardening to improve household food security. *Food, Nutrition, and Agriculture* 22: 4.

443. Hagenimana V, Anyango Oyunga M, Low J, Njoroge SM, Gichuki ST, Kabira J (1999) Testing the effects of women farmers' adoption and production of orange-fleshed sweet potatoes on dietary vitamin A intake in Kenya, OMNI Research Report Series No. 3. Washington DC: International Center for Research on Women.

444. Ayalew WZ, Wolde G, Kassa H (1999) Reducing vitamin A deficiency in Ethiopia: Linkages with a women-focused dairy goat farming project. OMNI Research Report Series No. 4. Washington DC: International Center for Research on Women.

445. Solon F, Fernandez TL, Latham MC, Popkin BM (1979) An evaluation of strategies to control vitamin A deficiency in the Philippines. *American Journal of Clinical Nutrition*. 32: 1445-1453.

446. Greiner T, Mitra SN (1995) Evaluation of the impact of a food-based approach to solving vitamin A deficiency in Bangladesh. *Food and Nutrition Bulletin* 16 (3): 193-205.

447. Tang G, Qin J, Hu S, Hao L, Xu Q, Gu X, Fjeld C, Gao X, Yin S, Russell RM (2000) *Food and Nutrition Bulletin* 21: 161-164.

448. Scrimshaw NS (2000) Nutritional potential of red palm oil for combating vitamin A deficiency. *Food and Nutrition Bulletin* 21: 195-201.

449. Manorama R, Brahman GNV, Rikmini C (1996) Plant Foods. *Human Nutrition* 49: 75-82.

450. Narasinga Rao BS (2000) Potential use of red palm oil in combating vitamin A deficiency in India. *Food and Nutrition Bulletin* 21: 202-211.

451. Canfield LM, Kaminsky RG (2000) Red palm oil in the maternal diet improves the vitamin A status of lactating mothers and their infants. *Food and Nutrition Bulletin* 21:144-148.

452. Lietz G, Henry CJK, Mulokozi G, Ballart A, Ndossi G, Lorri W, Tomkins A (2000) Use of red palm oil for the promotion of maternal vitamin A status. *Food and Nutrition Bulletin* 21:215-218.

453. Gillespie SR, Mason JB (1991) *Nutrition-Relevant Actions*. ACC/SCN State-of-the-Art Nutrition Policy Discussion Paper No. 10. Geneva: ACC/SCN.

454. Jennings J, Scialfa T, Gillespie SR, Lotfi M, Mason JB (1991) *Managing Successful Nutrition Programmes*. ACC/SCN State-of-the-Art Series Nutrition Policy Discussion Paper 8. Geneva: ACC/SCN.

455. Gillespie SR, Mason JB, Martorell R (1996) *How Nutrition Improves*. ACC/SCN State-of-the-Art Nutrition Policy Discussion Paper No. 15. Geneva: ACC/SCN.

456. Government of Tamil Nadu (1989) Evaluation of TINP-I. Madras, India: Government of Nadu.

457. Habicht J-P, Victora CG, Vaughan JP (1999) Evaluation designs for adequacy, plausibility and probability of public health programme performance and impact. *International Journal of Epidemiology* 28: 10-18.

458. Dicken K, Griffiths M, Piwoz E (1997) Designing by dialogue: A program planner's guide to consultative research for improving young child feeding. Health and Human Resources Analysis for Africa project. Washington DC: USAID.

459. Klemm RDW, Puertollano EP, Villate EE (1997) Nutrition communications to improve infant feeding: A planner's guide. Manila, Philippines: Hellen Keller International.

460. Bhattacharyya K, Murray J, Amdi W, Asnake M, Betre M, Freund P, Kedamo T, Kereta W, Winch P (1998) Community assessment and planning for maternal and child health programs: a participatory approach in Ethiopia. Washington DC: BASICS Technical Report, USAID.

461. BASICS/WHO/UNICEF. 1999. Nutrition Essentials: a Guide for Health Managers. Washington DC: BASICS/ USAID.

462. Gillespie SR (1999) *Supplementary Feeding for Women and Young Children*: Nutrition Toolkit Module, Number 5. World Bank Nutrition Toolkit. Washington DC: The World Bank.

463. Griffiths M, Dickin K, Favin M (1999) *Growth Promotion*. Nutrition Toolkit Module, Number 4. Washington DC: The World Bank.

464. Favin M, Griffiths M (1999) *Communications for Behavioral Change in Nutrition Projects*. Nutrition

Toolkit Module, Number 9. Washington DC: The World Bank.

465. del Rosso JM (1999) *School Nutrition.* Nutrition Toolkit Module Number 10. Washington, DC: The World Bank.

466. WHO (2000) *Complementary feeding: Family foods for breastfed children.* WHO/NHD/00.1. Geneva: WHO.

467. WHO (1999) A Critical Link: Interventions for Physical Growth and Psychological Development: A Review. Geneva: WHO.

468. Grantham-McGregor SM, Pollit E, Wachs TD, Meisels SJ, Scott KG (1999) Summary of the scientific evidence on the nature and determinants of child development and their implications for programmatic interventions with young children. *Food and Nutrition Bulletin* 20 1: 4-6.

469. Shekar M (1991) The Tamil Nadu Integrated Nutrition Project: A Review of the Project with Special Emphasis on the Monitoring and Information System. Cornell Food and Nutrition Policy Program, Working Paper No. 14. Ithaca, New York: Cornell University.

470. Gillespie SR, Measham A (1998) Implementation Completion Report of the Second Tamil Nadu Integrated Nutrition Project. Washington DC: The World Bank

471. Holmboe-Ottesen G, Mascarenhas O, Wandel M (1989) *Women's Role in Food Chain Activities and the Implications for Nutrition.* ACC/SCN State-of-the-Art Series Nutrition Policy Discussion Paper No. 4. Geneva: ACC/SCN, WHO.

472. Behrman JR, Deolalikar AB (1990) The intrahousehold in rural India: individual estimates, fixed effects and permanent income. *Journal of Human Resources* 25: 665–696.

473. Bengoa JM (1971) Significance of malnutrition and prioritization for its prevention, national development, and planning. Proceedings of an international conference held at Cambridge, MA, USA. Cambridge MA: MIT Press. (In Press).

474. Habicht J-P, Martorell R, Yarbrough C, Malina R, Klein RE (1979) Height and weight standards for preschool children: Are there really ethnic differences in growth potentials? *The Lancet* 1: 611-615.

475. Delgado H, Palma AP, Fischer M (1991) The use of the height census of schoolchildren in Central America and Panama. *Food and Nutrition Bulletin* 13: 17-19.

476. Adair L (1999) Filipino children exhibit catch-up growth from age 2 to 12 years. *Journal of Nutrition* 129: 1140-1148.

477. del Rosso JM, Marek T (1996) Class Action: Improving School Performance in the Developing World through Better Health and Nutrition. Directions in Development. Washington DC: The World Bank.

478. Bundy DAP (1990) Is the hookworm just another geohelminth? In Hookworm Disease: Current Status and New Directions, ed. Schad GA, Warren KS. New York: Taylor and Frances. 147 – 164.

479. Hlaing T (1993) Ascariasis and childhood malnutrition. *Parasitology* 107(Supplement 1): S125-36.

480. Awasthi S, Peto R, Fletcher R, Glick H (1995) Controlling parasitic infestation in children under five years of age: giving albendazole in conjunction with an Indian government vitamin A supplement program. Philadelphia: International Clinical Epidemiology Network 1995, Monograph 3.

481. Bundy DAP, Guyatt HL (1996) Schools for health: focus on health, education and the school-age child. *Parasites Today* 12: 1-16.

482. Gillespie SR, Mason JB, Kevany J (1991) *Controlling Iron Deficiency.* ACC/SCN State-of-the-Art Series Nutrition Policy Discussion Paper No. 9. Geneva: ACC/SCN.

483. MotherCare (1997) *Improving the Quality of Iron Supplementation Programs: The MotherCare Experience.* Arlington VA: USAID/MotherCare.

484. Achadi EL (1995) Reducing anaemia in Indonesia. *Mothers and Children* 14 (1): 11.

485. Sood SK (1988) Prevention and treatment of anaemia in women: oral supplementation with iron, parenteral administration, diet and fortification. Paper presented to the INACG workshop on Maternal Nutritional Anaemia, Geneva, November 14-16, 1988. Washington DC: International Nutritional Anemia Consultative Group.

486. Kim I, Hungerford D, Yip R, Zyrkowski C, Trowbridge F (1992) Pregnancy nutrition surveillance system, 1979-1990. *Morbidity Mortality Weekly Report* 41 (Supplement 7): 25-41.

487. Government of India (1989) Report of a meeting on prevention and control of nutritional anaemia. New Delhi: Ministry of Health and Family Welfare and UNICEF.

488. WHO (1990) Iron supplementation during pregnancy: Why aren't women complying? Geneva: WHO. WHO/MCH/90.5.

489. Schultink W (1996) Iron supplementation programmes: Compliance of target groups and frequency of tablet intake. *Food and Nutrition Bulletin* 17 (1): 22-26.

490. Ridwan E, Schultink W, Dillon D, Gross R (1996) Weekly iron supplementation in pregnancy. *American Journal of Clinical Nutrition* 63: 884-90.

491. Galloway R, McGuire J (1991) Determinants of compliance with iron supplementation: Supplies, side effect or psychology? *Social Science and Medicine* 39: 381-390.

492. Horton S (1999) Opportunities for investments in nutrition in low-income Asia. *Asian Development Review* 17 (1,2): 246-273.

493. Jonsson U (1997) Success Factors in Community-Based, Nutrition-Oriented Programmes and Projects. In *Malnutrition in South Asia: A Regional Profile*, ed. Gillespie SR. Kathmandu, Nepal: UNICEF.

# APPENDIX 1

## PROFILES OF SOME COMMUNITY-BASED NUTRITION INTERVENTIONS IN ASIAN COUNTRIES, FROM THE ASIAN DEVELOPMENT BANK REGIONAL TECHNICAL ASSISTANCE (RETA) PROJECT 5671 ON "INVESTING IN CHILD NUTRITION IN ASIA" AND OTHER RELEVANT PROJECTS AND STUDIES

Summary details are given here, by country, of some recent and ongoing nutrition-related programmes in Asia.

### BANGLADESH

The Government of Bangladesh implements several programmes which aim to address undernutrition. The Bangladesh Integrated Nutrition Project (BINP), which started in 1996 and planned to cover 40 rural thanas by 2000 (i.e., 8 million population or 8.6% of total rural *thanas*), is the only community-based nutrition project in the country. The BINP is implemented by the Ministry of Health and Family Welfare (MOHFW) with financial assistance from the World Bank and technical assistance from UNICEF. It has three major components: national level nutrition activities, such as strengthening of existing nutrition activities, information, education and communication, programme development and institution building; community- based nutrition (CBNC); and intersectoral nutrition programme development.

The CBNC addresses protein energy undernutrition, LBW and micronutrient deficiency. PEM is addressed: in the short run, through supplementary feeding to growth faltering and severely malnourished children; and in the long run, through behavioural changes related to the major problems of caring (for example, low levels of exclusive breastfeeding, delayed complementary feeding, and inadequate maternal nutrition during pregnancy) and through improved food security from intersectoral subprojects. The BINP attempts to address LBW directly, and the increased likelihood of infant mortality and morbidity associated with it, by providing pregnant women with the calories needed for proper weight gain during pregnancy. Micronutrient deficiency is combated through supplementing pregnant women with iron and folic acid, by motivating families to consume iodized salt, and by providing mothers with vitamin A capsules within two weeks of delivery.

The CBNC operates through Community Nutrition Centres (CNCs) which are each staffed by one volunteer Community Nutrition Promoter (CNP) who, with the help of an assistant, provides nutrition counselling, conducts growth monitoring and oversees feeding of infants and women. At present there are two ratios of CNCs to population: in one-half of the project, one CNC to 1,000 persons and in the other half, one CNC to 1,500 persons.

The CNPs report to Community Nutrition Organizers (CNOs) each of whom oversees 10 CNPs. CNOs in turn report to the thana manager who coordinates all BINP activities within the thana. At the central level, the project is administered through a Project Director, Deputy Project Directors for Management Information Systems, Training, IEC, and Administration, along with national consultants for MIS and Programme, Training, IEC, and Intersectoral Activities. At the village, union, thana, and national levels, Nutrition Management Committees, comprising community leaders and representatives of related sectors (e.g., health, agriculture), provide inputs to project activities.

The BINP uses the food-health-care conceptual framework of the causes of undernutrition. The CBNC activities address caring practices directly and the intersectoral component BINP component contributes to food security, but there is no direct BINP activity concerned with health care. The BINP activities are designed and planned for rural areas only.

Among other programmes in Bangladesh, the Campaign for Promotion and Protection of Breastfeeding, Nutritional Blindness Prevention Programme, Antenatal and Postnatal Care, Expanded Programme on Immunization (EPI), Family Planning, Control of Diarrhoeal Diseases, Control of Acute Respiratory Infection, and Water and Sanitation relate to nutrition service delivery and are supported by the Ministry of Health and Family Welfare (MOHFW). The Vulnerable Group Development Programme, Rural Development Project, and Micro Credit programmes that all relate to 'social safety net' initiatives, are managed by other government sectors and NGOs.

The MOHFW is responsible for providing health services in rural areas and has a well established organizational structure down to the village level. The Ministry of Local Government, Rural Development and Cooperatives has responsibility for delivering health services in urban areas, where 20% of the population live. Urban health care delivery is relatively less organized, and most of the services are provided by NGOs and the private sector.

The government service delivery programmes are vertical. Except for the EPI, the utilization rates of the programmes are poor: mainly due to inadequate mobilization, communication and service quality which, in turn, are due to nonavailability of sufficient quantities of drugs and lack of trained manpower. The nutrition effects of these programmes are further limited by their poor nutrition focus.

## CAMBODIA

In Cambodia, programmes with nutrition components are limited in scope and scale and uncoordinated, with nutrition not articulated explicitly as an outcome. The one exception is the UNICEF-assisted Community Action for Social Development (CASD) programme which is integrative, large scale and has an explicit nutrition goal. The CASD programme supports the establishment of village development committees (VDCs), as instruments for community development. In 1998, 552 villages in 8 provinces had VDCs. The model used by the CASD derives from UNICEF's global experience with integrated, community-based

programmes and the holistic UNICEF Nutrition Strategy. The CASD is a cross-sectoral programme, implemented with support from several ministries, notably the Ministries of Planning, Rural Development, Women Affairs, Agriculture, Education, Health, and Interior (in charge of local government). The focus is on enhancing community capacity by working towards basic social goals, through VDCs, civic organizations, and NGOs. This process of "building from below" is supported by national, provincial, district and commune structures of government in the relevant ministries. The process of VDC formation, through a gender-sensitive, free and fair election, and the training of VDC members, was adopted as the model approach by the Ministry of Rural Development in 1997. The development of Village Action Plans (VAPs) through which services are delivered, makes the approach demand driven.

The CASD Programme, with an annual budget of US$ 4 million for the period 1996-2000, uses nutrition as the outcome indicator and has six components: Capacity Building; Community Education and Care; Food, Water and Environment; Health, Hygiene and Care; Protection of Vulnerable Children and Women; and Credit, Employment and Income. Together, these address the three main food-, health- and care-related determinants of nutrition. The UNICEF-supported Multiple Indicator Cluster Survey (MICS), first conducted in 1996, provides a foundation for a national level, nutrition information database.

Regarding other relevant programmes in Cambodia, the United Nations Development Programme (UNDP) supports the CARERE programme, which is similar in concept to the CASD programme, in five provinces covering 380 villages. The EU-sponsored PRASAC programmes work with more than 600 VDCs. The Basic Health Services Project, initiated in 1996 and supported by the ADB, aims to strengthen the basic health care system as well as to improve management capacity in five provinces which lack a basic health care system. Numerous international and local NGOs are also working at the village level in community development.

Numerous donor-financed investment programmes are addressing the issue of household-level food security. The World Food Programme provides major support to the Rural Development Ministry for an extensive, national 'food-for-work' programme. The Australian development agency AusAID is actively engaged in developing agricultural extension programmes for small farmer support. The World Bank supports the strengthening of the central Agriculture and Rural Development Ministries, with a large social funds project, and is in the process of developing an integrated rural development initiative for neglected areas. The ADB supports programmes in agriculture and rural development that include rural roads, small irrigation development, employment generation and microcredit.

Programmes to address care and health considerations are more diffuse. As the health care system is being rebuilt, much of the emphasis of donor-assisted programmes is on communicable disease prevention and control, combined with strengthening the Central Health Ministry. NGOs support a wide variety of health and integrated programmes but these have not yet been systematically reviewed for lessons learned. Maternal and child feeding and nutrition practices are being addressed largely through UNICEF and NGO programmes.

With regard to micronutrients, universal salt iodization (USI) was expected by end of 1998, through UNICEF, Helen Keller International and United States Agency for International Development (USAID) support with substantial funding from the Canadian International Development Agency (CIDA), (through the Micronutrient Initiative), Kiwanis International, and the US National Committee for UNICEF. The only component of a national VAD control programme is vitamin A capsule distribution, supported since 1995 by UNICEF and HKI and linked to National Immunization Days (NIDs). Regarding IDA, it is reported that all health units have iron and folate supplements available as part of their minimum package of services. However, there is no specific information regarding the use of such supplements.

All nutrition-specific interventions are thus supported by, and largely driven by, agencies and/ or NGOs. Moreover, the human and organizational resources provided by the government for such programmes cannot operate without external assistance. Current and future nutrition-relevant programmes need to be coordinated in order to improve complementarity, share experiences and lessons and develop best practices. The ADB's RETA 5671 country report argued that a community-based strategy, supported by national level strategies, offers the best basis for progressive and sustained nutrition improvement in Cambodia. In order to achieve the overall national nutrition objectives of the National Nutrition Plan of Action (NNPA), the strategy should be to move the current small scale, community-based programmes that have nutrition-relevance to a larger scale.

# PEOPLE'S REPUBLIC OF CHINA

The health care system is the most prominent organization involved in the delivery of direct nutrition programmes in the PRC, and it is in a state of transition. Prior to the 1980s, it was one of the most progressive and effective health care systems in the world, achieving basic health outcomes at low cost. Since the 1980s, however, following economic reform measures, the rural health service delivery system has disintegrated. A lack of coordination of health programmes, coupled with escalating health care costs, has caused a crisis here in health care. Duplication of services strains government health budgets. Competition between maternal and health services and the vertical family planning programme, together with distinct western and traditional medical facilities, have resulted in inefficient resource allocation and poorly coordinated services.

Nevertheless, the health infrastructure in the PRC remains one of the most impressive in the world and the government is in the process of adopting major health system reforms, including: revitalization of community financing schemes; increased public financing of public health interventions; development of regional planning models; and improved health care pricing policies.

Direct nutrition programmes comprise both vertical and community-based programmes. Vertical programmes include the Baby-Friendly Hospital Initiative (BFHI) supported by UNICEF and now covering over 6,700 hospitals, and the National IDD Elimination Programme (NIDDEP), co-financed by the World Bank, UNICEF and UNDP since 1993. The main elements of the NIDDEP comprise: establishment of a multisectoral organization and management framework; revision, promulgation and implementation of relevant legislation; salt iodization and distribution; iodized oil supplementation to remote areas; and mechanisms for training, monitoring and evaluation. By 1994, a law mandating nationwide salt iodization was in place. By 1997, iodized salt coverage was over 80% in 23 provinces and autonomous regions and iodine content of the salt was adequate in 16 of 31 provinces.

For more than a decade, UNICEF and the Government of the PRC have developed jointly an area-based approach to nutrition problems. During the period 1985-1989, commune level programmes were introduced to 18 rural townships in seven provinces. A key management strategy for this project was the establishment of township and county committees, to manage activities related to nutrition. More than 11,000 field workers were trained during the five-year period. Intervention components focused on: promotion of home gardening and animal husbandry; nutrition communications, emphasizing breastfeeding and complementary feeding practices; disease prevention and management; anaemia control, through iron supplementation of pregnant women; and fortification of foods. In 1990, an enhanced, community-based, Child Nutrition Surveillance and Intervention Programme was initiated. This covered more than 120,000 preschool children, in 700 villages within 101 poor rural counties. A subsequent evaluation showed reduced levels of anaemia and stunting and made recommendations for management; e.g., the need to strengthen further local organizational capacity.

# INDIA

The most important national nutrition programmes in India are the Integrated Child Development Services Programme (ICDS), the Targeted Public Distribution System (TPDS), food-for-work, the National Mid-Day Meals Programme (NMMP), and micronutrient (iron-folate and vitamin A distribution, and salt iodization) schemes. These programmes aim to address significant segments of India's undernourished population: poor households, through the TPDS and employment schemes; young children and mothers, through the ICDS and health efforts; and school children through the NMMP.

The ICDS provides six services for 0- to 6-year-old children and mothers: supplementary feeding; immunization against the preventable diseases of childhood; health check-ups and referral; health and nutrition education to adult women; and preschool education to 3 to 6 year-olds. Although the 0-6-year-old population in areas covered by the ICDS is already 63 million, and the population of pregnant and lactating women is 13.6 million, only 30 million children and 5.2 million mothers are actually covered by the supplementary feeding, and 15 million 3-6 year-olds by preschool education. Coverage figures are not available for the other services. The ICDS also includes, in fewer than 10% of the, 4,200 programme blocks, schemes for adolescent girls' nutrition, health, awareness and skill development. In some areas, it has also been linked with women's income generating programmes. All ICDS services are delivered through a village centre, the *anganwadi*, by a trained village woman who is assisted periodically in the health tasks by an Auxiliary Nurse Midwife (ANM) from the health subcentre.

The ICDS is targeted at poor areas and increasingly at poor households, largely as a result of self-targeting rather than design at poor households.

Programme guidelines call for the food supplements (which are limited to 40% of the expected beneficiary population of an *anganwadi*) to be given preferentially to children and pregnant women from households at high risk of malnutrition: those of landless labourers, marginal farmers, scheduled castes or tribes. The adolescent girls' and women's programmes are intended to improve health and nutrition over the longer term through improvements in the roles of women.

Evaluations of the ICDS have found its impact on nutrition status to be limited. Among the reasons for this are: inadequate coverage of children below 3 years of age and at greatest risk of undernutrition, and of women and children living in hamlets; irregular food supply, irregular feeding and inadequate rations; poor nutrition education of mothers or families, to encourage improved feeding practices in the home and other relevant behavioural changes; inadequate training of workers, particularly in nutrition, growth monitoring, and communication; *anganwadi* worker (AGW) overload, and weak and unsupportive supervision of the AGW, resulting in the neglect of crucial nutrition-related tasks the mobilizer/community ratio of around one per 200 families is grossly inadequate; top-down management; lack of community ownership, particularly women's participation; and poor linkages between the ICDS and the health system.

In general, the quality of ICDS services has been low. Although the services are much in demand, they have been generally poorly delivered and uncoordinated. Worker training, in-service supervision, community support, and indeed community involvement in any sense; remain major gaps. Although there are exceptions, *anganwadi* facilities and environments are sorely inadequate and the programme does not inspire the good health, hygiene and nutrition-related behaviour that is so essential to changing the status of children and women in poor households. To make a significant impact on nutrition and health, a great number of changes are needed in the ICDS.

With regard to household food security, both national and state governments have made substantial efforts in designing and implementing food distribution and nonfood programmes to ensure household food security. However, IEC was found to be the weakest link in most of these programmes. The limited involvement, if any, of the community in programme design and implementation was the major cause for poor community response and lack of ownership.

Multiplicity and frequent changes in programmes to alleviate poverty have created confusion, making their monitoring difficult. Poor targeting of poverty alleviation programmes, with consequent substantial wastage of scarce resources, is the major area of concern. Many evaluations indicate that the poorer sections of the society could not benefit much from the safety net provided by the Public Distribution System (PDS). The PDS has been fraught with problems of leakages and with inefficiencies in storage and distribution, particularly in poorer states where undernutrition is very high. Only 22% of the total expenditure on PDS was estimated to reach the poorer sections of society, defeating the basic purpose of this safety net. The revamped TPDS, launched in 1992, has not managed to overcome these constraints.

The NMMP has the dual objective of improving both school attendance and child nutrition. It has had more success with the former, which is not surprising considering that the age group targeted is older than those who would benefit most readily in terms of growth. Progress with the micronutrient deficiency control efforts has been patchy: little success with anaemia control, some success with VAD control, and definite progress with salt iodization and IDD control.

## PAKISTAN

Pakistan has community-based and service delivery programmes, designed to improve child and maternal nutrition directly, and programmes with components to improve nutrition .The community-based programmes provide nutrition-related services to mothers and children in the community. Service delivery programmes may provide nutrition services in the community, but they may also be centered at institutions outside the community, such as hospitals, or may deliver a service through national level programmes such as food fortification. Community-based programmes also differ from indirect programmes which may provide training to medical and support staff, health services such as the EPI, or poverty alleviation efforts that affect nutrition indirectly.

The community level programmes include the Rural Child Survival Project, the Prime Minister's Programme, the World Food Programme, and two NGO programmes: Health and Nutritional Development Society (HANDS) and the Aga Khan University (AKU) School Nutrition Programme. Two noncommunity-based service delivery programmes are the IDD Elimination Programme, and the BFHI. They vary considerably in coverage, intensity, and unit costs. There is evidence for success of community-based programmes which employ local women as community health workers. The HANDS and AKU Programmes in Sindh combine education and nutrition, and have a special focus on including

girls in the process. Improved education and literacy is empowering and correlates strongly with the ability to assimilate information and to improve the use of available resources, leading to improved child nutrition. The HANDS programme covers 35,000 under-12 year-old children in 50 villages. The AKU programme covers 72 schools in 5 districts. Both have shown positive results, but neither has been successful in all communities. These projects are small, and are possibly difficult to replicate on a wider scale.

The small scale, pilot UNICEF-funded Rural Child Survival Project, which covers 28 villages in Islamabad Capital Territory, has a similar community-based focus. This project made an explicit link to the Ministry of Health (MOH) infrastructure, although there were problems of turnover and lack of interest by MOH staff, and the absence of a link to traditional birth attendants (TBAs or dais). An evaluation of the World Food Programme-supported supplementary feeding programme in Sindh suggested that its contribution to nutrition of the under-two year-old child was limited by problems of targeting and by irregular food supply.

The Prime Minister's Family Planning and Primary Health Care Programme represents a major attempt to use community health workers in order to provide some of the kinds of services of NGOs. "Lady Health Workers" (LHWs) can provide the linkage, and community responsiveness that basic health units are unable to provide. The LHWs' nutrition promotion activities centre on communications, in areas such as optimal feeding and caring practices and preventative, home-based, health care education. They are also given the tasks of mobilizing the community and of forming community organizations that can eventually take charge of their own health. Several pilot projects indicate that the programme can be successful, but no large scale evaluations of the national level effort have been done.

In 1999, a Women's Health Project was initiated in 20 districts, with support from the ADB. This has a specific focus on improving compliance with micronutrient supplementation and dietary quality during pregnancy, through counselling undertaken by LHWs.

The BFHI and the IDD programmes are not community-based, but provide important nutrition services. Both are reasonably effective, but need to extend their services more effectively to the community level, and to form linkages with existing services. The IDD programme has attempted to reach a number of education and health providers, doctors, and school children to spread the message about the importance of IDD. However, they are apparently not supported very effectively by front line MOH workers in emphasizing the importance of iodine.

The BFHI has been quite successful in its work with hospitals. However, since the vast number of women do not deliver in hospitals, the initiative would be more effective if it could work at the community level, providing information for TBAs and encouraging exclusive breastfeeding and timely complementary feeding.

## SRI LANKA

There are several ongoing efforts to strengthen the community-based nutrition approach in Sri Lanka. At present, there are four special programmes, implemented with substantial support from the state. The Participatory Nutrition Improvement Project (PNIP) is being implemented by the communities, in selected *Grama Niladhari* (GN) Divisions in 25 District Secretary's Divisions (DSD), with the assistance of multiple sectors and Ministry of Plan Implementation, and UNICEF support for coordination and monitoring. Basic nutrition programmes were implemented by the Janasaviya Trust Fund (JTF) in the 1990-1994 period and thereafter by the National Development Trust Fund (NDTF) which replaced the JTF. Another nutrition-oriented programme was implemented under the Samurdhi Programme, in 25 Divisions. The *Thriposha* Supplementary Feeding Programme, introduced in 1973, covers 32% of its target group, including pregnant and lactating women and under 4 year-old children who meet certain eligibility criteria. *Thriposha* is a blended fortified food that is distributed as a take-home ration, through Mother and Child Health clinics.

In addition, there are several NGOs working in the field of nutrition, using the community-based approach. The largest NGO programme is the Early Childhood Development programme of Sarvodaya that covers 6,000 villages. It does not have specific nutrition-related objectives but it incorporates nutrition interventions, in the form of a food aid programme for preschool children and nutrition education of mothers, through preschool teachers.

The coverage of such community- based programmes is as yet very limited. Excluding the North and Eastern Province, there are approximately 12,000 GN units of which the community-based programmes cover only about 5%. The three main programmes, as well as the individual programmes of NGOs, function independently of each other. Although the programmes have drawn on each other's experience informally, there is no formal or institutionalized arrangement for the regular and systematic exchange of information and knowledge.

The interaction between workers of the community-based programmes and the health workers who deliver services to mothers and children is limited, and is not structured and institutionalized in a regular and systematic way. There is no sharing of information between the two groups for purposes of regular monitoring. The community-based programmes such as the PNIP, have not yet installed an adequate information and monitoring system, with necessary documentation for their own work programme. One of the major problems of most of these programmes is sustainability, when the supportive agencies withdraw from the communities.

Despite these limitations, the models that are being developed in these programmes, particularly the model of the PNIP, address directly the issue of capacity building at community and household levels, for reduction of undernutrition. These programmes help to fill gaps within the state delivery system, which is not able to intervene adequately at the household level so as to promote desired behavioural changes.

Under these programmes, women's groups from the community are functioning as informal teams and are engaged in frequent dialogues with mothers on issues such as breastfeeding, complementary feeding and growth monitoring. Women leaders have developed their own indicators for monitoring nutrition activities and have continued to monitor changes in the community. Participatory development of communication materials and other methods of raising awareness (e.g., as role playing, skits, short dramas) have become very popular. Focus groups have developed their own thaemes and dialogues and have involved their family members, including their children, in these dramas, aimed at disseminating nutrition messages. House visits have been used to monitor informally the adherence to practices suggested through education. The growth chart is the main instrument around which the education programme is built. There appears to be a general awareness of the interrelatedness of nutrition with poverty and other factors, and a concern for safe water, sanitation, caring practices is reflected in many of the programmes. There have also been efforts to develop and to implement a system of monitoring and evaluation, with the use of simple indicators.

The persistence of a high level of undernutrition appears to be rooted in conditions that cannot be overcome entirely by the existing combination of interventions. The strategy for reduction of maternal and child undernutrition has been based essentially on the delivery of services, when the mother visits the clinic or when the public health midwife (PHM) visits the home. It is a top-down process in which the involvement and responsibility of households and the community for monitoring and management is limited. The hard core problems of undernutrition do not seem to yield to this top-down process. This was substantiated in the ADB's RETA 5671. The following were among the critical gaps and shortfalls identified. LBW infants are a highly vulnerable group requiring special attention. Yet programmes of maternal and child health which monitor the growth of preschool children do not appear to follow up LBW babies systematically and to monitor their later performance. Moreover, although growth monitoring is an essential feature of the system for child care in Sri Lanka, this confined largely to MCH clinics, without full parental and family involvement. The services provided by the clinics have achieved only very limited coverage. The number of weighings of children 1-2 years is available but without any percentages and any reference to their nutrition status over time. The data suggest that clinics do not obtain information on preschool weighings after 2 years. Generally the links between disease and undernutrition are not monitored and managed, and there is no information on growth monitoring cards on episodes of illness.

The present delivery system is encountering problems of implementation that are related first to nonutilization and nonparticipation by households, and second to lack of understanding of the causes of undernutrition at different levels. Such a complex interaction of a wide variety of processes requires a community-based approach to child undernutrition, capable of identifying the diversity of the real situations and different combinations of the variables that operate at community and household levels. A much more intensive and sustained effort is therefore needed to address the problem of child undernutrition at the place of its occurrence; i.e., in the community and the household.

## VIET NAM

In Viet Nam, 24 nutrition and nutrition-related programmes and projects, implemented by government institutions, ministries, nongovernmental organizations and international agencies were reviewed in the ADB's RETA 5671. A general summary follows here.

The main national programme is the National Programme of Protein Energy Malnutrition Control for Viet Namese Children, initiated in 1994. This targets under-five-year-old children and pregnant women, with a core package of services revolving around growth monitoring and promotional activities, carried out by community-level volunteers and mobilizers. Other directly relevant national level programmes include those focusing on the control of the three main micronutrient deficiencies (iron, iodine and vitamin A), breastfeeding promotion, EPI, control of diarrhoeal and acute respiratory diseases and household food security. In addition, there are several small scale, pilot projects.

The following lessons emerged from the RETA 5671. The national PEM control programme should emphasize preventative over curative approaches and become more household-focused, in order to improve caring practices for women and children.

The micronutrient interventions are well justified and should continue, as they have had a demonstrable impact on VAD and IDD. The anaemia control programme, which has lagged behind largely because of poor compliance with supplementation, needs increased prioritization.

National vertical programmes that address the diseases that contribute to PEM should be continued, while recognizing their limitations. Current household food security interventions, which focus primarily focusing on income generation, through food production diversification, employment generation and kitchen gardening and animal husbandry development, need to be better targeted geographically, with respect to need. Caring practices which address the central underlying causes of PEM are clearly in need of more attention, support and financing. Water and sanitation issues will remain a central concern for at least the next decade. The underutilization of health centres, due to poor service quality is serious and requires urgent remedial action. Interventions that address the education-related basic causes of PEM also have room for expansion and improvement.

As ongoing market liberalization continues to marginalize a fraction of the population, interventions that alleviate poverty and hunger through credit and other support will remain essential. Moreover, social mobilization is indispensable to sustained, nationwide success in nutrition. People have to get involved in assessing, analyzing and taking action on the determinants of PEM. Community-based growth monitoring, with the emphasis on growth promotion, is one avenue to explore.

## ACC/SCN Nutrition Policy Papers

1) **Nutrition Education: A State-of-the-art Review**.
   R.C. Hornik, 1985 (SOA No. 1)

2) **Delivery of Oral Doses of Vitamin A to Prevent Vitamin A Deficiency and Nutritional Blindness**.
   K. West Jr. and A. Sommer, 1987 (SOA No. 2)

3) **The Prevention and Control of Iodine Deficiency Disorders**.
   B.S. Hetzel, 1988 (SOA No. 3)

4) **Women's Role in Food Chain Activities and their Implications for Nutrition**.
   G. Holmboe-Ottesen, O. Mascarenhas, and M. Wandel, 1989  (SOA No. 4)

5) **Malnutrition and Infection - A Review**.
   A. Tomkins and F. Watson, 1989 (SOA No. 5)

6) **Women and Nutrition**.
   J. McGuire, B. Popkin, M. Chatterjee, J. Lambert, J. Quanine, P. Kisanga, S. Bajaj, and H. Ghassemi, 1990 (SOA No. 6)

7) **Appropriate Uses of Child Anthropometry**.
   G. Beaton, A. Kelly, J. Kevany, R. Martorell, and J. Mason, 1990  (SOA No. 7)

8) **Managing Successful Nutrition Programmes**.
   Edited by J. Jennings, S. Gillespie, J. Mason, M. Lotfi, and T. Scialfa, 1990  (SOA No. 8)

9) **Controlling Iron Deficiency**.
   S. Gillespie, J. Kevany, and J. Mason, 1991 (SOA No. 9)

10) **Nutrition-Relevant Actions — Some Experiences from the Eighties and Lessons for the Nineties**.
    S. Gillespie and J. Mason, 1991  (SOA No. 10)

11) **Nutrition and Population Links — Breastfeeding, Family Planning and Child Health**.
    S. Huffman, R. Martorell, K. Merchant, R. Short, P. Ramachandran, M. Labbok, B. Edmonston, and B. Winikoff, 1992 (SOA No. 11)

12) **Nutritional Issues in Food Aid**.
    J. Katona-Apte, J. von Braun, G. Beaton, J. Rivera, P. Musgrove, and M. Toole, 1993 (SOA No.12)

13) **Effectiveness of Vitamin A Supplementation in the Control of Young Child Morbidity and Mortality in Developing Countries**.
    G. Beaton, R. Martorell, K. Aronson, B. Edmonston, G. McCabe, A.C. Ross, and B. Harvey, 1993  (SOA No.13)

14) **Controlling Vitamin A Deficiency**.
    S. Gillespie and J. Mason, 1994  (SOA No.14)

15) **How Nutrition Improves**.
    S. Gillespie, J. Mason, and R. Martorell, 1996  (SOA No. 15)

16) **Nutrition and Poverty**.
    S. Gillespie, N. Hasan, S. Osmani, U. Jonsson, R. Islam, D. Chirmulay, V. Vyas, and R. Gross, 1997  (NPP No. 16)

17) **Challenges for the 21st Century: A Gender Perspective on Nutrition Through the Life Cycle**.
    P. James, S. Smitisiri, P. Pinstrup-Anderson, R. Pandya-Lorch, C. Murray, A. Lopez, and I. Semega-Jenneh, 1998 (NPP No. 17)

18) **Low Birthweight – Report of a meeting in Dhaka, Bangladesh, June 1999**.
    J. Pojda and L. Kelley, 2000 (NPP No. 18)

19) **What Works? A Review of the Efficacy and Effectiveness of Nutrition Interventions**.
    L.H. Allen and S.R. Gillespie, 2001 (NPP No. 19)

## Asian Development Bank Nutrition and Development Series

1) **Investing in Child Nutrition in Asia**.
   Joseph Hunt and M.G. Quibria (eds.). Asian Development Review Vol. 17, Nos. 1 and 2, 1999.

2) **Manila Forum 2000. Strategies to Fortify Essential Foods in Asia and the Pacific**.
   Asian Development Bank, Manila; Micronutrient Initiative, Ottawa; and International Life Sciences Institute, Washington DC, 2000.

3) **Improving Child Nutrition in Asia**.
   John Mason, Joseph Hunt, David Parker, and Urban Jonsson. Food and Nutrition Bulletin Special Supplement, September 2001.

4) **Attacking the Double Burden of Malnutrition in Asia and the Pacific**.
   Stuart Gillespie and Lawrence Haddad. Asian Development Bank, Manila; and International Food Policy Research Institute, Washington DC, 2001.

5) **What Works? A Review of the Efficacy and Effectiveness of Nutrition Interventions**.
   Lindsay H. Allen and Stuart R. Gillespie. Asian Development Bank, Manila; and United Nations Sub-Committee on Nutrition, Geneva, ACC/SCN, Nutrition Policy Papers No. 19, September 2001.

6) **The Nutrition Transition and Prevention of Diet-related Chronic Diseases in Asia and the Pacific**.
   Barry Popkin, Susan Horton, and Soowon Kim. Food and Nutrition Bulletin Special Supplement, December 2001.